BROKEN ENTRIES

OTHER BOOKS BY ROY MIKI

The Prepoetics of Williams Carlos Williams: Kora in Hell (UMI Research Press)

A Record of Writing: An Annotated and Illustrated Bibliography of George Bowering (Talonbooks)

Saving Face: Selected Poems 1976-1988 (Turnstone)

With Cassandra Kobayashi, *Justice in Our Time: The Japanese Canadian Redress Settlement* (Talonbooks/National Association of Japanese Canadians)

Market Rinse (DisOrientation Chapbooks)

Random Access File (Red Deer College Press)

BOOKS EDITED

This Is My Own: Letters to Wes and Other Writings on Japanese Canadians, 1941-48, by Muriel Kitagawa (Talonbooks)

Tracing the Paths: Reading ≠ Writing The Martyrology (Talonbooks)

George Bowering Selected: Poems 1961-1992 (McClelland and Stewart)

With Fred Wah, *Colour. An Issue* (West Coast Line)

Pacific Windows: Collected Poems of Roy K. Kiyooka (Talonbooks)

JOURNALS EDITED

Line: A Journal of Contemporary Writing and its Modernist Sources (1983-89)

West Coast Line: A Journal of Contemporary Writing and Criticism (1989-)

BROKEN ENTRIES
Race Subjectivity Writing

Essays

Roy Miki

THE MERCURY PRESS

The publisher gratefully acknowledges the financial assistance of the Canada Council
for the Arts and the Ontario Arts Council, and further acknowledges the financial
support of the Government of Canada through the Book Publishing Industry
Development Program for our publishing activities.

Edited by Beverley Daurio
Cover design by Gordon Robertson
Author photograph by Cassandra Kobayashi
Composition and page design by TASK

Printed and bound in Canada
Printed on acid-free paper

1 2 3 4 5   02 01 00 99 98

Canadian Cataloguing in Publication Data
Miki, Roy, 1942-
Broken entries : race, subjectivity, writing
Includes bibliographical references.
ISBN 1-55128-059-0
I. Title.
PS8576.I32B76 1998   C814'.54   C98-932198-3
PR9199.3M4564B76 1998

The Mercury Press
22 Prince Rupert Avenue, Toronto, Ontario, Canada   M6P 2A7

this one
is for my
grandparents
Yoshi and Tokusaburo Ooto
whose imagined lives
became visible inside
the writing

At the side of the road are boulevards where ditches once stretched across languaged stories of rescue. The city is layered, splayed, even unrepresentable in categories where lawns are trimmed and grammars snooze in the late colonial sun. The rim is one horizonal sign—looking to the pacific through the crevices of discourse blocks. Blocks and blocks of civil legacies worn thin by the lyric in one's i. The seams in the social and linguistic folds disclose formations of some interest here. In the practice of writing, for example, who's there—

out there listening

Table of Contents

Acknowledgements 11

Redress:
A Community Imagined   15

"Shikata Ga Nai":
A Note on Seeing / Japanese Canadian   29

The Future's Tense:
Editing, Canadian Style   34

Inter-Face:
Roy Kiyooka's Writing   54

"Turn This Page":
Journaling bpNichol's *The Martyrology* & The Returns   77

Asiancy:
Making Space for Asian Canadian Writing   101

Sliding the Scale of Elision:
"Race" Constructs / Cultural Praxis   125

"What's a racialized text like you doing in a place like this?"
Reforming Boundaries, Negotiating Borders
in English and CanLit Studies   160

Unclassified Subjects:
Question Marking "Japanese Canadian" Identity   181

Can I See Your ID?:
Writing in the Race Codes That Bind   205

Bibliography 216

Acknowledgements

This collection of essays begins in the aftermath of the Japanese Canadian Redress Agreement, signed with the federal government on September 22, 1988. The redress movement depended, for me, on the identity formation, "Japanese Canadian" ("JC"), which was linked to both a legacy and a limit all too often (un)thinkable. Through the language of activism, though, its previously determined boundaries constituted by the markings of "internment," were radically transformed, and with many others I too was swept up in the resolve to redress the mass uprooting, dispossession, and displacement of the 1940s, my own family's among them. The redress settlement came in the nick of time, and offered to many JCs a symbolic narrative closure to the historical trauma of victimization at the hands of their own government. *Justice in Our Time* (1991), written with Cassandra Kobayashi, presented a documentary account of redress by tracking the social, political, and community processes that led up to the agreement. But even in the euphoria of this resolution of the past, there was, in the wings, already the pressure to rethink "JC" in what had suddenly become a post-redress horizon.

I have had the good fortune of knowing many writers and artists who have aspired to create generative approaches to the urgency of cultural and theoretical issues. In this period of heightened instability and change, it has been all the more important to maintain a shared openness to the shifting boundaries of racialization, identity, and positioning. The writing act, as integral to these contemporary concerns, has of necessity been social in its responses and responsibilities and vitally so in the alliances formed in friendship, collaboration, and coalition-building. The essays in *Broken Entries* reflect my participation in a selection of events from the late 1980s to 1997. Although they have all been revised to varying degrees for this collection, I hope they continue to bear the signs of their occasions.

□

The occasions which prompted the writing have been so instrumental in shaping the history of the essays gathered here that some acknowledgements are warranted and perhaps useful for readers. "Redress: A Community Imagined," presented here as two parallel texts, was initially two separate speeches given at JC community events: "Redress: The Personal Inflected," for one of many redress celebrations, this one sponsored by the Lethbridge Japanese Canadian Association, April 12, 1991; and "A Community Imagined: The Meaning of Home Coming," for "HomeComing '92," Vancouver, October 10, 1992, a conference that recognized fifty years since the mass uprooting from the west coast. "'Shikata Ga Nai': A Note on Seeing / Japanese Canadian," written on the invitation of Bryce Kanbara, was part of the opening for the art exhibit, "'Skikata Ga Nai': Contemporary Art by Japanese Canadians," Burnaby Art Gallery, April 6, 1989. "Inter-Face: Roy Kiyooka's Writing," was undertaken on the invitation of Kate Rimmer at Artspeak Gallery and Nancy Shaw at Or Gallery, for an exhibition catalogue, *Roy Kiyooka* (1991). "The Future's Tense: Editing, Canadian Style" was delivered as a paper, in response to a request from Fred Wah, one of the organizers of the *Interventing the Text* Conference, University of Calgary, May 2-4, 1991. "'Turn This Page': Journaling bpNichol's *The Martyrology* & the Returns" was written as a journal to track some of the questions arising from a graduate seminar on bpNichol's *The Martyrology*, Spring Semester 1995, Simon Fraser University; its "Postscript" is an excerpt from "'TI' ME': And then there was Book 7," a talk prepared for a tribute to bpNichol, Vancouver, November 3, 1990. "Asiancy: Making Space for Asian Canadian Writing" was first presented at the conference, "Privileging Positions: The Sites of Asian American Studies," Association for Asian American Studies, June 2-6, 1993, Cornell University. "Sliding the Scale of Elision: 'Race' Constructs / Cultural Praxis" was written soon after co-ordinating, as Chair of the Racial Minority

Writers' Committee of the Writers' Union of Canada, "Writing thru Race: A Conference for First Nations Writers and Writers of Colour," June 30–July 2, 1994, Vancouver. Shorter speech versions were presented, first, at a conference organized by Smaro Kamboureli and Sneja Gunew, "Critical Multiculturalism: Between Race and Ethnicity," University of Victoria, January 28, 1995, and then as a public lecture in the Munro Beattie Lecture Series, English Department, Carleton University, February 3, 1995. "'What's a racialized text like you doing in a place like this?'" was given as a plenary talk at a graduate student conference, "Reforming Boundaries Conference," University of Calgary, March 9, 1996. "Unclassified Subjects: Question Marking 'Japanese Canadian' Identity" was delivered as a public lecture, on the invitation of Brook Thomas, for the Chancellors Distinguished Lecture Series, University of California at Irvine, April 3, 1997. "'Can I See Your ID?': Writing in the Race Codes That Bind" was presented on a panel, "Canadian Multiculturalism," with Fred Wah and Jeff Derksen, at the "Cross-Cultural Poetics Conference," University of Minnesota, October 18, 1997. It was also written as a critical response to "Sitelines," a writers' retreat sponsored by *West Coast Line*, October 11-14, 1996.

□

In more ways than I can unravel, the contents of *Broken Entries* have been influenced by the example of many writers, artists, and critical thinkers. It has been a pleasure for me to have had the opportunity to research and converse with them at events, in e-mail exchanges, in conversations, and in collaborative projects. For their friendship, knowledge, and encouragement I would like to thank Marie Annharte Baker, Pauline Butling, Jodey Castricano, Jeff Derksen, Smaro Kamboureli, Robert Kroetsch, Jacqueline Larson, Nicole Markotic, Ashok Mathur, Ellie Nichol, Mona Oikawa, Aruna Srivastava, Grace Eiko Thomson, Fred Wah, and Jim Wong-Chu. Graduate students at

Simon Fraser University have asked the pressing questions that made research a gratifying process of dialogue and discovery, for which my thanks to Karlyn Koh, Glen Lowry, Mark Nakada, Charmaine Perkins, and Geneffa Popatia. Scott Toguri McFarlane and Kirsten Emiko McAllister deserve special appreciation for prompting and stimulating me to rethink JC history and identity. Their research and our numerous discussions over the years have helped me see new possibilities in JC studies. I would also like to acknowledge the Japanese Canadian Redress Foundation for providing a research grant to document the redress movement. It was during this time in the early 1990s that I undertook some of the research incorporated in these essays. Thanks to Tony Tamayose, its Board Assistant, for his advice and friendship over the years. Finally, I have benefited immensely from the thoughtful editorial expertise of Beverley Daurio, who knows how to work directly with writers throughout the whole production process.

RM

August 31, 1998
Vancouver

ACKNOWLEDGEMENT OF PREVIOUS PUBLICATION:

Some essays were published in earlier versions in the following places: "'Shikata Ga Nai': On Seeing / Japanese Canadian," in *Fear of Others: Art Against Racism* (Vancouver: Artists in Action Society, 1989); "Redress— The Personal Inflected," in *The Bulletin: A Journal for and about the Nikkei Community* (October 1991); "A Community Imagined: The Meaning of Home Coming," in *Nikkei Voice* (December 1992 - January 1993) and in *HomeComing '92: Where the Heart Is* (Vancouver: NRC Publishing, 1993); "Inter-Face: Roy Kiyooka's Writing," in *Roy Kiyooka* (Vancouver: Artspeak Gallery/Or Gallery, 1991); "'TI' ME': And then there was Book 7," in *West Coast Line* (Winter 1992-93); "The Future's Tense: Some Notes on Editing, Canadian Style," in *Open Letter* (Winter-Spring 1993); "Asiancy: Making Space for Asian Canadian Writing," in *Privileging Positions: The Sites of Asian American Studies* (Pullman Washington: Washington University Press, 1995); "'Can I See Your ID?': Writing in the Race Codes That Bind," *West Coast Line* (Winter 1997-98); "'Turn This Page': Journaling bpNichol's *The Martyrology* & The Returns," *Open Letter* (Fall 1998).

Redress:
A Community Imagined

I'm rummaging among archival boxes on redress in my study: boxes stuffed into the closet with mounds of papers, newspaper clippings, essays, notes, memos, press releases, the whole frenzy of the years of daily involvement in that, now, historic movement called "redress." Despite that dazzling accomplishment by our community, the past still shimmers with the unknown. Our history still remains baffling as we continue to construct stories that evade completion.

Home coming, or speaking more actively, coming home, as if home were a place, like Powell and Gore, or a house one can stroll into, toss a hat on the rack, and say hello to one and all. As if home were the completed story.

If only it could all be that translucent.

In the batch of photocopied clippings from the *New Canadian*, I

This past winter I finally got to visit the small French Canadian town, Ste. Agathe, some twenty-five miles south of Winnipeg where my family was sent in May 1942 from their home in Haney, BC, a few months before I was born.

It was eerie, walking down its short main street, rue Principale, looking around at the houses in their snowy landscape. By all appearances, I thought, the town probably hadn't changed all that much since the 1940s.

I had driven there with a friend, the writer Robert Kroetsch, on a sunny Saturday afternoon, and out of curiosity, we dropped by the only service station to ask about any old people who could recall the war years here. The young guy at the pump, without hesitating, says yeah, Leon. Where he is? At the coffee shop down the road.

The coffee shop, Coin-du-Pont (Bridge's Corner), belongs to Leon's daughter and her husband. Yes, he was in Ste. Agathe in May 1942 when finally locate what I thought I remembered having, thinking ahead to today, the front page for this very day, itself a Saturday, October 10th, 1942— fifty years ago.

The headline reads, "Need Volunteer Teachers for Education by Mail." Both governments, the provincial and the federal have refused to provide education for the uprooted children, so JCs have to take on this responsibility, as "volunteers." At the bottom is an article on the 600 living in 100 tents in Slocan, and at the top left corner is a notice saying October 15th is the final date set by the BC Security Commission for JCs to be registered. On the left side is a report on the Vancouver *News Herald*'s hunt to expose the "Black Dragon Society" allegedly connected to Etsuji Morii then living in Minto, BC. The editorial below the headline encourages JCs to contribute to the volunteer work of educating the children in the camps.

What these details from history say nothing of, though, is the interior place, the ravaged heart, the tearing away from everything that

---

the Japanese Canadian family arrived, and yes, he remembered them well because his father owned the sugar-beet farm where they were confined in their displaced condition. After the harvest that first year, with the house in such disrepair, the family moved into town and became part of their daily lives— though back then, Leon says, people didn't speak English, as they do today. Back then, Leon spoke only French.

Excited by these "strangers" inquiring about his own local history, Leon improvised a tour through the town, leading us to the exact spot where he recalled the Miki family had lived. The house was gone but the one next door, still intact, was constructed in the same design. Behind the empty lot, the land descended to the banks of the Assiniboine River, and for an instant a recollection stirred of that river in family stories. (Later, in a drive back with my mother and my brother, Art, I learned that Leon's memory had confused our family with the Hayakawas, the family of my had been associated with "home," the family, the community, all the nuanced network of the social, cultural, and spiritual life built by the issei and the nisei for over fifty years. That entire edifice, by the stroke of a pen in Ottawa, was utterly dismantled and thrown into disarray.

Those sansei, like myself, who were born in the uprooting, were born into a deracination they absorbed invisibly. All the anxieties, the hopes and fears of their parents, became the very fabric of their thoughts, dreams, and language. The hastily built relocated communities, at least to my child's imagination in Manitoba, were fragile places always seemingly threatened by nothingness, by wordless spaces that would come and go in all the unacknowledged silences— like shadows in search of names.

My earliest memory is of childhood days in North Kildonan, Manitoba. A small group of JC families had moved there in 1944, after the sugar-beet farms, while the restrictions against living within the city limits still held. The rundown shacks, back lanes and all, around

---

mother's best friend, Nori, who chose to accompany her to help care for three young kids— a fourth on the way. Our family house, on the other side of the street near the Coin-du-Pont, had been completely re-invented, though its former shape with the large front veranda could still be imagined. My mother also commented on the uncanny intersection of lives. Leon's brother— a fact I was never aware of before— was the familiar guy who owned the corner garage down our back lane where my father gassed up and repaired his cars all through the 1950s.)

I have photos of my mother and Nori with my two brothers and sister taken in Ste. Agathe. Now I realize that my father took them (with his box Brownie camera) on rue Principale. Standing in what may have been that same point of their perspective, I reflect on the spatiality of the dislocation they must have felt— contained by an "alien" geography and in a "foreign" linguistic environment, with obviously no Japanese spoken,

McKay and Edison, with the fields across, rabbits roaming wild, an image that has remained intact for me. My parents, with others in this makeshift community, got up before sunrise to make the trek on foot to the city limits, to ride the streetcar in, to work all day, and to leave at night— all according to regulations on their RCMP permits.

One early memory persists, a pre-school blues memory, of following my older brothers and sister to the local school, my faced pressed to the window of the classroom, still too young to attend. Locked out, so it seemed then, those lonely days for the few of us kids left to roam freely in and out of each other's homes, cared for by elderly issei left in charge, my own obaachan and ojiichan among them.

Then, in 1947, when the ban on living in Winnipeg was lifted, we moved into the city— to a house on Alexander Street— the year I began school. How strange to think the name of that street was the same as the street my father and mother once lived on in Vancouver— 521 Alexander there, 631 in Winnipeg.

---

but no English either. Their personal and communal lives had suddenly been transfigured, and they were forced to endure monotonous and back-breaking labour, at meagre wages, in a place with weather so radically more severe.

A month later, I had a chance to do some research in the National Archives, in Ottawa. There are hundreds of thousands of documents on the nitty-gritty details of the displacement of Japanese Canadians during the 1940s. (Many, including those displaced, persist in using the euphemism "evacuation"— manufactured by federal propagandists— to narrate the experience of expulsion. This normalization of language may buffer consciousness of the traumatic consequences of the event, but it has also covered over its violence. "Evacuees" move temporarily from dangerous sites and return when the threat subsides. Japanese Canadians may have been led to believe they would resume their coastal lives— but

Those growing-up years in Winnipeg, for me, were unsettling, confusing, all a rush, though of course I was inarticulate then, more like a sponge just soaking up the milieu in what was an unfamiliar place, immigrant children from all over speaking many languages, native and metis kids, a crazy mixture to say the least.

It was all pushing in— the classrooms with all white faces, the teachers who never seemed to understand anything I said, and who were always asking me about being "Japanese." I hated those days when some of us, from so-called "exotic" ancestries, would have to bring in show-and-tell things; for me it meant ohashi, or chawan, or even geta— which in turn meant the giggles and the playground teasing. It was then, I think, that the term "Japanese," which later turned into "Japanese Canadian," became more and more the way I was defined, or the way I defined myself, in relation to the "outside," i.e., the white community that appeared so omnipresent and monolithic.

The death of my grandparents, first my grandfather in North

---

the government's political strategists had no such "return" in their plans.) Here we can study the papers of the British Columbia Security Commission, established on March 4, 1942, to carry out the expulsion from the coast of all "persons of Japanese race." Here also are the papers of the Department of Labour, the government agency that took over from the Security Commission in 1943, the RCMP, and the Custodian of Enemy Property. The list of government documents goes on and on— a truly staggering amount of paperwork exists on the administration of the dispossession and dispersal "east of the Rockies," and the exiling of some 4,000 to Japan.

Beneath the officious matter-of-factness of the government's documents, any reader would have to be stone deaf not to hear the multiple voices of suffering and anguish— for example, innocent young men, many in their late teens or early twenties, incarcerated behind barbed wire in

Kildonan and later my grandmother in Winnipeg, was the first step cutting me off from the older world of the issei. As a kid, I spoke only Japanese to them, but once they were gone, their stability was replaced by the drive to assimilate, to become fluent in English, to "master" the dominant values of an Anglo-dominant society— remember singing the "Maple Leaf Forever" and dancing round the maypole tree? It was all part of growing up in Canada, and of leaving behind the remnants of internment.

By the mid-to-late 1950s, when the exile from the coast was receding into history, the integration process, like some magical potion, was working its wonders, transforming all of us, through the educational roadway, into mainstream kids— at least, on the outside, because inside, the estrangement, the dislocation, remained a nagging footnote to matters yet to be resolved. Somewhere buried within was some reserve of curiosity, some seed of resistance, some dream of justice that wanted— and that would eventually demand— the unfolding of a narrative.

---

prisoner-of-war camps at Petawawa and Angler, in Ontario, merely for protesting against the removal orders. These men were part of what was called the Nisei Mass Evacuation Group that wanted to co-operate with the government's order but opposed the breaking up of families and called for relocation in family units. In their petition to the Security Commission they wrote: "...we request you to remember that we are British subjects by birth, that we are no less loyal to Canada than any other Canadian, that we have done nothing to deserve the break-up of our families, that we are law-abiding Canadian citizens, and that we are willing to accept suspension of our civil rights— rights to retain our homes and businesses, boats, cars, radios and cameras..."

Despite the pleas for so-called "British fair play"— a phrase that young Japanese Canadians had absorbed in public schools— the Security Commission pushed ahead, interning the Mass Evacuation Group, and

The narrative of redress is a complex one that I'm still trying to unravel. Let me just say here that, as a sansei, no other event in our history had so much vitality, so much heart, so much purpose, so much fullness of meaning. I was glad to be part of that crucial movement that changed the course of our community's history.

Gomen nasai, demo heta no nihongo de sukoshi hanashitai desu. Watashi no tomodachi ni tetsudatte moraimashita. Watashi ga kodomo no toki niwa, nihongo dake ka issei no ojiichan to obaachan niwa hanasemasen deshita. Karetachi ga nakunatte kara wa, nihongo o wasuremashita. Dare ka ga watashi no naka ni haiite, zenbu keshite shimatta yoo desu. Hakujin no naka ni hairu tame ni, sansei-tachi wa jibun no ichiban chikai mono made nakushimashita— sore wa nihongo desu. "Redress" no toki wa, issei no hitotachi ni nihongo de setsumei dekinakatta koto o zannen ni omoimashita. Kyoo wa watashi no ojiisan to obaasan, sore kara otoosan, shoshite kodomo no toki no

---

splitting up families. Men were shipped to road camps, and women and children ended up in the filthy livestock barns in Hastings Park on the PNE grounds where thousands were cooped up, sometimes for many months. The voices of hardship, confusion, and outrage, in the apparent quietude of the indifferent archives, goes on and on. It is as if all these voices were trapped in the limbo of inarticulateness, caged in the government's filing systems.

Like other sansei born in the fray of uprooting, I remember growing up in the shades of the injustices, through stories from our parents and grandparents, and through conversations with relatives and friends. The names of the "ghost towns" in the BC interior used as internment sites were repeated so many times in my childhood that they took on mythic proportions in my imagination— Lemon Creek, Popoff, Slocan City, Sandon, New Denver, Greenwood.

nihonjin shakai no koto o omoidashimashita. Zannen na koto ni, minasan wa "redress" owaru mae ni nakunatte shimaimashita.

[I would like to say a few words in my weak Japanese. I had a friend help me compose this in Japanese. As a child I spoke only Japanese in the home to my issei grandparents. After they died there was so much pressure on us kids to become proficient in English, that I began to lose my ability to speak in Japanese. It was as if someone had simply entered my mind and erased everything clean. Many sansei, myself included, wanted so much to be integrated into white society that we lost what was closest to us, our mother tongue. During the redress movement, so many times I despaired that I couldn't explain myself in Japanese to the issei, that I had to speak through the barrier of translation. For this I am truly sorry. Today, I am thinking of my grandparents and my father, and so many members of my childhood community, all dead for so many years, so many years before redress.]

I visited these sites for the first time, in 1967, while my wife Slavia and I drove from Winnipeg to Vancouver to settle on the coast. It was mesmerizing to walk around those historic places, and later to live in Vancouver. I spent endless hours around Powell Street, at Steveston, in the Fraser Valley, stopping by Haney to see my parents' house and my grandparents' house, side by side, still there— in their original shape, though run down.

Wherever I turned, so it seemed, these places reverberated with (almost invisible) traces of the lost community— on Powell Street, for instance, the fading, and now obsolete, name "Maikawa" on a building that was once the Maikawa Department Store of pre-war "Japantown" or "Nihonmachi." Passing by Oppenheimer Park, I could hear my father talking, in my own childhood, about Powell Street, Alexander Street, Main Street, the legendary neighbourhood map of his own growing up. During

For sansei born during the mass dispersal from the BC coast there is no "homecoming" as such, not the kind of "homecoming" shared by the nisei who lived here before the war. There is nothing to "come back to," nothing other than the memories of absent places, an absent community, of a history that was disrupted by dispossession, by exile. Our roots are very much the product of rootlessness, so that everything of intimate value relates directly back to the family unit itself, dropped in what was an "alien" place.

Only recently, while working in the National Archives of Canada, did I finally come upon the file containing some bare details of my family, sent to Ste. Agathe in Manitoba from their home in Haney. There among all the banal bureaucratic data on people sent to Manitoba, I found the RCMP reports on women allowed into Winnipeg to have their babies at the Winnipeg General Hospital. There was my own mother, Shizuko Miki, with her registration number prominently placed on the form, given permission to enter

----

my first year in Vancouver, I often used streets and places known only through memory to locate myself in the city. Slowly, though, the place I was fabricating gave way to the urge to reconstruct, in the specificity of daily lives, the social formation of Japanese Canadians.

As early as 1960, just after starting university, I had done some research on the wartime history, but only sporadically. In Vancouver, with the remnants of that past strewn like pieces of a puzzle, I found myself wanting to know more about my familial roots. In 1969, Slavia and I went to live in Japan, naively intending to live, work and study there for at least five years. We bought one-way tickets with only vistors' visas, with no means of support there. Luckily we found jobs in Tokyo, teaching English.

We lived in Japan for only sixteen months. I soon discovered I would never become "Japanese." I remember going to Fukuoka to track down information on my grandparents, and spending a number of days with a

the city, alone. There I learned she stayed in a hostel for one week before giving birth to her child, as it turned out, on my own birthday, October 10, 1942.

So I would like to end with this poem for my mother, initially written after finding the document about her, as a tribute to her, and as a tribute to all JCs who have come through, fifty years later:

Japanese friend there who spoke fluent English. My knowledge of their lives in Japan was so flimsy and so vague that we were unable to trace their personal histories. It struck home that the attempt to reclaim my "roots" (in the lingo of the day) was fraught with contradictions, and even a diversion from the more inevitable job of understanding "Japanese Canadian identity," whatever that term could come to signify.

Back in Canada, during the 1970s in Vancouver, others were also beginning to question the treatment of Japanese Canadians during the 1940s. I even joined a group of sansei, young nisei, and new immigrants who formed the Japanese Canadian Centennial Project (JCCP) Committee to mount a photographic history of our community. "A Dream of Riches: Japanese Canadians 1877-1977" became a national project for the 1977 centennial. A year later, it was published in book form.

Then, in 1981, a small group of us from the JCCP, along with other

single file

for my mother
who was there

at the back
of the library

the national
mind you

capital quiet
archive hush

working wish
no distraction

---

like-minded sansei, established the JCCP Redress Committee to raise the issue of redress for past injustices. We published a pamphlet, "Redress for Japanese Canadians," which attracted media attention and stimulated discussions amongst Japanese Canadians. At the time we eagerly followed the hearings of the US Commission on Wartime Relocation and Internment of Civilians to investigate the issue of redress for Japanese Americans incarcerated during World War II. Couldn't there be redress for Japanese Canadians?

I've always looked upon the redress movement as an inevitable act of reclaiming our history, and this made the process of editing *This Is My Own* a strange and haunting experience. Studying and assembling the letters, articles and speeches written in the heat of the moment, finding unpublished manuscripts with stories on Muriel Kitagawa's nisei generation, I was drawn into a language sphere that I had thought did not— or

the distillation
memory bank

brittle paper folds
spare trees snow

covered outside
the bland report

of the bus ride
from ste agathe

one week delay
alone at the hostel

---

could not— have possibly existed, given the absence of such documents in print. And most engrossing and powerful of all were the series of letters Muriel wrote to her brother Wes Fujiwara in Toronto from December 1941 to May 1942.

I first read the originals of these letters in the home of Joy Kogawa, whose novel *Obasan* first lifted Muriel's words out of their archival tomb in the National Archives of Canada. I spent one long afternoon turning the pages of the letters, some written, some typed, Muriel always talking at top speed, recording, assessing, perceiving, recording, narrating— and suddenly I was caught in the fluidity of the words revealing the day-by-day immediacy as her community was violated. Later, I tracked down other writing by Muriel, in the National Archives in Ottawa, in the personal files of her husband Ed Kitagawa and her brother Wes, and in the community papers, like the *New Canadian*, where she wrote as Sue Sada, TMK, and Dana. Then there were the interviews with her brothers and sister, with

putting in time
for the birth day

(who said what &
where is not there

tho the turning out
of a son is unrecorded

by name nevertheless
the stat made its way

to be documented
& then stolen by me

---

friends in her pre-war community, and slowly the shape of *This Is My Own* became apparent.

The process of editing Muriel's writing became a sustenance— an intellectual engagement that served to counteract the more demanding political and community work in the redress movement. Muriel came to signify the voice of the personal transformed, in the very act of writing, into a mouthpiece of lives so utterly affected by forces of malevolence beyond their control.

Okay we move. But where? Signs up on all highways... JAPS KEEP OUT. Curfew. "My father is dying. May I have permission to go to his bedside?" "NO!" Like moles we burrow within after dark, and only dare to peek out the windows or else be thrown into the hoosegow with long term sentences and hard labour. Confiscation of radios, cameras, cars and trucks. Shutdown of all business. No one will buy. No agency set up yet

weight ago
don't let go

wait ago
don't let go

way ta go
don't let go

---

to evaluate. When you get a notice to report to RCMP for orders to move, you report or be interned. "Who will guard my wife and daughters?" Strong arm reply. Lord, if this was Germany you can expect such things as the normal way, but this is Canada, a Democracy! And the Nisei, repudiated by the only land they know, no redress anywhere. Sure we can move somewhere on our own, but a job? Who will feed the family? Will they hire a Jap? Where can we go that will allow us to come? (From a letter, Muriel Kitagawa to Wes Fujiwara, March 4, 1942, *This Is My Own* 92-3)

"Shikata Ga Nai":
A Note on Seeing / Japanese Canadian

Who knows but that the next time will be made easier for the plunderers because we shrugged and said: 'Shikata ga nai.'
— Muriel Kitagawa, *This Is My Own* 216

i'll be damned if i'll let the word 'shikataganai' fall from my lips again
i thought, thinking of all the hostages of other malevolences...
— Roy Kiyooka, *October's Piebald Skies & Other Lacunae*,
  in *Pacific Windows* 283

Hear/say "shikata ga nai" and JCs, like me too, will quickly shift to the 1940s internment— the stripping of citizenship rights, the confiscation of belongings, the branding of "enemy alien" in this place of birth. To many the event was so awesome in its fury that it appeared to be governed by the stranger, "Fate," a force that mercilessly ruled over one's life and against which one was so helpless that resignation was the only pragmatic means of survival. "Shikata ga nai."

Leaving the question of fate aside, along with the profound implications of "resignation" in the philosophical and religious traditions of Japan (a topic far beyond this note), for JCs who found themselves grappling with the wounding that can be traced to internment, "shikata ga nai" had become a sign of a bounded state.

Anticipating the exhibit *"Shikata Ga Nai": Contemporary Art by Japanese Canadians*, I find myself turning and moving, again, around this— now more enigmatic— phrase: "shikata ga nai." How it resists transparency of reference, even in the face of the Burnaby Art Gallery's press release, where readers are offered the unproblematicized translation, "it can't be helped." Who knows, it may even be twisted, even occluded, by JCs themselves in various appropriations depending on the subjective effects of estrangement, generational positioning, and angle of familiarity with a JC vernacular.

The gesture of naming in Japanese, especially so in a dominant English-language milieu, risks the ambiguity of semantic disturbance, perhaps even the loss of communicational security, though this may be one of the routes toward an "involved" reading of "shikata ga nai." The phrase may then resonate with associational depth to some JCs, while others might begin to hear the subtle machinations of recuperated cliché.

For non-JCs the phrase, even with the aid of an English gloss ("can it be helped?") will likely remain without immediacy— without, in other words, the non-semantic undertones (for JCs) of its performance in such instances as family gatherings and conversations on responses to the war years. Or more, the foreignness could install a barrier alienating them from the artworks even before they have laid eyes on them. Of course, that linguistic distance could entice some while distracting others, though paradoxically, either response can trigger a search for meaning that draws them into the perceptual space of the exhibit where JC artist eyes are caught up in the passing scenes.

I dwell on the word "passing" because it conjures a process of passage, of a willful absence of willfulness, of a resignation to a flowing, what some would call a negative state. "Shikata *ga nai*." The artistic imagination, as a field of desire, thrives on receptivity, that ability to take in— to breathe in— the influx of events as they occur without the imposition (or the exploitation) of the will. It necessarily trusts in process. "Shikata ga nai?" Perhaps I'm stretching the phrase beyond belief. Nevertheless— never the less— the drift of this kind of entanglement may get us somewhere.

The mass uprooting and dispersal from the west coast— that historical trajectory— infiltrated my consciousness from birth and over time has taken on mythic dimensions. The hypothetical "original" unity, the blessed geography of the coast— "hey you could get a

salmon easily in the creek behind the house"— was torn apart by a
systematic series of racist orders-in-councils. It was by the brutal but
indifferent letter of the law that JCs were absorbed into the many to
become strangers in their own place, scapegoats forced to incorporate
and hence disguise the relentless power of an underlying violence
(here) towards otherness in all its forms.

The imagination formulated by the imposition of race signs
inhabits— in varying degrees from forgetfulness to awareness— the
unresolved, so disturbed, twilight of denial. In the mundane and the
daily, it acts out and re-presents what is expected, side-stepping
confrontation and thereby appeasing the turbulent memory of violation. Who among JCs in my own generation can forget the unspoken
constraints in the post-war years, the 1950s and 1960s, the social and
familial pressures to assimilate, to remain invisible, to be model citizens?
And who can forget those times, even when the rebellious "i" said no
to the constraints, how they surfaced in the imagination to prohibit—
but prohibit what? There were no words, no images, at least then. The
tabula rasa of erasure, of absences supplanting images— "we'll never
get back to the coast"— became a symptom of a restlessness which
seemed to coincide with my own birth.

The imagination, grounded as it so intimately is in the specific,
needs room to weave figures, and when the intersections are closed
off, it makes do with whatever is at hand. What is unspoken gets
reproduced in overlaid forms; what is unseen gets lost. Writing and art
become a scarce resource at the deepest reaches of a bound subjectivity.
The self-denial of JCs, the move away from the disrupted edges of
their perceptions— a necessary survival tactic of the 1950s— must have
had something to do with the paucity of writers and artists among
post-war JCs scattered all over the country.

In my own education through to the late 1960s, the concept of a
Japanese Canadian writer or artist had no public body, even though, of
course, a few JCs were writing and producing art. My memory locates
names such as Tak Tanabe, Roy Kiyooka, and Joy Kogawa. I use the

term "concept" cautiously and tentatively because I speak out of personal limitations shaping my own thinking at the time.

I recall the first strong stirrings in me that the silence of past injustices had to be broken, somehow— but how it could be done appeared altogether too immense to unravel. "Shikata ga nai?" Perhaps so, but the silences would not remain silent. Figures circled the air in the spaces left empty by the former community, and the desire to articulate the silences became more and more urgent. Joy Kogawa was one of the first JC writers to name victimization, in *Obasan*, a novel that moved down into an emotional whirlpool and spoke of the "cutting off of tongues" that occurred in the internment. Naomi's search for her mother in the narrative— in the decade of the 1970s out of which it arose— is the search for mother tongue to make audible the muting of JCs. The writer was swept up by history and could herself have been lost in the whirlpool but for the mirror of subjectivity she located in the voice of Muriel Kitagawa, buried in the national archives with the rest of her community. The lost and found manuscripts of Muriel set up a co-respondence that offered Joy a bridge to connect with the past. "Shikata ga nai"— it couldn't be helped.

Political acts, though, begin on the premise that conditions can be changed, that individual and communal will can alter the course of history, and that the process of seeking justice can become a healing process. The JC redress movement, though played out in the political arena of this country, included much more. The social struggle folded into the elusive notion of the "authentic"— an authentic history, an authentic story, an authentic language— to clear space and to open up time. So I hear the words of Gerry Shikatani:

> silence is bitten
> here, there
> and rooting in the mouth
> the reversal of dream
> trying forever

to find its way
back.
(*A Sparrow's Food* 143)

So I am drawn to the words of Joy Kogawa:

Forgive me.
I am obsessed with history
and always scratching for clues.
(*Woman in the Woods* 58)

So Roy Kiyooka brings us "home":

i had meant to write about a pear tree i knew as a child

when i lived over the mountains in a small prairie town but
the language of that pear tree belonged to my mother tongue . it
bespeaks a lost childhood language one which the pear tree
in our backyard in chinatown has a nodding acquaintance with.

how many languages does a pear tree speak?
(*Pear Tree Pomes*, in *Pacific Windows* 208)

The Future's Tense:
Editing, Canadian Style

This conference, "Interventing the Text," has been designed to address the implications of critical issues arising from the current production and reception of writing as text. Fred Wah's invitation to speak on editing contemporary Canadian writing is, for me then, an opportunity to reflect on the poetics informing some of the decisions I make as a practising editor. As a rule, I try to avoid working by "rule," or by a prescriptive agenda, while putting together journal issues, often two issues simultaneously— except, of course, when there is a special issue. Decisions arise in what could be described as a pre-conceptual way of thinking, not unlike the attention operative in any creative act. Such an editorial inclination, in which materials retain their textual surfaces without collapsing into predetermined categories, remains a crucial methodological strategy for the editing and reception of contemporary writing and criticism.

Today, though, because of this conference's focus on interventionist strategies, the occasion calls for a more self-reflective consideration of the why in the doing. Why edit at all? Or what is at stake for contemporary writing? What I have to offer are some notes on editing, I suppose "Canadian style," because of specific geographic, social, and cultural conditions. I am thinking, here, primarily about writing in Canadian English.

I

While it may be obvious to many, it's worthwhile reminding ourselves that editors have exerted a powerful influence in the making and shaping of establishment CanLit, more so in this country with its geographical spread, its small population of readers, its long history of anti-intellectualism, its colonial protestant ("puritan") ethic, and its attitude that literature is primarily recreation, and not (to borrow

34

Margaret Avison's perception in "Snow") "re-creation" (27). In the post-war years especially, the products of their "tastes," not only the literary journals but also the plethora of anthologies, have been instrumental in the canonization of writers and critics, and in governing what comes to be judged of *national* relevance. No one involved in the production or reception of literary texts— from the writer to publisher to bookseller to reader— is free of the boundaries that get drawn by editors in privileged positions.

Think, for instance, of Gary Geddes' anthologies of Canadian poetry. First was his *15 Canadian Poets* (1970), co-edited with Phyllis Bruce, at the time a kind of pseudo-canon with the imprint of the staid Oxford University Press, and for many years the text used in Canadian universities to introduce students to poetry— and probably the tastes of a significant portion of one generation were formed by it. Then came *15 Canadian Poets Plus 5* (1978), again co-edited with Bruce, and finally, as if to mimic the schema of movie sequels, multiplication has eclipsed simple addition in *15 Canadian Poets X2* (1988), edited by Geddes alone. The escalation of "representative" Canadian poets may reflect the growing and aging population of poets, but it also confirms the exclusionary tactics common to canon-making anthologies, which now includes the editor. By editorial fiat, a number of old-timers like E.J. Pratt and F.R. Scott have been brought in to "historicize" the group, thereby constructing the frame for a "national tradition." Not unexpectedly, then, Victor Coleman, whose work is aligned with the language-based poetics of US writers Louis Zukofsky, Gertrude Stein, and Jack Spicer, has been removed from the auspicious group, silently. The anthology also conspicuously excludes non-white poets (Michael Ondaatje is the exception, though he too is normalized as one of the "same"), First Nations poets, and others who have not paid lip service to the centralist power base of the CanLit industry, poets like Daphne Marlatt, Fred Wah, bpNichol, Gerry Gilbert, Robin Blaser, and Roy Kiyooka.

In the introduction to *15 Canadian Poets Plus 5*, the editors say that the first anthology was "conceived in 1970 to meet a very specific need to provide a representative selection of the best post-war Canadian poetry in English..." (xiii). Notice that the word "best" is used instead of "relevant," a common signal that the editor's taste and biases have determined the contents. The popularity of the first anthology, readers are told, led to its fattening. Unfortunately, the latest in succession, "X2," no longer reflects a "need," but instead has become a territory of the chosen poets. Though ostensibly representative of Canadian poetry, the editors' inclusions advance a literary stance favouring conservative poetic forms and values belonging to the ideology of positivist humanism and its colonialist legacy.

Such a stance is a familiar justification for denying the place of a materialist or textualist poetics in Canadian writing, a move that is more explicit in Geddes' decision to remove the section of "concrete" texts from his other academically popular anthology, *20th Century Poetry and Poetics*. He explains the excision on the basis of his own subjectivity: "...in the intervening years between the first and third editions my own tastes in poetry have altered somewhat... I have lost some of the innocence and catholicity that once made me smile favourably on poetic fashions that I now regard as interesting but of limited significance. Imagists, Beats, Black Mountain poets, and Concrete poets have all had their say... The token section on Concrete poetry has been dropped..." (xvi). Here the editor, in the dis/guise of "taste" and maturity (always a dangerous sign for editors), and with an off-hand (reformist) gesture of disregard, erases a line of poetics— the only trace of the avant-garde in the earlier anthology.

I have dwelt in some detail on the editor Geddes because he has established himself in the CanLit industry, and in his post-catholic stage has been doing some house-cleaning, shutting out an "open form" poetics which many like-minded nationalists (i.e., centralists) see as US contamination— and not as the product of a larger post-war breakdown of belief in rationality and formal closure. The issue of open form extends beyond the historic frame of the New American Poetics of Charles Olson and others. It includes, in contemporary writing, those writers who work within de-stablized and ex-centric language forms that disrupt the centrality of the autonomous lyric voice in a great deal of CanLit. In this sense, Geddes' tastes may be a symptom of a dominant, socially homogenizing mode of reading that sustains itself on poetry that seeks to tame and "order" experience— and poets as well. In his Preface to *20th Century Poetry and Poetics* (dated March, 1985), Geddes offers the observation that he is "not convinced that poets in public offices would act other than as politicians; the shambles of their domestic and financial lives suggests that they would not. However, we can trust the *best* of them with our language, which seems a sufficiently enchanting and exacting *mistress* to keep them in line" (italics added; xvii-xviii). *Our* language? Whose language? Language as an "enchanting... mistress"? Someone to keep poets "in line"? These sentiments could use a strong dose of feminist and post-structuralist serum. The formalism implicit in Geddes' editorial stance is reinforced by an a-historicism of approach. The editor simply decides in terms of what is the "best," as if such a rule were not subject to the inevitable politics of representation.

2

When Frank Davey, in "Surviving the Paraphrase" (1974), first challenged the ascendancy of "thematic criticism" as a front for centralist nationalism in Canadian critical practice, he called for reading and criticism that attended to language, style, and form— to the textual particularities of the literary work. At the time, this was an effective interventionist manoeuvre, especially in the wake of a growing number of academics who were launching careers in CanLit. Nevertheless, Davey's essay— and I say this without diminishing in any way its importance as a sign of the move from theme to text— still fell short of proposing a theory of textuality to account for the contextual relationship of literary works to social, cultural, historical, and linguistic constraints— constraints which, on the one hand, make them possible, and on the other, assign them value in literary institutions. I read *Reading Canadian Reading* (1988), Davey's recent book of critical essays, as both a deconstruction of his earlier "formalist" (concern for the work in and of itself) approach and as a challenge to critics and editors who have, for too long, assumed that critical thought was immune to bias if it appeared neutral and objective. The editor who begins by saying that his/her journal will publish the "best" of contemporary writing is not divested of interest, but may (unwittingly or not) be subscribing to the standards of prevailing social and institutional expectations. Writing that actively "intervents," or subverts those habits, through the dislocation of grammar, syntax, and other characteristics of normative "literary language," will not appear in that journal. By such exclusion, much that may be of relevance to cultural processes in Canada will remain at the least marginalized, or at the worst suppressed through omission (our usual "Canadian" way of doing things!). In *Reading Canadian Reading*, Davey recognizes the post-structuralist approach to textuality which situates the writer and reader in the historicity of the writing and reading act.

3

In the late 1960s and the early 1970s, a far-reaching transformation took place in contemporary Canadian writing, evident in part through the appearance of text/books, or books as texts, which were loosely called "long poems," the vagueness of the term reflecting, as it perhaps still does, the apparent resistance to generic classification and a willingness, even a delight, to work polyphonically with multiple genres and subject positions in the writing process. The lyric voice found itself alongside a textual I, alongside prosaic discourses, alongside strategies of fiction-making. It was Robert Kroetsch who, using an exemplary critical method in "For Play and Entrance" (1981), prominently foregrounded the textuality of the "long poem." Two statements are especially apropos:

> The problem for the writer of the contemporary long poem is to honour our disbelief in belief— that is, to recognize and explore our distrust of system, of grid, of monisms...(118)

> We try to read, not what is in the book (that failing), but the book itself. The poet, then, not as maker, but as bookmaker. (129)

Kroetsch's essay is both an announcement of a new kind of text in contemporary Canadian writing, as well as an acknowledgement that the liberal humanist assumption of transcendence in literary works had become obsolete— or more, a reactionary turn away from the historical and cultural exigencies forming contemporary subjectivities. The signs were operative, in numerous texts listed by Kroetsch, that explorations by a generation of Canadian writers and poets in the materiality of language provided a theoretical way through to the heterogeneity of stances in this (potentially) empty space that has been nominalized as "Canada." As the road to the contagious margins opened, writers and readers could begin to articulate the textual constraints shaping the creation and reception of writing. This, in turn, led to an awareness of the politics of literary form, for instance, in feminist and so-called "ethnic" (more often than not the euphemism for "race") writing. Included also was the wave of interest in prose texts where the substance of language undergoes radical displacements and transformations, as well as the opening into what has been termed "life writing," writing in which the assumed wall between an auto-biographic "I" and a fictive "I" has become permeable to create a textualized "I." In these sites of writing, the reader is no longer the passive consumer of pre-packaged contents, and hence no longer a stable point of reference, but becomes an active producer of signifi-cances and values relative to the daily effort not to be brainwashed by homogeneity of thought and perception. Literary journals occupy an opportune position, at this crossroads of literary activity, to participate in what is still germinal, what has not yet been defined— the future tense of writing.

4

At this moment, I would like to recognize the "pioneering" (to adapt an older narrative vocabulary) work of the TRG, the Toronto Research Group, namely the dialogic duo, bpNichol and Steve McCaffery, who were working at the edge of writing theory in its Canadian context. Few academics, critics, and readers in the CanLit world would have been following the series of TRG reports in the 1970s (in *Open Letter*), but Nichol and McCaffery, from the late 1960s, had been working against a predominantly lyric stance of much Canadian poetry, and towards a theory of writing as a semiotic procedure. The writing they researched in their reports— collected in *Rational Geomancy* (1992)— allowed for the rupture of thought in the very materiality of signifiers and the release of energies aligned with the kinetics of the body. Their research drew them to the analysis of the book as machine, which helped blow wide open the concept of what constitutes publication and what constitutes a text. The traditional notion of a book as innocent vehicle for the subject/writer's expressiveness gave way to a transgression of publication boundaries.

I have in mind, for instance, McCaffery's *Carnival*, in two texts, *Carnival, the first panel: 1967-70* and *Carnival, the second panel: 1971-75*, the former a series of amazingly complicated typewriter texts, and the latter making use of the photocopier, by which the writer could, to use McCaffery's own words, in a bibliography of his works by bpNichol, "demonstrate writing inside its own disintegration" (73). These were published in bound form, but the binding can be undone and the separate pages placed together to form a large panel, or "page"— so the linearity of the bound text becomes another text in its spatiality. In the reading experience, the reader deconstructs temporality and constructs a textual space wherein the subjective "I" is dispersed in the materiality of the signifiers. Or think of bpNichol's first big publication, *bp*, also referred to as *Journeying & the returns* (1967), a boxed text made up of separate texts in various forms: the conventional poetry book, *Journeying & the returns*, bpNichol's farewell to the lyric stance of his early poems; *Letters Home*, an envelope of visual poems/objects; *Borders*, a recording with sound poems; and *Wild Thing*, a flip text, which the reader, after reading, is invited to destroy by fire. I don't believe criticism has sufficiently caught up with the theoretical implications of the things Nichol and McCaffery were doing in that early period of their writing lives, but their TRG reports are key documents in the thinking about textuality in a Canadian context.

5

Let me be speculative, given that these are provisional notes, and propose that we appear to have entered a post-McLuhanesque cultural phase wherein a writer can no longer rely on the truthfulness of "one's primary experience," i.e., of a point of origin for the "I" that produces clarity of meaning to dispel the obfuscations plaguing contemporary daily life. We are bombarded by a literal siege of non-hierarchic texts, from graffitti to newspapers to whatever, all randomly distributed according to the accidents of place and time. Indeed, the contemporary self is so thoroughly textualized that the "i" can no longer sustain its former capitalized status and has become a floating signifier with no transcendental signified— except for those frames of reference that are constructed as a refuge from the non-articulate silences constantly threatening to sweep our signifiers away— and not under the rug.

Post-structuralists like Jacques Derrida, Michel Foucault, and Julia Kristeva have offered the methodological frame for understanding the primacy of texts in the constitution of knowledge, perception, and language. In our own Canadian context, it was George Grant who, years before, in *Technology and Empire* (1969), exposed, with a certain degree of fear and anguish, the de-materialization of place that occurred in the territorialization of space (empty, to the European mind). The initial, historically bounded violation of this space was actualized, both symbolically and technologically, through the power of the rail line— with the powerful closure, like the sealing of a text, in the national myth of the last spike— the empire's ex-clamation mark to proclaim the continent its colonized place (think of the subsequent obsessive and violent drive to erase the culture, language, and place of First Nations, and think as well of the confinement of their bodies). So the oral historian/poet of Daphne Marlatt's *Steveston* (1974) witnesses the extension of such technologizing of matter by the Imperial Cannery in the fishing town of Steveston, BC, a power that appropriates both the matter of fish and the matter of human lives to stuff them in the most violent of all formalist closures: the sealed can. In the empire's form, which became the nation's form, settlements (like metaphors) cover over the emptiness, excluding whatever does not fit in, initially the indigenous peoples, and then later those who did not arrive through the eurocentric funnel, my own personal examples, those Japanese Canadians in Marlatt's poem and the Chinese Canadians who built the railway, who were controlled by a centralized power distant from the localism of their lives.

6

Imperial form works from the stability of a centre outward to the colonies. It resembles the kind of form that survives as long as the circumference keeps expanding, yet when the expansion stops it will try to maintain its power through stasis, through its resistance to change. Derrida exposes such closed forms when he talks about a "centred structure" which is "constituted on the basis of a fundamental immo- bility and a reassuring certitude, which is itself beyond the reach of play" (279). However, when the centre disintegrates and a transcen-

dental signified no longer stabilizes the structure, it enters the immediate flow of time, history, and the endless play of signification. Derrida
sees such a move as liberating— "the affirmation of a world of signs
without fault, without truth, and without origin which is offered to
an active interpretation" (292). In such a space-time continuum,
chance and indeterminancy become operative, and no particular site
is privileged; instead, all sites exist through their localisms. Here we
have a model for a sense of textuality that relativizes the functional
interplay of writer, reader, and text.

The contemporary, as it is created in textuality, is not a segment
of linear history, but the very actuality out of which writing, criticism,
and theory are constructed. So literary texts, both those written now
as well as past texts, are all conditioned by their reception in the present.
"Interpretation," as such, becomes a productive process drawing on
the contingent relations of difference, dissemination, and plurality in
the on-going immediacy of embodied change. Critical consciousness
is forced to negotiate its way through a shifting field of interactions that
do not coalesce into a totality— or to adapt some words by Mikhail
Bakhtin in *The Dialogic Imagination*:

> Through contact with the present, an object is attracted to the
> incomplete process of a world-in-the-making, and is stamped with the
> seal of inconclusiveness. No matter how distant this object is from us
> in time [and space?], it is connected to our incomplete, present-day,
> continuing temporal transitions, it develops a relationship with our
> unpreparedness, with our present. (30)

7

Bakhtinian "inconclusiveness" mirrors the cultural condition of Canada in the post-war era. The dislocating shift, first apparent in the early
post-atomic bomb years, was the collapse of humanist history into the
contemporary forever— a period which Eli Mandel so aptly said was

haunted by "its nostalgia, its longing for history, its impulse to define a Canadian past and to create a usable tradition" (81). For a brief time, in the anticipation and then the hiatus created by the 1967 centennial, there was an insurgent nationalism that attempted to construct a "usable tradition" to fill the void left by the loss of the centred structure called "Canada" (see George Grant's *Lament for a Nation: The Defeat of Canadian Nationalism* [1965] and Dennis Lee's essay, "Cadence, Country, Silence: Writing in Colonial Space" [1972/1974]). The wave of nationalist concerns— the drive towards unity forever— waned in the 1970s, and more recently has become a defensive strategy.

Robert Kroetsch delineated the limits of nationalist form in "Unity as Disunity: A Canadian Strategy," the text of a paper given in 1985 at a conference of the British Association for Canadian Studies. In his opening paragraph, he posited the coincidence of two "narratives," both dated 1885: the completion of the CPR railway, the "national dream," and the hanging of Métis leader Louis Riel, a force of resistance to that "dream" (21). These two narratives embodied the coincidence of form violently imposed on colonized space, and the rebellion from a localist perspective— a rebellion snuffed out through the ritual excision of the marginalized Riel from the centralized body politic. The example of ritual expulsion and scapegoating would be enacted many times again in Canadian history, a modern instance of which was the mass uprooting, dispossession and dispersal of Japanese Canadians from the west coast in 1942.

Drawing on Jean-François Lyotard, Kroetsch cites a passage from *The Postmodern Condition: A Report on Knowledge*, a report on the state of universities in the western world commissioned by the Quebec Government. Lyotard defines the postmodern in terms of the demise of "meta-narratives"— or for nationalists those "master narratives" through which the ruling powers attempt to impose unity on their citizenry (think here of the failure of Meech Lake, a metaphoric strategy to impose unity by the federal government, defeated by the power of the metonymic eagle feather in the hands of Elijah Harper, a First

Nations MLA in Manitoba, Riel's home place). Lyotard writes, "The narrative function is losing its functors, its great hero, its great dangers, its great voyages, its great goal. It is being dispersed in clouds of narrative language elements..." (xxiv). Canada, for Kroetsch, has become a place where the demise of meta-narratives has brought out the relevance of the marginal, the local, and the heteroglossia of texts that do not privilege master narratives. The issue of appropriation of an other's story through a literary work, which has stirred such controversy, is part of this mistrust of national unity and identity. *Unity and identity at whose expense?* is one of many questions being asked by writers who reject any definition of "Canadian" that cannot accommodate the multiplicity and plurality of voices, texts, and readers that do not merge into a unified whole.

8

While it is always dangerous to generalize, especially when one constructs a historical frame for a phenomenon, two books associated with Canadian "thematic criticism" both traced their lineage to Northrop Frye's account of the origin and substance of CanLit in his essay collection *The Bush Garden* (1971). The centralist bias of these studies was kept at bay, and never allowed to emerge as a constraint on the credibility of the thematic method.

In her introduction to *Survival* (1972), Margaret Atwood constructed a critical narrative in which a pronominal "I" had begun writing criticism after having undergone a subjective discovery. The "I" was projected through a personal voice that spoke out of a kind of messianic revelation: i.e., once "I" didn't realize such a thing as "Canadian" writing and culture existed, but now "I" do, but so few others do, so "I" have decided to write a "guide" to reading "Canadian" books; and because "I" am a living example of "Canadian," "I" can speak for the "we." In the assumption of a transparent shared "nation" of values, what was left unquestioned was the constituting "myth" of expansion through centralization which had excluded those who were other than British or European. Indeed, in *Survival*, many of these outsiders became the objects of categorization, never subjects who spoke out of their critical confinement.

D. G. Jones, in *Butterfly on Rock* (1970), shied away from the subjective "I" and gave the illusion of "national consciousness" through his liberal use of the communal "we," but he was even more determined than Atwood to possess space in this country through the master narrative of western expansion. So he began his introduction:

> Having reached the Pacific, Canadians have begun to turn back to themselves, to create... Canadian culture... more than ever before we have arrived at a point where we recognize, not only that the land is ours, but that we are the land's. (3)

Both Jones and Atwood moved easily from the personal to the national, and by resorting to "themes" rather than material texts, they could just as easily move from the particular to the general. Jones wrote:

> This book... is not primarily a survey, nor does it attempt to deal fully with any single author or work. Rather, by isolating certain themes and images it attempts to define more clearly some of the features that recur in the mind, the mirror of *our* imaginative life. (Italics added; 3)

Atwood, too, once she had established the tie between her subjectivity and her country, could propose a centralizing "theme"— her transcendental signified— to totalize the literary texts she had selected as representative. And like Jones, she too held the positivist belief that things are subordinate to ideas and systems. So she could argue:

> I'd like to begin with a sweeping generalization and argue that every country or culture has a single unifying and informing symbol at its core...

The symbol, then— be it word, phrase, idea, image, or all of these— functions like a system of beliefs (it *is* a system of beliefs, though not always a formal one) which holds the country together and helps the people in it to co-operate for common ends. (31)

For "Canada" this symbol was "survival," and this thematic centre allowed the writer of *Survival* to string numerous books on a critical clothesline without ever approaching them as texts whose significance depends very much on the contextual constraints— the social, cultural, ethnic, and historical constraints— which limit both writer and reader, including the language within which the exchange between them occurs.

9

My comments are not only meant to show up the limits of thematic criticism. On the contrary, the books by Jones and Atwood, though reductive to an extreme, are intellectually stimulating, and there is no doubt that they were written out of a genuine passion to construct a cohesive rationale for CanLit that could help unify the disparate and otherwise chaotic spread of titles. A whole generation of university students have been introduced to "Canadian" writing through their books. Indeed, the danger may reside in the illusion they, and similar "guides," created of authority and the bibliographic security of apparent canonization.

What is not sufficiently emphasized is that Atwood and Jones, while using thematic criticism, have advanced and made academically acceptable a platonic disregard for the materiality of texts. They have fostered and re-inforced a reading habit that approaches texts as if they are merely the transparent reflection of themes and images under the umbrella of some "national mind." The leap from the phenomenality of the particular— the text as specific in its materiality— to the generality of theme is a manoeuvre that could succeed only by eliminating multiciplicity and difference. It was, finally, a critical strategy that ignored the limits of a reader whose subjectivity is saturated by the bias of colonial history.

To summarize briefly, then, the use of theme as a critical device displaying the apparent unity, or the sameness, of a diversity of works, provided a methodological tool for a nationalist criticism, and perhaps it was useful in a specific phase of Canadian literature. What contaminated the charm of generality, however, was the activity of writing itself— an activity that situates itself at the intersection of the finite self (which should include the critic who is him/herself mortal) and contemporary history. It was the removal of the critical "I" from historic exigencies that made the demise of thematic criticism with its nationalist objective an inevitability— which is not to say, of course, that thematic criticism is not alive and well in many Canadian classrooms and critical journals.

As an antidote to the temptation of national identity in the 1960s and early 1970s, there was, again, the post-thematic reader, Robert Kroetsch— a kind of centralist drop-out— who revelled in the act of falling back into the indeterminate zones of "borders," as he wrote in his 1985 essay: "The centre does not hold. The margin, the periphery, the edge, now, is the exciting and dangerous boundary where silence and sound meet. It is where the action is" (23).

10

The Kroetchean alternative is evident in those contemporary texts that undermine generic boundaries and classifications, and which challenge the readability of consumable books where form is merely the beast of burden carrying its load of goods to the reader. The writing that is struggling to retain the on-going tension of that interface between subjectivity and history has become, to borrow from Julia Kristeva's *Desire in Language*, "the ridge where the historical becoming of the subject is affirmed..." (97-98).

Such writing proposes the critically challenging notion of an unreadable text that explodes the assumption that reading is simply the recuperation of a referential signified. It is writing that Steve McCaffery, in *North of Intention*, sees as "a departure from consumption to production, presenting the domain of its own interior, interacting elements (Barthes' 'magic of the signifiers') as the networks and circuits of an ultimately intractible and untotalized meaning" (143).

II

In the late 1940s, while Northrop Frye evoked the fearful "primeval lawlessness and moral nihilism" (146) of Canadian nature and constructed his master narrative of colonization, the dualistic model of the struggle between culture and nature, one writer was working in an opposite direction: Sheila Watson, born in New Westminster, BC, and self-educated in the modernism of Wyndham Lewis, Gertrude Stein, James Joyce, and Ezra Pound, was literally writing her way through the deracinated cultural condition of her country. The distances she had to cover in her poetics can be glimpsed in comments from a rare interview in *Quill and Quire* by George Melnyk.

Watson mentions two works, *The Double Hook*, and a previous manuscript of a novel written in the 1930s, *Deep Hollow Creek* (finally published in 1992). The earlier work was, for Watson, a "failed" text because it was governed by the conventions of referentiality in "realist" novels where the narrator is an "external observer" removed from the "immediacy of the experience." So Watson "decided to take narrators out of my writing altogether. That threw me into the dramatic dialogue form of *Double Hook*" (15). And it also threw her into the realm of a textuality that restricts authorial intention by infusing writing with the element of compositional time. Form is no longer transcendent but transient, i.e., governed by the immediacy of the blank page and the ritual framing of language which becomes the physicality of the book.

Watson describes the narrative texture resulting from the removal of the narrator's controlling perspective:

> What I tried to get is the tension between the characters which created space, an environment that operated on their lives. That emotional environment is as much a part of their lives as anything else. So is the verbal climate in which they live. Your environment is the language in which you live. Words aren't neutral like magnetic tape. They create the qualities of an experience. (15)

What amazed the young poet bpNichol about *The Double Hook* when he accidentally found it in the Salvation Army book bin in Winnipeg in 1965— he would have been 21 years old then— was the texture of its prose. The opening words, each word, as word, appearing on the space of the page, together working their way down the page, the narrative constructed as a "concrete" text, through the linguistic frame of the trickster coyote whose speech enacts the opacity of writing:

> In the folds of the hills
>
> under Coyote's eye
>
> lived

For bpNichol the writing discovered in the throwaway bin proposed a counter-tradition to the dis-taste for formal disturbances and opacities in mainstream Canadian writing. *The Double Hook* declared itself as a text written out of a recognition that language and subjectivity are closely aligned. "Your environment is the language in which you live." By de-throning the narrator of her work, Watson in this sense enacted the "death" of the author as a unifying centre and in "its" place created the writer writing and being written by the text.

Watson pointed bpNichol towards the notion of writing writing, a Canadian example of how it could be done.

Watson was completing the manuscript of *The Double Hook* in 1954, though its beginnings can be traced back to the late 1940s, and perhaps even to the early 1940s. However, it took another five years for the manuscript to be accepted (there were many rejections) and published in 1959, by McClelland and Stewart. F.T. Flahiff, in his Afterword to the most recent edition of the novel, 1989, comments on the first review in the *Globe & Mail*, May 16, 1959, with the crass title, "Left Hook, Right Hook, KO!" The novel is "obscure," "eccentric," "difficult," "permeated by an odd atmosphere of unreality," and "it cannot be described as entertainment in any sense of the word" (119-120). The first critical readers of the novel, working out of the thematic mode, were intent on making its textuality transparent to a central theme, e.g., Margot Northey read the novel as a Christian parable (1976) and Beverley Mitchell, applying Frye's theories, located its real "meaning" in its biblical allusions (1973), and there were other examples of such referential readings, collected by editor George Bowering in *Sheila Watson and* The Double Hook (1985). In his "Afterword," Bowering points to the effect of Watson's radical narrative strategies: "Mrs. Watson disrupted the 1959 reader's reading habits, so that he was made aware almost of a kind of threat, of at least a laughter beyond the reach of the reading lamp" (189).

12

I would conjecture that the need for the security of referentiality and the legitimation of a literary work through extra-textual sources, based on the assumption that meaning is locatable as an entity separable from the text's specificity, comes out of a deep uneasiness in western protestant society with the experience of language as material— Daphne Marlatt's "what matters"— language that is other than reasonable, decodable, merely a vehicle of communication— language as "a living body we enter at birth" (45) and that surrounds the transiency of the daily. Transparency of meaning in the reading act upholds the humanist illusion that books can be consumed, that the "signified" is valued over the material "signifier," that consciousness can absorb objects, in the same way that technological form consumes the environment. This is ostensibly for the sake of species "survival," but the obverse is that such power is a way to erase— and ward off— the possibility of meaning's disintegration, of meaning's meaninglessness, and of language prior to rationality. Language, in the domain of literature, is "no longer communication," as Kristeva says, but "transformative, or even mortal, for the 'I' as well as for the 'other'..."(103).

In writing as text, the contemporary moment becomes the transitional site where history and the finite "i" intersect. It is the desire to recuperate the value of the everyday, the quotidian life where the doubles, theory and practice, writing and reading, thinking and activity, are intertwined, or entwined, twinned. Like the double helix of the DNA? One might hope so.

Paul de Man reminds us:

> In the everyday language of communication, there is no a priori privileged position of sign over meaning or of meaning over sign; the act of interpretation will always again have to establish this relation for the particular case at hand. The interpretation of everyday language is a Sisyphean task, a task without end and without progress... (11)

Editing in a Canadian context, then, is itself bound up in the problem of representing the contemporary, the "present," which appears and disappears in the flickering sights, sounds, and silences of language. The contemporary is never at rest, and never visible in a stability of relationships, but it is what inaugurates the desire for freedom from the tyranny of imposed systems of thought. Within its immediacy, the relationship between signifier and signified is always indeterminate and fluctuating; perspectives are always multiple, with

there is no right answer

no centralizing vanishing point; the marginal translates into a variety of localisms; and writing— literature— survives as a mode of critical attention.

Here, at this (hypothetical) bend in the making of contemporary Canadian writing, one would want to start a journal, as a critical and creative act, to map this shifting terrain, not as a territory, but as a (future) place, a texual place where literary and cultural conversations can perhaps begin.

Inter-Face:
Roy Kiyooka's Writing
A Commentary/Interview

On the road map of designated sites along the transCanada canonical way, there won't (likely) be a sign for the writer-Kiyooka, even though the painter-Kiyooka has now been inscribed in Canadian art history. Even that latter endorsement, however, is often without recognition of the multi-disciplinary stance which, to a handful, has taken on a certain legendary glow over the years. The sign "Kiyooka" is not singular but plural— many "Kiyookas" enacting various phases of the imagination— as painter, as sculptor, as photographer, as film-maker, as musician, as poet and writer. As poet and writer, Kiyooka produced a number of stunning books— from his first, *Kyoto Airs* (Periwinkle Press, 1964) to *Nevertheless These Eyes* (Coach House, 1967), *StoneDGloves* (Coach House, 1970), *Transcanada Letters* (Talonbooks, 1975), *The Fountainebleau Dream Machine* (Coach House, 1977) and most recently, *Pear Tree Pomes* (Coach House, 1987)— all of which, in form or content or both, project the interface between the necessities driving the artist and the necessities driving the writer. Such a fined-tuned, chiasmatic relationship between two domains of the imagination is a rare achievement in contemporary Canadian writing, yet, except for a few sideways glances in his direction, Kiyooka remains a neglected figure.

In part, the dazzling plurality of Kiyooka's engagement of diverse artistic media may have made him a slippery writer to comprehend, especially because his texts resist the formal expectations of anglocentric Canadian taste by undermining the customary lyric stance of much canonical poetry. More tellingly, though, the arbiters of critical standards continue, by and large, to inhabit a eurocentric historic tunnel which allows no space for "Asian Canadian," and other non-white, writers.[1] This cultural and "race" bias of the Canadian literary establishment has been a roadblock for Kiyooka, but it did not prevent him from producing a number of texts that outshine, through sheer formal accomplishment, so much of what is considered dominant Canadian poetry. A text like *StoneDGloves* is still a rarity.

The act of writing— and the determination to shape language into articulation— was a central and abiding preoccupation for Kiyooka, more so because of his background. From childhood on, language, both spoken and written, was the vital and irresistible material for exploring and graphing the bilingual conditions of his own upbringing in the shadow of a hegemonic WASP society. Like those other minorities, in like conditions, he had his mother tongue, Japanese, the familial language of childhood and family, overlaid by the English language of the anglo-mainstream. Learning "english," then, was tied to the need to be accepted and the pressure to conform, i.e., tied to the erasure of the specific and the local. For the young Kiyooka, growing up in east Calgary in the 1930s, becoming adept in the use of "english" was a matter of survival in a predominantly white world: "Oh yeah, to me it had to do with surviving— survival. At some level I needed to be able to come to an articulateness by which I could stand in this world of literate people, and hold my own. I had that as an actual drive" (Miki, "Roy Kiyooka" 59). This drive placed him in that paradoxical but generative situation of having to construct a subjectivity through what Kiyooka has deemed an "inglish" inflected by the memory of speaking his mother tongue.[2] Kiyooka's "inglish," in turn, transformed the push toward literacy into a desire for literature, for writing as a means of coming "to an articulateness" in social spaces where he had literally to inscribe himself— as if from scratch.

It was George Bowering, in a discussion of Kiyooka's writing, who foregrounded "his accuracy. Accuracy of perception & accuracy of rendering it" ("Roy Kiyooka's Poetry" np). In the midst of a cultural morass of stale perceptual habits, where language and thinking retreat into conformism, the kind of accuracy found in Kiyooka's writing is a gift. It is the sign of an alert intelligence that refuses the already categorized, the already catalogued. The surfaces of his words are

stripped of the verbiage, and the whole attention is drawn to the
internal necessity of writing as articulation— park all that phony
"poetic" language outside. So we read in *Kyoto Airs*, the product of
Kiyooka's 1963 trip to Japan and his first meeting with Mariko, a sister
who had been separated from the family:

> the song is
> about tortoise
>
> and not the hare

In Kiyooka's writing, there is no headlong rushing to get to the
goal-line of meaning. Each word, like each stone in the "rock garden"
at Ryoanji in Kyoto, has its own weight in a syntax of measure enacting
the rhythms of daily experience in all its transiency and evanescence,
off the beaten path where the mundane, that darkest and most invisible
of phenomena, resides. The warp and woof of that insistence textures
all of Kiyooka's work and gives a sheen to the forms his "inglish" takes
on the written page. In a letter/text written to *The Capilano Review*,
Kiyooka pointed to the ongoing participation between the "i" and the
contexts of its movements—

> a
> sustaining vision of
> the intricate palimpsest-of-relationships
> supporting every living/dying
> thing ought to inform an enlightened polis:
> to imagine oneself interacting
> with everything (imaginable) at a strategic
> moment: pen, brush, spear to hand
> is simply what it's always been about
> ("Notes Toward" 80)

Certainly, the "ought to form" implies an awareness of failure in the body politic, of a lack of care for "every living/dying thing," at the tail end of which appear those "ghost-writers paid to pump platitudes into politics" ("Notes Toward" 82).

Kiyooka's life project was to live, as intensely as possible, in relation to what was immediate and near at hand— and to articulate that intimacy in his art and writing. So he commented in an interview for *Roy K. Kiyooka: 25 Years* (1975), the catalogue for a major exhibit at the Vancouver Art Gallery:

> Gertrude Stein in one of her many books sez, 'The business of art is to live in the *complete actual present*, that is the complete actual present, and to express that complete actual present.' If we take our cue from her words, the ones i've italicized, the impossible answers should be right under my nose. ("Intersection" np)

In the same interview, when asked to locate the beginning of his artistic life, Kiyooka could find no origin in memory. It had always been there, at the edge of his shifting perceptions; frame after frame of childhood and early adolescence was imbued with the power and reach of the imagination, of the image-making capacity spilling out in all directions. There was, nevertheless, out of that unrecoverable beginning, a later bifurcation into the attraction of image and the struggle for voice, i.e., a doubling into the movement towards both art and writing as extensions of the lived moment. "Call it inter-face. Painting gave me a face, writing, a voice; but its not a matter of choosing. Its more like fate" ("Intersection" np).

"Inter-face" is a term that conceptualizes the "crossing over" zone between the necessities driving the artist and the necessities driving the writer. It is here, in this transitional space, that the imagination of Kiyooka resides. In the pragmatics of survival as one of a beleaguered minority, though, writing also became the most effective mode of articulating the personal, familial, and communal conditions of being Japanese Canadian.

□

Roy Kenzie Kiyooka was born on January 18, 1926, in Moose Jaw, Saskatchewan, but his earliest retrieved memories of the restless childhood "i" forming belong to the sidestreets and lanes of his neighbourhood in east Calgary during the 1930s. Kiyooka is nisei, the second generation, Canadian-born progeny of the issei, the first generation, immigrant parents. He was the third of six children born to Harry Shigekiyo and Mary Kiyoshi Kiyooka, who ran a vegetable stand in a multi-ethnic city market. The young Roy quickly developed resources to fend for himself in the anglophone milieu of the majority, his native tongue sealed in the confines of the familial and internalized by the racism dominant in his society. The movement between those two "worlds" may have eventually transformed into a workable dialectic— given an uninterrupted developmental process— but one event would intervene to radically transform the shape of Kiyooka's life: the mass uprooting of Japanese Canadians in 1942.

The Kiyooka family, living in Calgary, were not among the 23,000 Japanese Canadians— 95% of the whole Japanese Canadian population in Canada— expelled from the "protected area" 100 miles from the west coast. The political wave of racism, however, reached beyond BC and affected Japanese Canadians all across Canada. Even those living far from the coast were branded "enemy alien" and, overnight, found themselves the target of bigots who took advantage of the wartime crisis to press for the removal of Japanese Canadians from BC and who passed the Orders in Council to prevent them from moving back.

In casual conversation outside the parameter of this interview, Kiyooka suddenly recalled the personal impact of the bombing of Pearl Harbor on December 7, 1941— an event which abruptly ended his schooling, his adolescence, and thrust his family into a rootless turmoil:

I was three months into my tenth grade at Western Canada High School. I heard of Pearl Harbor, after we had been playing hockey down at the city dump, and the bunch of us had come back and gone to a corner grocery store called Switzer's. It was a soda bar, and sold fruits, vegetables and things on the side. We sat there and had Coke, and they had their radio on with this sputtering voice, hysterical almost. That was the first time I heard it. Up until that moment it never meant anything to me, the war, in a curious way, because we only had access to it by radio and newspaper.

Then I remember going to my social studies high school class, just following Pearl Harbor, and there was a German kid in the class who up to that point I only knew of— I was not friends with. He came up to me, we were sitting at the back of the class, and said, do you know what happened yesterday? I told him I had heard about it, but he made it 'real' only to me because he had heard about it and, of course, the German in him spoke to who was 'obviously' one of the Allies.

Kiyooka's family life swiftly disintegrated in early 1942. His father, and older brother, George, who both worked for a hotel, lost their jobs, as did other Japanese Canadians in Calgary. With no means of income, the Kiyooka family moved to Opal, Alberta, a small Ukrainian town where they were able to live by farm work.

The traumatic experience of being branded "enemy alien," and having his canuck birthright erased, had a profound impact on the imagination of the young Kiyooka. As he recalled, writing to the Japanese Canadian Redress Secretariat, the government office established after the Japanese Canadian Redress Settlement on September 22, 1988, to receive applications for individual compensation:

In and through all the ideological strife we avidly attended via the local paper and the radio a small 'i' felt as if a punitive fist kept clenching and unclenching behind my back but each time I turned to catch it flexing it would disappear into the unlit corners of our small log house. ("Dear Lucy Fumi" 125)

The permanent disruption of his public-school education and the radical estrangement from the country of his birth became two strands of a founding moment that later conditioned his writing. From 1942 to 1946, the urban-bred kid was initiated into the physicality of farm life:

I milked the cows churned the cream fed groomed and harnessed the horses rode the plough walked behind the disc and harrow cut each winter's supply of wood and hauled it home from the govt. wood lot. I helped birth pigs and calves and I helped the hired stallion hump our mares each spring. ("Dear Lucy Fumi" 125)

This exile from normal life, though on the surface a retreat from overt racial violence, was all the more painful because of his older sister, Mariko, born in Japan and living there, who wrote "to tell about her appalling hardships. And I clearly recall how those precious letters had been slit and the contents scrutinized and stamped by a nameless Censor" ("Dear Lucy Fumi" 125).

Immediately after the war, Kiyooka entered art school, and his life in art and writing began to take root. It would be during the crucial 18-year period from 1946 to 1964 (the year *Kyoto Airs* was published) that the transformation from novice to artist and writer occurred.

□

On April 9, 1991, we talked in Kiyooka's house on Keefer Street, in Vancouver's Chinatown. We began by addressing the place of writing in his life, especially during his beginnings as an artist.

Miki: Roy, in the late 1950s and early 1960s you were working primarily as an artist, and didn't think of yourself as a writer.

Kiyooka: I didn't think of myself as a writer until *Kyoto Airs*— which was not my first writing, but it was the first writing that I felt was adequate. It got through to something in terms of language. In retrospect it seems comparatively simple-minded, but it took a lot for me to get there. So with *Kyoto Airs* I took on the notion that I could potentially be a writer of some sort, and from that point on, the writing activity, though it went on parallel in the 1960s with other things, started taking over in actual fact. That's what started happening, though I had no poetics of any sort.

M: Was that sequence of poems an attempt to clarify or articulate something in your experience that was only available in words, and on the printed page?

K: Well, I'll have to do some groping in this area, but— let's see now, one previous writing, from the mid-1950s when I was in Mexico, is actually my first writing in a way. I put it together as a lecture when I came up from San Miguel to teach at Regina College. The Mexican experience was very vivid in my mind at that point and I wanted to see if I could grasp what it was essentially about in some way that was speakable. That's the first writing actually, and it was given as a lecture. I still have it.

M: Did you see yourself then as an artist who perhaps might write?

K: Yes, oh, yes, because I had read an awful lot of writing by artists, all down through the years. That gets into, for instance, *The Fountain-*

ebleau Dream Machine; one of the poems that quotes Delacroix goes directly back to those years when I was reading the literature of artists. I was fascinated by those artists who wrote. Some part of me, of course, had got bored with reading the art historian's more formal approach to an artist— and it still does that to me, in terms of the immediacy of art. I mean, an art historian's perspective can be profound, but it's always hindsight, and never relative to a one-to-one experience of looking at something intimately. I remember reading Michelangelo's sonnets. I was profoundly moved by those!

☐

As luck would have it, soon after beginning Kyoto Airs *while in Japan, Kiyooka returned to Vancouver just in time to catch the influential 1963 Poetry Conference at the University of British Columbia, organized by Warren Tallman, which introduced the New American Poetics to the Canadian west coast. Charles Olson, Robert Duncan, and Robert Creeley were there, as well as Allen Ginsberg, Denise Levertov, and Margaret Avison, plus numerous other writers, local and from the US. At the time Kiyooka was on faculty at the downtown Vancouver School of Art (now the Emily Carr Institute of Art and Design).*

K: I had organized a series of poetry readings at Emily Carr, which as far as I know, were among the first public readings any member of the *Tish* group had given at that point. George [Bowering] was a participant in it, and Daphne [Marlatt] had read there. What is curious about this is that I had an active interest in poetry then, but no abstract sense of language as something that could be studied. I didn't have that, but I had been an active reader, and some part of me, even then, just loved to hear poetry live.

M: What kind of poetics did the conference appear to offer you?

K: One of the things I found amazing is how utterly particular the articulation of each of the guys that were there was. It seemed to me that here was language in the works, as it were— I mean the world that Allen, or Olson, or Creeley, or any of the others, articulated, or attempted to. It was the peculiarities of their speech that I was really fascinated by.

M: That's a weird word to use— "peculiarities." They were Americans, or speaking American, weren't they?

K: Yes, I know, but it didn't sound like anything that I knew as English, as a Canadian English. It definitely didn't have that at all, so that was fascinating.

M: You mentioned being in Japan before the conference.

K: Allen Ginsberg and I were both in Japan immediately previous, in June. He had been on his India trip and had come back slowly through southwest Asia and ended up in Japan. He was already a kind of a cult figure among the speedy Japanese kids. And Gary Snyder and Joanne [Kyger] were ensconced in a little house attached to Daitokuji Temple.

M: You saw them there, too?

K: Yes.

M: How long were you in Japan?

K: That summer I was there for seven weeks. So Allen ended up there, and he was going to Vancouver because he was invited to the poetry conference. I had to come back because of family, teaching, and one thing or another. We came back 48 hours before the conference.

M: So you were influenced by the new American poetics in a very direct, personal sense?

K: Oh, yes. There was Cid Corman, in 1963 in Kyoto. He'd already been in Japan a few years at this point, so I saw quite a bit of him, and then as now, Cid's a great talker. He can talk your ear off.

M: Was this influence affecting your work as an artist?

K: No.

M: There was a clear division?

K: Oh, yes. Basically it comes down to this: the syntax of colour, which is what painting is about, can't be accessed through language, not really. Theoretically it can be talked about, but the experience of painting and the use of colour is much closer to the experience of reading poetry, rather than writing it, because the language has to be performed. That's what you do when you paint, except the medium of your performance is colour— and I don't mean colour towards a representational end, like the colour of a hat. No amount of the study of language gives anybody access to that. For me it doesn't overlap, and it's quite clear to me why because, whereas writers certainly with frequency write *about* painting and *about* painters, I see the writer being given ostensibly a subject matter around which he can create an articulation. But paint as paint, or colour as colour, for the painter— it has to be seamless, it is silent, it has no language of a linguistic sort by which you can define its parameters. Quantities and qualities are entirely measured through the eye.

M: So it's of another order?

K: Well, it's maximized, of course, in that it's older than language. I think homo sapiens in prehistory inscribed an image before they spoke one. That's my thought. It's not difficult for a painter to live without language.

M: Why, then, did you need to write?

K: I wanted to claim some kind of articulation for myself. That's what it really meant.

M: Perhaps this desire to articulate was a way of constructing for yourself a verbal context to understand your practice— or perhaps your "self," maybe that was more important?

K: Well, that's closer to it.

M: Your "self" was more important, so that precedes. What I'm trying to say, Roy, is that you project, just as we're talking, someone who understands that there's a measure in art which is non-verbal— other than language— and it's obviously something that you consider a ground. As you said, it's prior to speech.

K: But it's also for me, the writer, prior to my speech, my language. Modes of perception that for me occur in language, and the way I say things, came about in the years that I was a painter, simply because of the kind of attention a painter gives to things. A painter will look at this [points to the teapot on the table], and not a word will pass between you and him, but for him, he can see the syntax of colour in his mind's eye, and it's not anything like that simple-minded notion of representation, of making it look like a teapot, or anything like that, because one knows it's an artifice as soon as you take up colour and start putting it down on the surface.

M: Perhaps this same kind of thing occurs in writing, where language takes on its own materiality and surfaces?

K: Yes, that's how I understand the "language poets," in a way. They get hooked into the language and it almost fills a void— it moves them.

M: Couldn't we take that further? It seems to me that writing has clearly become more and more a part of your daily life, as you get older and accrue more experience. You're doing a lot of various types of texts right now— poems, diaries, letters, fiction, even making your own books.

K: I'll tell you what though, Roy— this is going to be a truncation, but I have come to a place where I want to walk away from language again.

M: Right at this moment?

K: No, within the next year or two. Something tells me, though I'll go on writing, that I think I've proven to myself that I had a writing to accomplish, and it had to do with being a Japanese Canadian. I didn't know this at the time I wrote *Kyoto Airs*.

M: That's interesting.

K: *Kyoto Airs* is my first book, and it's about Japan; the first long piece in *Transcanada Letters* is about Japan, and it's prefaced by the photograph of my grandfather with my mother. So all my texts have started in Japan. I don't know why that is so but that's true.

M: Yes, there's a lot of work that's written in Japan.

K: Sure, and I can still ask myself why, with the exception of a very few people in the Japanese Canadian community of my generation, they haven't had even the desire or the inclination to work to that kind of articulation. I would say that most nisei are therefore, as they tend to get characterized anyhow, comparatively anonymous. You know, their own discretions, and one thing or another.

M: They haven't made a public stance within language. There have been artists but writing makes a different demand.

K: Who is there? There are more writers when they get to be your age, and younger, because the ground for speaking oneself has been in some ways articulated and one can come into it, and simply do it. I feel that I was given a tract of land that had to be cleared, for myself in the first instance, but for a generation in another instance.

M: Can you talk about the constrictions that were holding the nisei psyche back from language?

K: The only thing I knew was that here was a whole generation of us of whom I knew very very little in actual fact, except for those who were immediately around me. The *New Canadian* was for many years the only community newspaper, and what I knew of my fellow nisei I only knew in and through that kind of source. I know their silence, I had that in me. It was a feeling of something repressive, that one couldn't finger, and something very Japanese about being reticent about "self."

M: What you're saying is that it was also difficult to say whether the reticence was a prison, or whether it was a sense of experience that you lived with— i.e., whether you're at ease with the reticence, or you're uneasy thinking, I'm being reticent right now when I should be saying something or doing something in language, and putting myself in that form so that I can be heard, or at least be challenged, or I can challenge. Is that the kind of situation you're talking about?

K: Yes, in a way. Of course, the other thing here is that I did have a sense, when I was quite young, that to survive in this culture was essentially a quest for language as the modality of power about which you could be present in the world. I had a sense of that quite early, through my teachers, and those I knew as friends who were articulate. I had a very lovely Jewish boy in my life, David Sidorski. He was a genius, an amazingly brilliant kid. He had a sister who was a graduate in mathematics from the University of Alberta, and though he was ten to twelve years younger, there he was already, by the time we were in grade eight, completely fluent in trigonometry. But he wore this with a lot of grace. We, his friends, thought of the Sidorskis as that kind of very scholarly inclined Jewish family, though we didn't know what their scholarship consisted of. That was there as a model— there were those kinds of little things. And my own parents were, for their own generation, educated people. My mother and dad both finished high school— this would be at the turn of the century. Dad, in fact, came over to North America with the intent of going on to study. It never worked out for him, but he was always a bookish person himself. He was among the very few issei that I knew who was an avid reader. But he never spoke of these things, you know what I mean.

M: So you were aware of a barrier, something that had to be overcome. The English language was itself a system of power, and you had to gain access to the world through that language.

K: I was born into the final fade-out of Victorian English colonial attitudes. They persist to this day, but I'm talking of the fade-out of the glorious kind of thing, because of course all my models around me in Calgary at that time were white Anglo-Saxon protestant (WASP), all my school teachers were, and visiting dignitaries— and I could clearly see they all talked in a kind of a fancy way, and that the quality of their speech was ingratiating or persuasive or meant to make a point.

M: All the rhetorical forms they had down, and what were you coming out of, a street language?

K: Sure, a street language. It was a ghetto: Jewish, Hungarian, Chinese, East Indian, and Native Indian. That was the kind of area it was, at that time.

M: All of you were marginalized.

K: We were all immigrants, or immigrants' children.

M: In a talk you gave in Seattle you said you can see yourself as "a white anglo saxon protestant with a cleft tongue" ("We Asian North Americanos" 117). I thought, that's a strange way of putting it. I would never see myself as a white Anglo-Saxon protestant. I've been imbued with the values of that world, and we've had to go through the hoops to survive in that world, but I never thought that I was *of* it. I just figured I had to get *through* it. Anyway, the notion of "cleft tongue" is very intriguing. It suggests a kind of perversity within the form—

K: Oh, yes—

M: — perverse not in an immoral sense but as a disruptive force. You upset language, so that once you gain access to it you can do things with language that can open up your own experience of language.

This is what I'm hearing in so much of your recent writing, say in the last ten years, which especially comes through in *Pear Tree Pomes* where it reaches an incredible kind of delicacy. The street language now has this beautiful form.

K: I haven't the same kind of scholarly curiosity about the sources of my own things. I know what they are intuitively, but my own notion of how all these things occur in time is really, I would call, osmotic.

M: It just sort of filters into you?

K: Yes, yes, yes... because not being really a child of academia in any way, after all I didn't get past grade ten, I was never particularly beholden to them.

M: But you do have a strong sense of your own articulation within the language.

K: Yes, I do. I mean, one has been published enough now to be able to get words down, and say, hey, there they are out in the world. Sometimes I say to myself, that's just as good as so and so's, and other times I say, oh god they're terrible. Having them out in the world is an awful thing! I don't think I'll ever get over that. I have none of the Bowering-like confidence in my writings, not finally, no, I don't. I know the other necessity of having done them, and to put something to myself that was even pursued, in many ways, naively.

M: I'd like to push that further. You mentioned that, being Japanese Canadian, writing took on a certain importance. Language was more important for that side of your experience— so there was the need to construct some understanding of that part of your life.

K: My first public, and it has always been true for me, has always been my family. I've got a large family, and in terms of Japanese Canadians, it's quite exceptional because there are three artists in our family. So the family has always been the first public, and that's true in both ways, because I see myself as being in my particular way a voice for them, my three sisters who are voiceless, and my brothers are not necessarily so, but they are not literary people, so that there's no questing on their part for recognition through literature. But I myself have always felt that somehow, and my mother plays a key role here— to think that if my life had taken a slightly different turn when I was younger I could have grown up and learned to read and write Japanese as fluently as English, but that never occurred. Then when I did become a writer, I found myself writing in a language my mother cannot read. So here I have written all these things, and a lot of it is about her. She only knows this by one of her children who, having read the text, would explain it to her, but she cannot read it. If you grow up in that kind of "inter-face," it's very poignant, because not to have been able to write in Japanese is to never have been able to have demonstrated to my mother that... well—

M: In a sense your texts are sealed off from her in a very immediate, fundamental way, yet she recognizes that the language in those works is still an extension of your familial experience, though now it's been translated into this form, in English.

K: Yes, so there is all that kind of stuff.

M: Do you feel that you've worked your way through all that?

K: Oh, yes, I do. From now on, I don't have to write anything to prove anything to myself.

M: Where do you think this— not a comfort, or anything like that, but a feeling of being able to work within the language— started to happen?

K: Well, starting from nothing, with only what I had an intuitive grasp on, I had to claim every inch of the language that I've come to, literally syllable by syllable. So I feel that the 20-year stretch that I've given myself over to writing and photography has been an initiation, and of course the curious thing about a person like myself is that it has been a self initiation. No one could initiate these things for me.

M: You're saying that you had to claim each thing as you went along.

K: Yes, one has the authorial look of what gets published, but if you're like me, you know how vulnerable you are in terms of what it costs you to be able to say what you have been able to say, and knowing that once you go through that ground you never look back. You can't, because it was sort of crawled over.

M: Do you have any sense of bitterness over that?

K: Oh, no, because I feel that that has been the name of what my life has been about as an artist— that growing up in this country and being beholden to the white culture, its institutions, I have nonetheless grown up athwarted. Oh, yes, I have.

M: "Athwarted" is an interesting word. What do you mean by that?

K: You are of it, and you are not, and you know that very clearly. See, what you can do in academic life— I know only a small handful of my generation who came to any real excellence in academic life. For one reason, I'm a member of the 1950s in the years following the war, and the taint of racism was still left. Academic life was not really a choice for most nisei, not really. There was an implicit racism that came out of the war that affected white Anglo-Saxon academic life, and I think there was a number of casualties among nisei whose lives never reached any fruition because of that. But be that as it may, I came through the back door anyhow. I didn't finish high school. I had no degree. I got into teaching because in the 1950s there were only two institutions in the whole of Canada in which you could get a BFA degree. It wasn't until the 1960s that the whole flourish into the arts opened out, and all these degrees of all sorts came into being. But in the 1950s, no, they were barely inscribed, so any institution that had an art department, or was thinking of opening one, didn't have a body of university-trained artist/historians to draw upon. The job pool—there wasn't one. The only ones that were around were people like me who had gone to art schools, and had excelled in that. The whole notion of what was lacking academically was put aside. That's how I came into it. I would have never been there otherwise. I had nothing to qualify me. When I came into it, the first years of teaching were amazingly intent because I didn't even know what I was about!

M: So you were learning day by day.

K: Oh, yes!

M: The idea of being an apprentice and working your way through, and finding yourself now actually teaching others, i.e., telling others how to do it, must have been a very strange thing— resistance to power, eh?

K: Well, even until last week, when I gave my last lectures, I still had that feeling. I mentioned it to one of my groups, my graduate class, I said I feel quite subversive standing in front of you, and I tell them why. Here they are trying to get straight As and be worthwhile candidates for the Master's program, and I said, I don't even have a degree, you're all better educated than I am— what are we doing here together? But, of course, I have a terrific advantage because I've come to pedagogy largely through practice. Everything that I can teach I know— I have done.

M: You matured in a cultural time-period in this country when things were opening up, right?

K: A great period. I would not like to come into maturation in the 1980s or 1990s. I think it's a shitty period, in that way. A traffic jam. There must be 10,000 painters and 15,000 poets in this country now. In those days, no. I mean, what was Prairies writing in the 1950s? Sinclair Ross' *As for Me and My House*. There were a few texts—

Frederick Grove. I came to the possibility of the arts in this country at a great moment, because it was uninscribed.

M: Out of curiosity— I remember talking to you years ago, and you said you never ever thought of yourself as a "Japanese Canadian writer," that term didn't mean much, but that you are a writer who is Japanese Canadian. There weren't non-anglo writers who were getting any attention. If they were, they just fell into narrow ethnic categories, and a lot of the stuff they were writing maybe wasn't that interesting, because they were working only with content. But you were always doing things in your writing— the formal quality of your writing had strong influences from your painterly side, especially in the way your texts were constructed, in their form, the "objective" quality of your books and your language, and the way you did things with the page. Nobody was paying any attention to that.

K: I'm the kind of artist that any culture finds very difficult to deal with, because I don't feel beholden to any school. I don't even feel beholden to my own generation, actually; most of my generation are just a bunch of old fogies. I can't even stand them! And because I've been multi-disciplinary, most of my life, people don't know how to get a handle on me. I think the most critical thing about my activity is the inter-face between myself as a painter and myself as a language artificer. But what has to be understood is how the two inform each other. There are any number of people who are terrific writers and who even write about painting, but I don't feel that their writing per se is *informed* by painting, a prolonged study of painting as such, but everything I do is. It can't be otherwise.

M: Can you explain that inter-face?

K: It's a mode of attention— that's how I see it as. I don't see the attention to language, sitting down to my computer, as being different in kind from my attention to paint when I was a painter. It's a form of being concentrated, open, and not too self-censorious in the beginning, you have to give yourself a chance— it's that kind of thing.

M: I notice that in your writing you place something concrete in front of you. It's either a form or an idea or an image, like the pear tree, and it remains there, so you can't just go "through" it—

K: No, I have to write myself through it sequentially.

M: That resembles the way a painter might work, in a serial form.

K: That's how I work as a photographer, too. I've always been a serial artist. My books are always whole entities. They're not made up of discrete things. That's how I photograph, too. I can hardly claim to be the kind of photographer for whom each photographed moment is an exemplary moment, and you frame it, and say, this is like a beautiful poem. No, I'm not that kind of photographer. I need a number of images to articulate what it's about, so I tend to work in sequences. That's so deeply a part of my practice that I don't even think of it. I painted that way, too.

M: When you talk about mode of attention, then, say you're in the initial stage of writing a text, you might have something that's grabbing your attention and holding you there, and you keep coming back to that, and work it through and see what occurs?

K: Yes. In the early years when I was a painter and trying to really make it in a big way, you could say that I was both product- and deadline-oriented. I had shows to get done, and other things. But because I had started teaching almost at the same time as I came to art, I discovered that teaching would bear the burden of my material needs. I would go on teaching and pay my way, and not expect my art to do so, and that was clear to me from the start. So I've never compromised that way, never have. And my writing is not product-oriented either. I never get anything done in less time than it actually takes to get done. It has nothing to do with meeting a deadline, because clearly that wasn't a venue that was open to me. There was too much involved in terms of self-education, all that kind of stuff, which you can only think of as an encumbrance. It's been part of my life, so I've never aspired to that other kind of thing, never have, really.

M: So the compositional time of a text might be a month, or it might be five years. If a text is not working itself, you can leave it and put it aside?

K: Oh, that's what I do.

M: Do you have a number of things going all the time?

K: Oh, sure, I've got six incomplete texts, and I pick them up every so often and I sit down to them, and if I can, I really get into them. That usually means a prolonged working period. I can't do anything over a weekend. I've never been able to do that kind of writing, never, because I don't have that kind of facility. I literally don't. It's always an anguish for me.

M: It's that mode of attention again— the thing holds you there, and you have to be authentic to that.

K: I haven't established any hierarchy of writing. There are people who are really facile, and they can say, oh well I'll do this this weekend, and then I'll do this the next. I've never had any of that— never, never, never had that.

M: Well, when do you know when a text is over with?

K: I abandon it. That's what I do, really.

M: You abandon it, then it's completed, well it's not completed, but it's over with.

K: Or it abandons me, either way.

M: That's an interesting notion of closure, abandonment.

K: Oh, I think if you were to ask a lot of writers, a number of them would tell you something like that. It's a kind of a wrestling with one's own psyche and with the language to come to some sort of clarity. But I always think of clarity as provisional anyhow. It's clear at this moment, but if I walk away from it and come back three months from now?

Painting has an element of that to it. What you do with painting is you work on it over a period of time, and it's always a movement towards clarity. Ideally one wants the utmost complexity, along with that clarity. A simple kind of clarity is very easy to come by. That's also a process that can only be realized in time. And coming to a painting, day by day, is like coming to a poem, day by day, in a way. You stand it up and you look at it, and you wonder what you've done— well, it's deeply intuition, yes that's what it really is. I think there are all sorts of levels of it that are subliminal.

NOTES

1. As noted above, *15 Canadian Poets X2* (1988), edited by Gary Geddes, is a good example of the canonization process, Canadian style. Of the thirty included, Michael Ondaatje is the only non-white poet. Looking at the poets' photographs on the cover, all arranged in alphabetical order, the reader ostensibly sees the "representative" poets of this country, but the excluded faces— the inter-faces, as it were— are missing.

2. In "Kumo/Cloud/s," for instance, Kiyooka uses this term in the following passage:

> i filled 3 notebooks full of
> an oftimes indecipherable 'romaji' alternating
> with pages of cluttered 'inglish' (*Pacific Windows* 260)

Kiyooka's "inglish," then, stands for his own transformation of anglocentric "english" into a language that could articulate the networks of a subjectivity nurtured in another mother tongue, in his case the vernacular, childhood "japanese" which he absorbed through his mother. For a more recent discussion of this term in Kiyooka's poetics, see my afterword to *Pacific Windows: Collected Poems of Roy K. Kiyooka* (1997), "Coruscations, Plangencies, and the Syllibant: After Words to Roy Kiyooka's *Pacific Windows*." For Kiyooka's ties to the "Japan" of his mother, Mary Kiyoshi Kiyooka, see *Mothertalk: Life Stories of Mary Kiyoshi Kiyooka* (1997), edited by Daphne Marlatt. Both works were in process when Roy Kiyooka died in early January, 1994.

"Turn This Page": Journaling bpNichol's *The Martyrology* & The Returns

If, in the poem, language becomes its own image, doesn't this mean
that poetic language is always second, secondary? According to the
common analysis, the image comes after the object. It is the object's
continuation. We see, then we imagine. After the object comes the
image. 'After' seems to indicate subordination. We really speak, then
we speak in our imagination, or we imagine ourselves speaking.
Wouldn't poetic language be the copy, the dim shadow, the transpo-
sition— in a space where the requirements of effectiveness are
attenuated— of the sole speaking language? But perhaps the common
analysis is mistaken. Perhaps, before going further, one ought to ask: but
what is the image?
— Maurice Blanchot, *The Space of Literature* 34

It is from the site of death as the place of my irreplaceability, that is, of
my singularity, that I feel called to responsibility. In this sense only a
mortal can be responsible.
— Jacques Derrida, *The Gift of Death* 41

the undated poem is
found and
forgotten

passes
— bpNichol, *The Martyrology, Book I* np

February 12

At the entrance to Book 5, the road as site of journey, of walking, of
writing, beckons:

a road

a rod

The elision of "a," first letter, prime letter, enacts the transition from site to measure, though "rod" also invokes an instrument of invocation, of authority, a symbol of ancient powers, and a part of (bp's) "automobility" (Chain 3). Process as presage passage and as incorporation— taking in while moving on— had become the internet of limit and provisionality, a goes without saying method(o log!)ical icon for the Martyr-poet who awoke late in the text's history, in the middle of the night, and turned to Ellie to ponder: why process?

The road in a (hot) rod— is a rood? One letter at a time demarks space, or in Steve McCaffery's words, it can be "the remotivation of the single letter as an agent of semantic distribution" (65-66). The attention, then, says stay tuned to word as interior with no exterior. No reference to co-sign this application. This eventuality of letters in alphabetic disarray— Cocteau as the gatekeeper to Book 5's "The greatest literary masterpiece is no more than an alphabet in disorder." It is dérèglement again, or the social body forming in a reign of signs (sigh) in their production (semantics) capacity as consumptive identities (taken in from the rain by a hunger for stabilized transactions). But nesting the proliferation of— is it still semiotic?— the dispersed, "life's a sign / beneath which signifieds slide" (Chain 3, Book 5).

□

In Book 5 the semiotheological procedure ("a road / a rod" = a dive / a divine) prompts the cursor to dial up stories of humanist recoveries. "Loo, what sholde a man in thyse days now wryte, egges or eyren" (William Caxton, cited in Book 5). Is the minotaur then being slain? Do all the roads / rods lead home? Even as the textual "rime / of coincidence" (Chain 1)— say in Chains 1 and 3, the two longest chains— interweave a pattern of connections linking writing, the poet's "i," the immediate spaces of living (Toronto's "annex"), familial history, the death of friends, national history, and pre-colonial history, the insistence of recovery itself begins to nudge out the insistence of "the precision of openness" called for in Book 4.

□

Charles Bernstein, from "Matters of Policy" (in *Controlling Interests*):

> On a broad plain in a universe of
> anterooms, making signals in the dark, you
> fall down on your waistband &, carrying your
> own plate, a last serving, set out for
> another glimpse of a gaze. (1)

bpNichol, from "from the Chronicle of Knarn" (Book 1):

> i'm holding my hat in my hand
> standing awkwardly at the entrance to their shrine
> wishing i were near you.
>   were they like us? i don't know.
> how did they die & how did the legend grow?

The figures of the saints, the paragrammatic event of an origin that is not an origin, a beginning that is not a beginning, a lineage that is not a lineage, can be read as a linguistic stratum for a textual machine. The probable system of a poem that is itself a probable system. Or how do you invent a cosmogony and get away with it? Think of the lyric stroll down memory lane as a barf in the brain, hemorrhaging its way into vessels in space, cloud-town dispersed as a distantiation, as a loss of measure, as non-narcissus, as narcosis. To ask the question, "how did they die & how did the legend grow?" is to arrive only in language's darkness when fun and games flip into spun and blames, i.e., why was "i" born anyway? And does it all matter in the end— less the blanks left in history where nothing occurs? "As to what auguries attended his birth nothing is said. Perhaps it was simply that nothing of importance happened" ("The Martyrology of Saint And," Book 1).

You can see (i.e., play) the machinations at the rim of the published text in the manuscripts. There dis/cards earlier dealt are exiled to the non-historical realm of the archive, saved from dissolution by institutional capture. To recall a refrain in Lola Tostevin's essay, "Is this where the poem begins?" (137) In the detritus of undated pieces, in the manuscript drafts, in the first edition, in the second edition published in one volume with Book 2? What to make of the fiddling to make something narrate— while the imagined future beckons, "a future music... w g r & t" (Book 1)? Or is it this that seeds the intent to invent make-shift strategies no matter how clumsy, cumbersome, off the wall?

The machinery functions as mediating screen on which the unharvested bundles of desire clothe themselves in the artifice of a pseudo-Catholicism:

> t he
> hee hee
>   ha ha
>
>   ho ho
>   tho i know its no laughing matter some days
> a sum of ways
> weights the measured writing of the poem (Chain 3, Book 5)

So the joke's on "i," so the yoke's on "i," so the laugh is in slaughter, after all is said and done. St And, St Reat, St Ranglehold, St Orm. "random brain stranded in the station." "i'm tired of fingering these old poems / stringing them into beads" (Book 1).

February 15

Why *The M* makes for obfuscating encoding (aside, that is, from its textual opacities which may be governed by the seams of its textual expansions, dispersals, and extensions):

a) No matter the rationalizations that retain the separation of text and scriptor, *The M*'s interior spaces were bound by the exigencies of time, process, and history. The assumption is that change on its contemporary edge could reconfigure or reread— even in the shifting theoretical frames of reading— its project from its so-called origins in that inaugural act of dismembering the word at its "s t" alphabetic arbitrarianist matrix. The sudden and unexpected death of the penned body (a unicorny figure by now) inserted the st asis rendering impossible the then historicized models of readings. The open-ended project, a martyrdom of form, in form, and by form— a "life sentence" (Eli Mandel)— theoretically demonstrated its own withdrawal from humanist history, leaving those blanks, those _____, and _____, or _____, but ____, which could not be remotivated by the fictional insertion of "bpNichol, author" as the hypothetical floating signifier. Or if that's done, as we do do do in the hold that textual presence has over the reader, the author appears in the apparitional form of absence. No way to read or to be read. Echo of "is this where the poem begins?"

b) The project's termination in the death of the scriptor freezes the frame in the same way that the reader, in history, is framed by the text. Open-endedness would then require the abjuration, or perhaps at least a suspension, of an expectation of truth value as immanent possibility (as it would in the present tense of mortality), alongside an encounter with the problematic of re-readings that call forth questions more than answers. The notion of canonization, already an obsolescence (see the listing of the saints in Book 1 in which, even in shaking its historical cage, referentiality is siphoned off), cannot be pre-empted without recourse to the standardization of power hierarchies in the discourse of literary hegemonies. "What's a poem like you doing in a context like this" is a phrasing adapted that shucks that route of critical containment.

c) Do "we," if such commonality can be assumed even if provisionally, canonize by setting our critical sites on *The M*? The question, applicable in instances of institutional incorporation, has to be asked in all phases of inquiry and engagement, alongside "our" inevitable complicity in the formation of power networks. Reader positioning participates in the production of power—all the more urgency why the interrogation of "our" own subject limits should be woven into the discourses that circle the textual body.

d) The gendered body emits a masculinist semiology of quest, discovery, territorialization (the marking of urinic space). The operation of male desire, the otherization of the muse as "w omen," and the companionship of the male heterosexual saints set the perimeter of the familial geography that both temporalizes space and spatializes time. O Ca Na Da, the empty signified waiting for the signifiers to arrive on the noon coach (house?), plays into the eurocentric (nation construct- ing) westering of the east and the appropriation of history, legend, myth as the lost treasure in need of technologization. But where, then, does the text begin, if it does at all? And if *The M* does not begin, or no longer can begin in the removal of its prime mover, where does reading begin? And should it begin? And would it begin without a kick start?

March 5

Does *The M* enact the last ph(r)ase of the millennium— fulfilling by its 10th book, left on the shoreline, the prophecy of the beginning's orphanic voice awakened to the crisis of disbelief? In the haunting of an absence of edges, the "personal" is st umped by the demons of

poeisis— and all the saints fabricated as guides, as originals, as interme-
diaries, begin to appear as projectional, even that "late P" in Book 3
who falls into the mid-initial wake of the material signifier that
generates a speaking. So the text can be resumed as a technology, as
perhaps a typographical pneumaticism— but are "we" in the ra-
diogrammic or in hyperspace? Are "we" casting shadow lenses back
on time (*The M* as time capsule) or has inchoate road turned into an
information highway? Is the reader pro-positioned or pre-positioned?
The problem (is it still?) resides (yes the space of a dwelling) in the
status of suffering. Who suffers? Why is there suffering? And how to
represent suffering at the rim of the millennium?

>   two 'n one or
>   in one door & out the other
>   voices speaking
>   that this suffering is born in language
>   that that is true & that that is true
>   two true or
>   wholly to be believed but
>   who'll y' find to
>   believe it?

>   leave it
>   this pain words wear
>   carry within them like a spine
>   involves the very line its
>   twists & turns ("The Grace of the Moment," Book 6)

During life with *The M* in the poet's era "the texts" were in the
perpetual state of becoming, more the biogeographic performance,
which contained the hypothetical present of the future that could or
would continually keep rearticulating the shifty and shifting past. In
that fold— "friends as footnotes" (Book 2)— the living body with its

voice at the gate lawned the hauntings with the false security of the chronological successive. The referent for the Martyr-poet, "bpNichol" or "barrie" or "bp" or "beep," covered up the lack that saturated the text in a paradoxical longing for a beyond. The pushing for newness harboured within its rush the signing that only accrues to death (as a noun verb)— the unravelling of babel and also the other, the conundrum necessitating the dispersal of signifiers across the splayed reaches of textuality.

March 12

Somewhere— or at some irretrievable temporal or spatial location in the chaining of Book 5, enchained by the splitting apart of linear textual space into chains of thought, of writing, of reading— a doubling over occurs. It was a kind of double or nothing in which the wager of sin became the labour of signs. The nostalgic humanist revival of the walking body constituted itself in the labyrinthine semiotics of the "eyear." Caught in the minotaurian dawn of a post-Book 4 era, the poet proposes a mapping procedure, delineating space from the local centre outward but also resurrecting the mapping out of colonized space— in effect, drawing on linguistic spillage to decode, in "pataphysical tones, the normalized street names of to ront o! as a primal narrative of descent and recovery (see Chains 1 and 3 especially). The dis-played tactic of the appearance of form in the midst of dispersal and scatter reflects the emergence of a theogonic practice that spells out plot lines in the avenues of process. Do the epigraphs (for Book 5) *point to*, as signs indicating the way ahead, or are they theoretical openings, indicating the bridges crossed as t's in the whirlwind?

Book 5 operates as a textual turnstile— who can say what comes and what goes, or whether the wind takes or overtakes *The M* poet? Is it a drive or a driven? Or is the consequence understood as both, as middle voice, as mid-initial, as cruising with the top down?

Somewhere, here, agency arises and already, for the first time in what has also become the "history" of *The M* (or *The M* as itself assuming the guise of history), the "beyond" of the textual present announces itself. The machinery of letteral production has begun to speak the present of the future, so that the sequel (a new way of thinking about *The M*'s extensions) is in the works. There is more than can be contained etc.

Curiously, then, Book 5 signals a radical change for *The M*. To this point, the poem had continued in unexpected extensions through promptings that disrupted apparent closure:

★ Book 1 at one point was to be *The M* as a single volume, but then came Book 2.

★ Book 2 was to conclude *The M*, a two-volume long poem ending with the death of the father's law. The text was even misplaced twice and given up as lost, but like the proverbial cat it always kept coming back. So eventually Book 3 came into being, only again to apparently conclude just prior to the "Mid-Initial Coda" with the mirrored concrete vision of "me" and "we" and the lines:

> the emblems were there when i began
> seven years to understand
> the first letter/level of
>
> > martyrdom

★ But turn the page in the published text and there is what has been read as the pivotal moment of *The M*: the fall into the letteral that dethrones the father and deconstructs the capitalizing stance of *The M* poet who signs himself into the text, simultaneously dying into language and being reborn as bp— no longer the imperial / empirical Nichol but a textual entity. One life for another, for an other, one life:

> the late P

        destroyed

leaving only b

& n

beginning again

b n a

all history there

t here

opposed against the suffering
we have yet to bear

★ Though placed immediately after the "final" section of Book 3, the "Mid-Initial Sequence" was written in the spring of 1973, some two years after Book 3, when it was named "Coda" and attached as the closing section.

★ The breakthrough into the letteral, or the paragrammatic potential of writing, ushered in new directions for *The M*, but it took another two years before Book 4 was initiated with the line, "purpose is a porpoise."

bp converses with Pauline Butling in an unpublished interview:

...when Book 6 began, it began with "Imperfection: A Prophesy" before I had even finished Book 5. Up until then, *The Martyrology* had, as it were, always announced itself very discretely: I finished one book, and the next book began. Here I was, still writing Book 5, and damned if I'm not writing Book 6, so I decided to stick with it. The more I wrote on "Imperfection: A Prophesy," the more it was obviously— I was writing *The Martyrology*, but it didn't make sense to me for this piece to go in *The Martyrology: Book 5* that had chains in it. But, in fact, what happened in really quite a logical outgrowth was that the chains were all going off in different directions, so that certain thrusts that were finished with in Book 5 were not finished with in terms of topic matter. Hence, I had dealt with a lot of that Bran/Brendan/Brun stuff, and I was fascinated by suddenly finding new information, which spawned "Imperfection: A Prophesy." But it didn't fit in back over there in the way that it was wanting to be written, so I began that, and then once the chains were finished, I sort of began— no I also began "A Book of Hours" even before Book 5 was finished.

pb: That's "Book I" and "Book II" [of *Book 6 Books*]?

bp: Yeah, I began it. Now of course "A Book of Hours" was the last one I finished. It took me the longest time. The very final piece I wrote was "in place of Hour 28." So that became kind of a pattern for how they were working. I mean, if I were to publish it [Book 6] totally accurately, I would probably publish a chronological thing, and I would have to weave the other sections in between various sections— but it would be so broken up it would make no sense.

So accomplishment of Book 4 and the formal innovation of textual chains in Book 5 announced a new sense of agency— of a choreographic "making sense" in which *The M* poet, now letterally inscribed in what had become an on-going narrative, "a life long" work (see "Hour 2" of "The Book of Hours"), began to steer the course of the textual expansion. The gain was already there in Book 4:

> sense out of nonsense
> N on sense
>   (which is me)
> i spell out changes

realign essentials
as i thot to
sing a balance sing

But when the struggle is done, is *The M* as the project of a confusion already being done? Would the shuffle text concept that was abandoned in favour of the fat manuscript left in a folder, arranged for publication and called "gifts," be anything more than a capitulation to endless variations of the same? And is "gifts," the first book not to be named a "book," a narrative closure— all the loose ends, the exiled texts, the "lost" ones brought into the fold of the page, gifting the reader with the book of bookness, or booked &? Do "we" have an incomplete completion of which the "bard" project envisioned for Book 10 can be read as a barge project?

March 20

Read "Lazarus Dream" from Book 7 and wonder if the performance of text can allow for the resurrection of the already dead body. "Car Rue sew." Or "rue de rue de rue / d'awakening." Do rue the day i was dyed in song. If the voice issues in the "" no is' / 'e says" who remembers the awl (all owls) in the brain? The sound waves. The light wavers. Who is a pear there.

March 26

The transparency of the haunting instills the burden of memory—those surfacings in the linguistic trace of the dead sister, "Donna," the dna connective. Here a link there a link between her premature death and the "lung wage" that propels the subliminal (and protestant) guiltiness of narrative struggle. Why "Donna" dead dead dead, and not the mid-initial P? Is that a sign in the landscape or a mark on the page? Does the P age in the text? "The word erases itself. No it doesn't.

Well yes it does but only if i read it that way. And that's not real. except, of course, that it is real. i can literally point to it— *no* tation. So i'm pointing to something which is erasing itself even as i point to it" ("The "Pata of Letter Feet" 80). L or D, life or death? No tation for me, thanks. i think i'll pass. (On the railway tracks the detritus of the colonialist legacy gardens discourse. Rose bushes, a line of petunias. Some scattered marigolds. The sun of temptation rises in the mountain air. Surveyor surveying services the memory.)

Why the desire to re-member? Why "conscious always of that one beginning we do not remember / taunted by the things we'll never know"? Read the text on my back. The roads, streets, lanes, boulevards et al. Find your way home in the maze. E-mail your identity when you find the time. Find the time. Is this where the poem begins?

The letteral mark on the whiteness of the page inscribes the black (th) inkiness in the birth of the pro-testant cosmology: T, the cross, the black diamond, the static letters awakening in the reeds (the ear reads). In "Scraptures: 1st Sequence" (Book 7) the words "in the beginning there was the word" is a translation of the letteral O as beginning which then accrues as gOd, as ylnO, depending on the directional read (a word "spoken" into "speech"). The patriarchic logos F alls it on his F ace. "dogma i am god" (Book 3).

Which is to say, only, that *The M* constructs itself on the tail-end of the low ghost, its elaborate technique (like the enormous computers of the 1960s) a kind of memoried technocracy to produce scripted speech: "eech to each" (Book 2). Hear this, hare that, heir this, err that, so it is, in the wind tunnel of the "eyear," that "we" have a heart to heart. Hence a community?

Ear to the ground, i remember Eli Mandel's fond use of Groucho Marx's statement, i would never want to join a group that would accept me as a member. The fly in the oinkment, O Donna, the sound of valence in a nation that is a notion, a potion for "you" and a potion for "me."

□

Ok, i'm ok now, believe me, i'm o k. Think of repositionings, contexts of the "elsewhere" (Book 7) within and/or against which *The M* assumes either the posture of resolution or the resolution of the posture.

> It is the trope of our times to locate the question of culture in the realm of the *beyond*. At the century's edge, we are less exercised by annihilation— the death of the author— or epiphany— the birth of the "subject"... The "beyond" is neither a new horizon, nor a leaving behind of the past... Beginnings and endings may be the sustaining myths of the middle years; but in the *fin de siècle*, we find ourselves in the moment of transit where space and time cross to produce complex figures of difference and identity, past and present, inside and outside, inclusion and exclusion. For there is a sense of disorientation, a disturbance of direction, in the "beyond".... (Bhabha 1)

Was *The M* born too early? Is the absence of the "post" in nation formation, in colonialist stratagems, in gender constructs, a foreclosure? Or can the text now be re-read in the "beyond" that haunts its passage from its multiple beginnings to the manuscript of the opening of Book 10?

> Word structure reveals,
exposes, even as the speaker conceals,
even as the writer masks his or her intent,
still that unerasable trace of content
betrays them. Intentionality, meaning's dark lament,
keens forth. (10)

The M's reading— its sign of the times— has been narrated in the bounds of CanLit history, that linear progression from colony to nation to the postmodern, the long poem as a paradigm of cultural autonomy (read here ethnocentic state-sanctioned historiography with "Canada" as hero). Its own restlessness, even as the signatory of the biological bpNichol, has been sacrificed to a critical projectile of a synthetic grid, even in the influential essay by Robert Kroetsch ("For Play and Entrance"). There its "massive evasions" (123) are placed alongside Atwood's nationalist poem of exclusions, *The Journals of Susanna Moodie,* where the figure of Moodie is appropriated and inhabited for the sake of history conceived through anglo-colonial eyes. Foot notes as friends manufactured sense, talking their way through the bio-geograph of bpNichol, the moving signifier, who functioned as the absence of presence in a text that continually confused the boundaries of the living and the dead. The boundary, though, is an end that begins:

> mina d l abour
> arbor or (within
> — not a notion of—
> but &) so
> c

So the lines from "St. Anzas I" (Book 7) write themselves into the spaces of splayed discourses:

> caffin so seeing
> did & nothing
> not even thant
> repeat so repeat
> sounds open did
> ot
> nor

Is this where the poem ends?

□

In the gift of context where does the sign reside? From "Scraptures: 8th Sequence" (circa 1969) to the inclusiveness of Book 7, a book not of books but of sites, the end announces itself in the language of the already written. Can there be any where else to go in this space of the named, *The Martyrology*?

> so now i can tell you the breath is dead that brought forth the song (poem) long time gone old dear old poem yur a long time gone and i cannot do more now anything to bring you (him) (it) back no nothing no thing at all to bring the poem (song) back tho i cry for it to say a part of me has a hunger that will not be eased (again & again) by speech (an old form) no for the form is dead that brought it forth

> ACTUAL FACTUAL THE DEATH REPORTED TODAY TO ANYONE WHOLE WHO'LL LISTEN TO ME

> as a friend would say it is over beginnings and endings say nothing not even middles used to i have confused you my people my people who are you listen to me who are you i do not know who i am today

> maybe i will know now that the poem is dead

Book 7 ends, "erase even this," followed by a trail of "tabula rasa." Is this, then, the final gesture of the Martyr-poet, about to dump (as in computer lingo) the whole of *The M* into the void of erasure? Well, nearly, but for the concrete *tabula rasa*.

Perhaps the death of form was already impishly keening forth in the trace of an "other" voice appearing (and disappearing in a wink) as a sound effect in the otherwise constricted textual procedure of the opening section of Book 1, "The Martyrology of St And":

i've looked out your eyes years now saint and

how
i tell you
no

   things
cannot
   measure thee

       motion

Who is speaking the "and how," the "how" (the racialized and deformed salutary speech of the indian in white movies), the "noth-ings" that undermine the ponderous seriousness of the struggle for thought to begin? Is this where the poem beguns?

March 27

Each page of *The M*, as a reading, contains numerous localized constellations of letters, syllables, lines, and themes that compel a sense of streaking or spillage— generating a textual productivity uncontain-able by interpretation. To interpret seeks to reduce the incommensu-rate to the cache of knowledge. Affects in effects. Actual in factual. How, then, can *The M* be traversed as *a* text, i.e., can it ever be singular, i.e., be approached as itself the name of an identity? Stephen Scobie writes: "The most acute problem faced by the long poem is that of structure: of maintaining some kind of coherence whereby the reader may continue to hold the whole expanse of the work in her mind *as a single poem*" (108). *The M* can be entered, roamed in as spatiality, read in time, but never grasped as a "single poem." The whole expanse, which would include every nook and cranny of the text, evades exegetical satiation. To say the least that can be read: "i / cannot stop / singing tho the sheer quantity / balk..." ("St. Anza IV," Book 7).

April 1

The structures of textualized memory, despite our best intentions in gestures toward openness, retain a stubborn hold on the ear. What one hears, more so in the kind of tensile provisional reading necessitated by *The M* as an on-going weighty "continuing" writing project, accumulates a linear critical narrativity that is difficult to shake off. In other words, the programs— i use the plural to emphasize the relativity of "readings" of *The M* prior to the death of bpNichol in September, 1988— evolved in the occultation that conditioned its so-called "origins." In the emerging post-structuralist milieu in which "master works," i.e., works that supposedly represented a mainstream collectivity and/or culture, had lost credibility (and were beginning to be reframed within the ideological closures of nationalism, patriarchy, and bourgeois commodification), the fact of "*The M*" was simultaneously parodic, outrageous, cartoonish, and yet intensely desired. While the nationalist forces built transcendent garrisons called "Can culture," the contrary impulse toward localization, immediacy, and particularity sought justification for collectivities that accounted for process and change. *The M* proposed an exploration, a journalying in which the finite "i" is parachuted into the machinations of a textual disjunction— hence a pseudo-cosmogony constructed out of two conjoined letters, the "s" and "t," which seeded the project isle.

The margins, then, were constituted in relation to nation-bounded works that required the humanist lyric "i" in poems or the aestheticization of "Canadian" content in novels. The obfuscations of narrative, form, language, and lyric stance, particularly in the first two books of *The M* with the prominence given to "saints" constructed out of alphabetic rumination, located a rift that called for alternative strategies of reading. These were strategies in which the hierarchic binary of "author" over "reader" was dismantled and replaced by a process text that apparently democratized the relation between "author," now called "writer," and the "work," now called "text." The so-called "death of the author" in semiotic circles of the 1970s was understood loosely as a political position that advanced a materialist poetics (evident in feminist writing, theories of textuality, and emerging critiques of colonialist nationalism).

The M, especially Books 1 to 5, reflected its times but was also, in many ways, occulted because of the sheer labour required to de/en-code its expansion into books that made little sense in institutionalized readings of CanLit. Readers, at least the most vocals ones, were themselves writer-friends who formed the initial collective circle around *The M* and whose readings articulated the initial reading codes, more often than not bolstered by their personal ties with the living writer, bpNichol. The privilege of insider connections was a significant component of most of the influential commentary on *The M*; see, for instance, the two large collections by two journals associated with bp, *Read the Way He Writes* (1987) from *Open Letter*, and *Tracing the Paths* (1988) from *Line*, which by and large set the critical boundaries drawn at the time of bp's death.

The death of the author of *The M*, for *The M*, by *The M* sets up theoretical conundrums that complicate assumptions of life and death vis-à-vis literary works. We can absorb the notion of a work left incomplete because of an author's death, but it's not so easy to realign our relationship to a life long text written on the premise of literal (though perhaps also figural) open-endedness— and then to have the writer die so suddenly, so unexpectedly, and so young. It simply doesn't make sense, or it does make sense in not making sense. In life, the name "bpNichol," the biological writer of *The M*, was so interwoven with the name "bp" or "N" or "Nicky" inscribed in *The M*, that death itself (the "disrupter" in "The Grammar Trilogy" of "A Book of

Hours") now has to be read as f(act)iction. The letters "bp" become the equivalent of "st," as the authorial death undoes the knot of (prescribed) intentionality and gives the power to legitimize over to readers who, from this moment on, either abandon the project or continue the processes it has inaugurated—including response-abilities that account for, and even attempt to read through, the blind spots. The death of the Martyr-poet, in short, signals a constitutive baseline for *The M*. No continuing long poem, or life long poem, could function without that provision for mortality's rub.

April 3

Change—of clusters of readers, of theoretical frameworks—is inevitable, is a threat to comprehension, yet the only means by which an open-ended text can continue its formal existence. In the death of the signified, i.e., its location in the person of the living poet, significance appears as a critical act contingent on the politics of textuality and the positioning of readers, circa the late 1990s.

In the current critiques of ethnocentric patriarchy, canonization, colonialism and nation-formation, race, class and gender constructs, how does *The M*, as it were, "measure" up to readers for whom this long poem is only one of many texts? How can *The M* be articulated in fields of reception and institutionalization once these have also been exposed as sites of power? As a cultural document, that is, as a "post-1960s" long poem, *The M* reflects in assumptions its share of normative values—and these should, indeed must, be critiqued for blindnesses and limits. But how are we to construct the politics of blame in its case? To what extent can the Martyr-poet, or the textual "bpNichol," be held accountable for its theoretical shortcomings? To draw on Derrida's comments on the implications of Nietzsche's textualized name in *Ecco Homo*:

To put one's name on the line (with everything a name involves and which cannot be summed up in a *self*), to stage signatures, to make an immense bio-graphical paraph out of all that one has written on life or death— this is perhaps what he has done and what we have to put on active record. Not so as to guarantee him a return, a profit. In the first place, *he* is dead— a trivial piece of evidence, but incredible enough when you get right down to it and when the name's genius or genie is still there to make us forget the fact of his death. At the very least, to be dead means that no profit or deficit, no good or evil, whether calculated or not, can *ever return again* to the bearer of the name. Only the name can inherit, and this is why the name, to be distinguished from the bearer, is always and a priori a dead man's name, a name of death. (*The Ear of the Other* 7)

To embark on the long poem, a poem as long as *a life*, is already to have admitted the name of death (the "late P") into its textual spheres. The "elsewhere" (see the Hawkings drawing in Book 7) resides in here and not in here, out there and not out there— or in the borderblur lines of the poem. "i have this wish to write the world i can never realize" ("Hour 17," Book 6).

□

Close up, line by line, page by page, book by book, *The M* appears "monumental," a monument perhaps analogous to the "earthworks" in "Hour 17" (Book 6) from which "all reference [eventually] vanishes." In the current move towards consumer-lit in contemporary social appropriations of texts, and the backlash against linguistic opacities, the odds are against the continued material existence of *The M*. Blame, in this instance, returns not to the writer who is dead and/or death but to the reader whose own agency will realize textual horizons and determine the so-called "fate" of future alignments. The contexts of reception are political locations of opposition, contestation, and negotiation. By signing off in the loose sheets, the initials "bp: if" (Book

7) standing in for "body paranoia: initial fugue," the biological writer of *The M* returned the texts to the orphanic moment of Book 1: his now-deceased body re-placed in the body of the word/world.

> The poems are to be interleaved into the final bound copy of *Martyr* 7 &.
>
> — bp Nichol

The writer's intention, left in a notebook, partially transcribed and editorialized by Irene Niechoda for the posthumous publication of *Gifts*, is not honoured by the publisher. Instead, the loose sheets have been inserted in a pocket on the inside back cover— a double sign of the author's death and the birth of the power of others: of readers who can now appropriate or otherwise translate *The M* into still unrealized geographies of social and cultural formations.

NOTE
"Broken Entries" was written during a graduate course on bpNichol's *The Martyrology*, Spring Semester 1995, at Simon Fraser University. Thanks to my students— Kate Foster, Karlyn Koh, Glen Lowry, Mark Nakada, Carl Peters, Graham Sharpe, Chris Swail— for the stimulating discussions which are reflected in this re-consideration of *The M*.

Postscript

My last lengthy conversation with bp, by phone, occurred some time around the end of July, 1988, or the beginning of August (i can't be sure now). We talked again, briefly, at the end of August, when i was passing through Toronto and, as i often did, called him from the airport.

Barrie was in considerable pain when he came to Vancouver in June for the book launch of *Tracing the Paths*, and he had continued to get weaker. When he phoned me he said he wasn't able to move around much so, strangely, for the first time in a long while, he had time to think, to meditate, to day-dream, and he also mentioned being attracted to Stephen Hawking's thinking on time in *A Brief History of Time*. The drawing based on an illustration in Hawking's book (27) and inserted in *Gifts: The Martyrology Book(s) 7&* is dated June 12. What excited bp was a major transformation in his conception of Book 7. Laughing, he confessed to having experienced a real live, down-to-earth "vision," a term he used in a very mundane and pragmatic way. It had had to do with a much more inclusive awareness of time. Stated simply, he had this "vision" of the past and future bridged by the wider context of the immediate present in which all the events of his own personal past could be re-envisioned. Here i'm starting to "translate" his explanation, because his exact words are lost to me now. What he did conclude, though, was that the "vision" gave another dimension to the shape of Book 7. The earlier shuffle concept of form— i.e., a text made up of loose sheets that could be shuffled to offer a different arrangement for each successive reading— would be abandoned— and, in light of an expansion of temporal potentialities, Book 7 would retrieve two past works that had been previously excluded.

I would conjecture that Barrie's vision had to do with his troubled relationship to his personal and literary past. *Monotones* and *Scraptures* were written on the margins of the long poem, and so much of the previous books had been dominated— sometimes obsessed by— a preoccupation to dissolve the barriers haunting the loneliness of the mortal i. Book 7 appeared to be offering a means to retrieve "lost" contents and renew a past that had become static as the history of *The Martyrology* was constructed.

Hawking's figure illustrates the paradox of what he terms a finite universe with no boundaries. The two cones posit a past consisting of all possible finite events that have shaped the finite present, and a future containing all possible finite events that will shape a finite future. The number of events are finite but the possibilities are infinite— there is always (already) an "elsewhere" to the past and future cones. At the juncture of past and future is that p, for present, for Barrie the "mid-initial p"— the letteral p of his middle name, Phillip, also doubling as a mid-initial state of consciousness (first un-covered textually in the midst of Book 3, in the "mid-initial" sequence). Time in Hawking's drawing is conceived as a spatial site, so that all past events of one's life need not be compartmentalized through exclusions, excisions, and erasures. The past can be reshaped (and re-invented?) by the imagination of the present, and by this strategy of writing can even re-member the future (recalling a Kroetcheanism in *What the Crow Said*).

Aside from the cosmological and scientific implications of Hawking's drawing, for Barrie, this way of thinking offered the prospect of liberating contents from his past through the act of re-membering. I jokingly responded that perhaps he was finally working his way out of the "books of the dead," which meant that now he could get on with the "books of the living." No comment, except soft laughter.

I was pleased with Barrie's excitement— and it never occurred to me that we would never have another chance to speak about *The Martyrology*. I assumed our conversation would be followed by another and another— it was just part of an on-going process. Even here, in recounting this memoried anecdote, i remain uncertain of thought's credibility—

> turn this page? your'n. imagination
> of a future place & time, turning, over. an act of
> faith. stupidity. trust. the keys. turned over to you.
> (*Gifts: The Martyrology Book(s)* 7&)

Asiancy:
Making Space for Asian Canadian Writing

People who feel invisible try to borrow visibility from those who are
visible. — Robert Kroetsch (6)

In Margaret Atwood's best-selling critical guide to Canadian literature,
Survival, national literary politics located a methodological tool for
constructing an anglocentric history with Canada as victim of American imperialism. The privileging of the author's own subject position
as "English Canadian" reader, in effect, banished "racialized" Canadians from public space, a gesture that denied them "identity" in her text
of nationhood. In the climax to her critical narrative, at that moment
when a liberated future for Canadian writing is posited, an astounding
admonition appears in what is no more than an aside:

> ...the tendency in English Canada has been to connect one's social
> protest not with the Canadian predicament specifically but with some
> other group or movement: the workers in the thirties, persecuted
> minority groups such as the Japanese [sic] uprooted during the war.
> English Canadians have identified themselves with Ban the Bombers,
> Communists, the FLQ, and so forth, but not often with each other—
> after all, the point of identifying with those other groups was at least
> partly to distinguish oneself from all the grey WASP Canadians you
> were afraid you might turn into. (242)

The unabashedly unqualified erasure of Canadians of Japanese
ancestry unsettles: no attention whatsoever to the specific "Canadian
predicament" of their uprooting, dispossession, even deportation, as
the direct consequence of xenophobic Canadian policy— based on
that very "each other"-ness of which *Survival's* writer laments the
absence. The reference to Livesay's "Documentaries" in the paragraph

following implicates the dramatic poem, "Call My People Home," a poem that supposedly "documents" Japanese Canadian internment. Atwood critiques Livesay for dwelling on a minority, but they share more than meets the eye: both privilege a "thematic" reduction of texts and the normalizing power of English-Canadian nationalism.

The humanist binary— "subject" versus "object"— constitutes the discursive centre of Livesay's often-cited description of the Canadian documentary poem as "a conscious attempt to create a dialectic between the objective facts and the subjective feelings of the poet" (267), with the narrative functioning as "a frame on which to hang a theme" (269). In "Call My People Home" the narrative frame becomes a representational device that enables the translation of Japanese Canadian experience ("the objective facts") into a public discourse ("subjective feelings of the poet"), in this instance, a radio drama which displaces the specificity of internment through "thematic" abstraction. As Tejaswine Niranjana says in Siting Translation, "Translation... produces strategies of containment. By employing certain modes of representing the other— which it thereby also brings into being— translation reinforces hegemonic versions of the colonized, helping them acquire the status of what Edward Said calls representations, or objects without history" (3).

The hierarchic power relations in the poem are codified by the ubiquitous third-person narrator, the voice of hegemony that demarks, tames, and finally inscribes Japanese Canadian subjectivity, not in terms of a betrayal of democratic process— a violence woven into the fabric of white liberalism— but as a stain that can be rubbed clean through the (ultimate) absorption by "white" totality. This rite of assimilation awaits Japanese Canadians— in the words of the "The Student" at the end: "Home is the white face leaning over your shoulder / As well as the darker ones."

In Livesay's poem the documentary mode functions to turn Japanese Canadian subjects into racialized objects of white discourse. The appropriating gaze of the poem, operating under the guise of liberal empathy, excludes specificities of language, culture, history, and geography, effectively stripping away the subjectivities of those depicted. The thematic message conveyed to its non-Japanese Canadian readers (and listeners, since it was aired on the radio) is that internment and forced dispersal, despite the hardships, has "allowed" Japanese Canadians to assimilate. Rendered invisible and ahistoric, the sign "Japanese Canadian" is monumentalized and abstracted from the particularities of racism, political opportunism, and exploitation. Livesay's text, in other words, becomes itself another site of internment, a site of containment, by which the white majority re-identified "Japanese Canadians" as a model minority within a mainly anglocentric political space.

> As a kid in Winnipeg in the post-war years, the explusion took on the appearance of a gone world, as the prairies came to be seen as the confines of permanent exile. The dispossession, the dispersal from the west coast— where the salmon leapt from the Fraser River right into your arms and where the orchards were always filled to plenitude with fruit, ah yes in memory— meant a distanced relation to "place." Always somewhere to get away from, a "dis place." Nomadicity, maybe, but the terminological screens were still censored by white-outs. The "real" dropped from the sky in a packet of formulaic phrases, packaged icons, cultured institutions. On the streets it was all signifying, no signified, and the heteroglossia of warped tongues, of multiple accents, of babel syntaxes never found its/their way into the imperialized "class" rooms.

□

The pervasive power of "English Canadian" centrality— white and Anglo-Saxon— has acted as such a weighty cultural pall that the process of over-coming imposed representations, misrepresentations, and erasures has been an almost insurmountable obstacle for Japanese Canadians and other communities of colour in Canada, until only recently. Of all the "isms" that have surfaced in the past fifteen years, perhaps feminism and post-structualism together have been the most instrumental theoretical positions to resist and critique the power of patriarchic nationalist forms and the normative ahistoricism of humanist beliefs in universality.[1] Although the debates are often engaged on the borderlines of literary and public institutions where all "isms" of any sort are still treated as hot potatoes, there are signs that writers and cultural workers of colour have begun to create theories, texts, and visual works that foreground issues of representation, appropriation, race and ethnicity, and subjectivity.[2]

A brief example, May 1992: At the historic meeting of Canadian writers of colour at a conference, "The Appropriate Voice," the issue of "cultural appropriation" was aligned with, among other consequences of colonialism, racial oppression, and exploitation, the "misrepresentation of cultures and the silencing of their peoples" (n.p.).[3] Asian Canadian writers too have begun to interrogate and undermine representations of their communities manufactured by outsiders, often liberal and sympathetic white writers, artists, and film-makers whose intentions may be sincere but who fail to account for differences based on subjectivity, language, history, and the problematics of appropriation. Instead of assisting Canadians of Asian ancestry, these products of white assumptions and biases have all too often confirmed and reinforced the systemic racialization process through which privilege and power has been maintained.

American cultural critic Cornel West has pointed to an emerging theoretical awareness as "the new politics of difference" which has features including the desire "to trash the monolithic and homogeneous in the name of diversity, multiplicity and heterogeneity; to reject the abstract, general and universal in light of the concrete, specific and particular; and to historicize, contextualize and pluralize by highlighting the contingent, provisional, variable, tentative, shifting and changing" (19). Within this evolving "new politics" is the contestation for positioning and the necessity for writers and cultural workers of colour to assume responsibility for the frames of reference through which their subjectivities are reproduced in public discourses. In a time of imploding paradigms— and the temptation of riding on changing fads and fashions in theories and terminologies— the risk of compromise and co-optation hovers on the edge of every cultural fold. Who is speaking? For whom? Why? In the plethora of discourses formed to answer these simple but profoundly destabilizing questions, allegiances can become ambiguous, even misleading. For some establishment critics, the so-called "margin" (itself a critical construct for a prior "centre") may even take on a curious exoticism, as a comment by Linda Hutcheon reveals: "...in this age of the postmodern re-valuing of borders and margins as preferred sites of articulation of difference, many feel that the margins are indeed where the action is: that resistance and contestation make for more exciting art than centrisms of all kinds (ethno-, phallo-, hetero-, and so on)" (49). For those on the "borders and margins," for those oppressed by the "centrisms of all kinds," the question of preference is laughable at one extreme, and outrageous at the other. The paradigm of centrality in which the "other" is the necessary border/margin delimits the (assumed so unrevealed) discourse boundaries of Hutcheon's statement— a reminder of Trinh T. Minh-ha's warning to be wary of those from the centre who work from an authority that cannot leave a stone unturned and who, accommodating the language of humanism, may enact a kind of liberal "pilgrimage" (17) to borderline sites in order to extend its dominant forms of power.

□

Such a deterrent to the making of a historically situated cultural space for Canadian writers of Asian ancestry, as well as for other writers of colour, is all the more prevalent in a country such as Canada where the ideology of assimilation, despite the so-called "multiculturalist" lip service, still pervades dominant social values— reflecting, by and large, white, male, Anglo-European priorities. Whatever the varying contexts for understanding the federal government's "multicultural" policy, initiated in 1971 and enshrined in the Canadian Multiculturalism Act of 1988, at an explicit level it was meant to appease the rumblings of those "others" standing on the sidelines of the Bicultural and Bilingualism policy. Indeed, it was the latter policy that was so necessary to solidify the English- and French-Canadian power base, against the threat of growing demands for more recognition by Canadians who did not belong to those designated as charter ethnic groups. In Evelyn Kallen's words, the multicultural policy "was a technique of domination designed to entrench the power of the ruling Anglo élite when its superordinate, national position was threatened by Quebec's claim to political power, on the one hand, and by the growing numerical and economic strength and increasing cultural vitality of immigrant ethnic collectivities, on the other hand" (167-8).

However, by the early 1980s the strain and constraints of Canadian nationalist (read here "centralist") ideology with the "founding" priority given to the English and French colonist groups had become increasingly visible; the multiculturalism policy was perceived to be inadequate to deal with systemic racism and the specific problems of non-European minorities of colour who, in turn, had begun to confront racism by foregrounding the historical framework of colonization and eurocentricity still evident in Canadian institutions and public policies. That broader neo-colonialist perspective brought into view the inequality of representations of different subject positions in the body politic. The Japanese Canadian redress movement, a strategy to redress the injustice of internment in the 1940s, developed within that shift, perhaps even thrived on the changes going on. Other communities of colour, including Chinese Canadians, Afro-Canadians, and Natives, became more vocal in asserting their histories, which had thus far been neutralized, denied, or otherwise erased.

By the time of the Japanese Canadian redress settlement on September 22, 1988, the cultural spaces of Canada had radically transformed. In recent years, the new works and theories emerging from formerly excluded sites, from Natives, from writers of colour, including Asian Canadians, have opened a network of articulations and theoretical concerns that not only undermine assimilationist pressures but also allow for provisional spaces where writers of colour can navigate diversity within the specificity of histories, languages, and subjectivities. The struggle for such empowerment and liberation from the imposed signs of "race" is on-going, and may get even more tense in the years ahead. As the earlier rhetoric of a binary centre (biculturalism) with its subordinate "others" in the margins (multiculturalism) has exhausted its credibility, reactionary voices have arisen sounding the alarm of the country's cultural disintegration, often pointing fingers at minorities of colour as the cause. Indeed, the resistance of writers, cultural workers, and community activists of colour has created the possibility of explosive conflicts with establishment institutions, making all the more urgent the need for terminology and theoretical speculations that avoid the pitfall of simply re-circulating the old systems of power.

□

A one-dimensional oppositional positioning is hardly an adequate basis for new cultural forms which can represent the localized subjectivities of writers of colour. While such contests of will and confrontation may be a pragmatic strategy for certain instances requiring immediate interventionist action, they do not instigate the internal transformations necessary for moving beyond the constraints of racialization to make spaces where difference and diversity are constantly being (re)negotiated. For Canadian writers of colour— and here I speak in (personal) terms of Japanese Canadians— the internal "battle" to overcome the powerful effects of racialization may, finally, be the most formidable

*is this envisioning a co-existance
of differences where everyone gets
their own way?*

V.S.

opponent. Assimilationist assumptions, mostly unspoken, continue to
saturate the mass media, and the ideology of white, male, European-
based values still reigns in literary institutions, in granting bodies, and
in decision-making areas of the publishing world. In a climate where
difference is pressed into sameness, and where "universality" implies
white perceptions, many writers and artists of colour internalize the
propaganda of dominant aesthetic and cultural norms and never reach
that critical threshold of having to decolonize themselves.

For writers of colour, then, the new form of becoming invisible
may be less visible as an ideology, because of the official rhetoric of
multiculturalism, but it still requires conformity to dominant representations, to socially determined "tastes," and to transparent literary
expectations. Only the most vigilant can escape the temptations of
power relations that govern what gets to be judged of "national
significance" and of "consequence"— reinforced as they are by an
elaborate system of awards, rewards, media privileges, canonization,
and ultimately, institutionalization.

*So
true,
so true.*

Writers who become aware of the conflict between acceptance
through conformity and resistance to co-optation undergo a paradig-
matic internalized upheaval. Historically and even at present, the strain
of a domineering exterior on the interior of those in the state of
exclusion created/creates complicated networks of ambiguities, repressions, and compromises that infiltrate the language and geography
of their subjectivity. Such a state of boundedness, of inhibitions, of
imposed silences, at an extreme, kills creativity altogether— but when
interrogated, deconstructed, and entered, can constitute an exploratory
process which may even necessitate the creative act. It can be a
generative space analogous to what Trinh T. Minh-ha describes when
she speaks of that liminal consciousness betwixt and between, in the
transitional zone of an inside–outside confusion: "The moment the
insider steps out from the inside she's no longer a mere insider. She
necessarily looks in from the outside while also looking out from the
inside. Not quite the same, not quite the other, she stands in that

undetermined threshold place where she constantly drifts in and out" ("Not Like/Like You" 374-5). Certainly, the "threshold place" is familiar to many writers, but for Asian Canadians, and perhaps for other writers of colour, the experience of inner and outer is not merely an instance of a decontextualized, abstract binary, but vitally connected to a community-based positioning vis a vis— or contained by, or surrounded by— an overriding white majority from which it is estranged either by language, or by sociocultural values, or by the phenomenon of physicality, i.e., the appearance of the semiotic body as inscribed by the constructed signs of "race."

My father resisted reminiscences of his Vancouver youth around the Powell Street area, Nihonbashi ("Japantown"), "Japtown" for Anglo-Europeans in the lingo of the day. When pressed to imagine the city's sites, the one reference point that resurrected its architectural body in his memory was the master's piece on the corner of Hastings and Burrard, near the Pacific Ocean— the Marine Building. This structure, writes Bruce Macdonald in *Vancouver: A Visual History*, was "Vancouver's first modern skyscraper" (42). Construction began in 1929 within the aura of civic canonization and was completed in 1930, despite the market crash. A visible proof of wealth, a signifier— perhaps why my father would remember its imposing form— of the imperial signified that had such awesome power to identify his community as "enemy alien," to confiscate properties, and to destroy families, without accounting for prying eyes, except in the generalization and rule of racialized laws. The saturation of the contradictions and hypocrisies of Anglo-European democracy would contaminate the social values of Japanese Canadians. Rendered them unable to protect themselves from abuse and the posture of silences.

□

Françoise Lionnet says, while talking of the stance of post-colonial writers— substitute here, writers of colour, in a Canadian context— "the individual necessarily defines him- or herself with regard to a community, or an ethnic group, and their autobiographical mythologies of empowerment are usually mediated by a determined effort to revise and rewrite official, recorded history" (321). Let me, for a moment, consider the Japanese Canadian writer or artist as a case example to amplify the problems as well as the possibilities facing Asian Canadian and other writers of colour.

The necessary tie to community establishes that ethnically specific tension of inside and/or outside that Japanese Canadians have continued to inhabit as a matter of course. In the assimilationist, and even in the more recent integrationist model, on the one hand, the inside, or what in a familial realm of childhood might have assumed the shape of an interiority, is erased, rendered speechless, or so devoid of content that the subject does not or cannot even recognize its absence. For those who underwent the horrendous trauma of denial, estrangement, and ostracization during the internment period, the monolithic and unwieldy powers of the outside— the white Canadian public, the government, the media, and all the ethnocentric forces that together constituted the body politic of this country— decreed that Japanese Canadians were "enemies" in their midst who were incapable of speaking as subjects. The abrogation of citizenship and the subsequent degradation of subjectivity would have devastating effects on a community that had already suffered some fifty years of racism and exclusionist policies on the west coast.

The generation of Japanese Canadians who were interned adopted various poses in self-defense— silence, resignation (*shikata ga nai*: "it can't be helped"), and rationalization ("blessing in disguise": forced assimilation got us out of our ghetto so we could finally enter the white mainstream). These are reactions evident in Japanese Canadian nisei

(Canadian-born, second generation), a generation formed on the consciousness of doubleness: growing up between the ethnocultural and linguistic enclave of the issei (first generation immigrants from Japan) and the Anglo-Saxon "westernized" democratic values of the Canadian majority. Had their lives not been so utterly stymied by the mass uprooting of 1942, the nisei, as is the pattern in other immigrant communities, might have developed aesthetic, political, and cultural strategies to promote their own expressiveness in visual and literary texts, but the radical discontinuity of internment at the hands of their own government severely shook their faith in democratic values— and threw them into a double bind. Their ethnicity, the very cultural and linguistic skin inherited from their parents, as they "entered" the dominant society in their dispersed state, became a negative that had to be translated into a positive, if they were to be accepted/adopted within white culture.

Significantly, though, for many nisei, the disintegration of community did not erase all of its traces, but forced that allegiance, now removed from the geocultural place on the west coast, back into the privacy of familial ties, early friendships, local community organizations, all of which resulted in a "club" mentality. In other words, though the community bond was broken, community ties continued in diminished forms— even while, to all outward appearances, the assimilation process had occurred successfully. This is why many nisei see no contradiction in working with white Canadians all week long, then relating to their nisei friends in more intimate settings on the weekend. The two domains, though balanced in their minds, rarely coalesce in any significant way.

Such a doubleness does not characterize the sansei, the third generation, especially those born in internment, or in the immediate aftermath of 1949, the year the restrictions were lifted. These sansei grew up, for the most part, in closely knit families and were witness to the debilitating effects of the internment, but found themselves moulded by the dynamics of dispersal, the community in fragments,

111

the language disappearing— and the more open road of assimilation as temptation for their future. The touchstone of community had slipped out from under, so no framework existed for reproducing, even identifying in meaningful self-critical patterns, a shared history. Instead, the weakening of community-based values often led to self-denial, self-effacement, passivity, and a fear of politics, qualities that aided in the stereotype of Japanese Canadians as the "model minority." Hardly the position out of which vital writing could arise. Before that could happen, a reclamation process had to occur.

As a "JC" school kid in Winnipeg during the arborite 1950s, the non-existence of writers telling stories of "our" turbulent BC history remained unarticulated. Real history was always "over there"— in England and Europe. One exception to colonial rule, so we learned, was a prairie poem of the Depression, "The Wind Our Enemy," by Ann Marriott. Though supposedly valorizing "our" local place, for me the tension in the class radiated from the single line, "Japs Bomb China." Yes, of course, the day "we" read the poem out loud, the turn came for me at that line, and "i" then could not— had not the terminological apparatus— to resist the act of voicing the word that was anathema at home. No one exposed, except for the chuckle chuckle, this moment of linguistic anguish. The match between word and "me" struck a chord but the unspoken fluttered out the (open) window. Even "i" was numbed by the evacuated words.

Japanese Canadians, as an ethnic group, in the 1950s and 1960s were characterized by the absence of writers. The exception is the lone figure, Roy Kiyooka, who was carving a place for himself in the art/literary world. His first book, *Kyoto Airs* (1964), is a landmark publication: a serial text written during a trip to Japan, in which

Kiyooka confronts the manifestations of conflict and confluence between his Canadian-born mind and his Japanese ancestry. His text remains invisible, by-passed by his nisei peers and unknown by those sansei who might have been able to draw from it in the 1960s, and of course absent in national literary circles.

□

How, then, to begin to begin? At one extreme, in the tension between inside and outside, the inside can be so subordinated to the outside that it cannot recognize its specificity at all. Such a hierarchic determinacy almost inevitably results in an identity formation in which the dominant values outside come to censor, repress, or otherwise propagandize the inside. Once the foundation of this "self" is undermined, however, as it is when a subject begins to mistrust its conditioned reactiveness, a process of reversals can come into play. There is, initially, the recognition that both poles in the interchange, inside and outside, are constructs dependent upon each other for their existence, and bounded by social, psychological, cultural, political, and historical constraints characteristic of a body politics in which minority subjectivities are denied or otherwise contained.

Once doubts and questions arise in the subject, the passageway between inside/outside (suddenly) transforms into a place of static, of noise, of perceptual destabilizations, including what Gloria Anzaldúa refers to as "linguistic code-switching" (xxii), the disturbed subject/writer set adrift in a shifting space of vertiginous pluralities that awaken the desire to speak, to write. But where to begin? Feminist writer Gail Scott, commenting on the difficulty of articulating a female subject position that has had no space before, exposes an analogous beginning from scratch for writers of colour:

> We may use language our whole lives without noticing the distortions.
> Distortions and omissions. Surely the assertion of the inner self has

to start with language. But what if the surfacing unconscious stream finds
void instead of code? What if we often lack the facility to raise to the
conscious level our unconscious thoughts? Due to our slant relationship
with culture, therefore language, the words won't come. And without
the words, the self. No capacity for separation. (17-18)

It is, for instance, out of such an inaugural crisis that the writing of
Obasan by Joy Kogawa was "born," which is to say, called into being
by the urgency to reclaim a suppressed history— the urgency to speak
back to the barrier of a denied personal and communal past. Alongside
the overt narrative of the central character, Naomi, as she unravels the
riddle of "herstory" as a Japanese Canadian, is the covert drama of the
writer, herself the product of historical injustices, creating a fictional
vehicle to recover, through documents, memories, and tales, the
interior consequences of abuse and betrayal. The construction, then,
is itself a movement into the inhibitions, ambivalences, and erasures
that have underwritten the writer's psyche and which threaten, at each
point in the unfolding narrative, to suck her back into silence, i.e., into
the nothingness of non-speech. Much of the provisionality of *Obasan*
inheres in the writing itself, in the very textuality through which the
silenced history of Japanese Canadians is imagined[4] and re-configured.

As a novel written by an Asian Canadian, *Obasan* has enjoyed an
unusual popularity, receiving great praise by reviewers and three
awards, the *Books in Canada* First Novel Award (1981), the Canadian
Authors Association Book of the Year Award (1982), and the Before
Columbus Foundation American Book Award (1982). Indeed, *Obasan*
helped to make Kogawa into something of a celebrity, especially when
its narrative entered the catalytic milieu of the Japanese Canadian
redress movement which gained momentum in the early 1980s.
Academic articles appeared, magazines published profiles on the
author, and *Obasan* was studied in many university courses across
Canada.

In the Public Archives of Canada, the mass of sheeted language. Wade through documents on the systematic dismantling of the community. Two agencies collaborate in this elaborate dismemberment. The Custodian of Enemy Property and the BC Security Commission. The letterhead, Headquarters, Marine Building. So the Custodian, that misnamed representative, who was to care for their homes and belongings, wasted no time in manipulating policies to dispose of all. The splayed trust split them from the homebase, from the geocultural coast, syntaxed into the racialized discourses of the body of law. Mariners. Registered. Letterheads.

The consensus from its commentators, for the most part white academics and journalists, has been that *Obasan* is a relevant literary work because, with it, Kogawa has written her way through the silence of the past to come to terms with Japanese Canadian internment. Academics who analyze the novel in detail, despite differences of approach, all tend to incorporate a resolutionary (not revolutionary) aesthetics in their overall critical framing of the novel. The agreement seems to be that Naomi resolves her silenced past, so establishes peace with the human rights violations that caused such havoc and grief to her, to her family, and to her community. Much is made of the immediate aftermath of Naomi's hearing of the translated letter disclosing the "facts" of her mother's disappearance, as she leaves Obasan's house wrapped in her militant Aunt Emily's coat, and returns to the coulee— where the story began— where she sat with her uncle on the bank.[5] Here, as her grief is released to the landscape, the narrative ends with the faint scent of "wild roses and the tiny wildflowers" caught in a pose: "If I hold my head in a certain way, I can smell them from where I am" (247). Quiescence, quietude, the absent presence of her uncle, all in the hushed silence of the coulee.

Still, Naomi's gesture and its fade-out does not close the novel, as many readers assume; the heightened moment is followed by a matter-of-fact document asking the government not to deport Japanese Canadians, signed by three white men. Why is this document here? Is it referentially necessary for readers to understand Japanese Canadian history? Is it simply meant to be read ironically? Naomi's story, beginning and end, does have the symmetrical balance of aesthetic closure, a novelistic convention that *Obasan* fulfills, and which many readers see as a sign of Naomi's resolution of the injustices, but the end document has an asymmetric relationship to its counterpart, the opening proem written out of the depth of the writer's struggle to dispel the silences that haunt her. At novel's closure, then, following Naomi's own private resolution, the silence still haunts in the absence of a Japanese Canadian name on this political document submitted to the government. The implication, in the materiality of the document, is that nothing has happened to change the social and political background to Naomi's experiences.

Naomi's tentative hold on her (now) unrecoverable past— only a scent remains of the memory of plenitude— stands in sharp contrast to the objectivity of the document signed by three men from the same white society that inflicted such violations on her family and community. And their comment that the dispersal of Japanese Canadians has worked and that the government need not "fear of [their] concentration on the Pacific Coast as in the past" (249) sounds the eerie note of forced assimilation— not outrage at the destruction of the community, not outrage at the dispossession, only the objection to deportation of Canadian citizens who have not committed any crime or act of disloyalty. Is it not the social system talking back to itself, resolving its own contradictions through the disguise of petition and pleas? Where is the subjectivity of Japanese Canadians in this document? The last word is written in the rhetoric of dominant language. The silence of Naomi's gesture is speechless. It is as if, by clothing herself in Aunt Emily's warmer coat, she has absorbed her aunt's verbal outrage, in a sense drawing her voice back into silence. *Obasan*, then, instead of resolving the dichotomy between silence and speech, between repression and exposure, ends within a gap where private and public are dichotomized as a stasis. Japanese Canadians are still *spoken for*. "The voices pour down like rain but in the middle of the downpour I still feel thirst. Somewhere between speech and hearing is a transmutation of sound" (245).

☐

Language, the vehicle of power, is a contaminated site. Truth does not reveal itself in the voice of clarity and plenitude— so Asian Canadian and other minority writers, speaking out of the finitude of their subjectivities, have to be vigilant not simply to mime the given narrative, genre, and filmic forms through which dominant values are aestheticized. Minority subject matter, when encoded in forms adjusted to accommodate the expectations of the social majority, can willy-nilly lead to compromise, distortion, and misrepresentation. Formal disruptions, such as the generic crossing of fiction, history, autobiography, and documentary in *Obasan,* become strategies of resistance to norms. In terms of receptivity, these strategies relativize the reader's performance and draw her out to the subjective limits (hence the otherness) of the text where minority perceptions are encountered in what could be thought of as their foreignicity.

Gilles Deleuze and Félix Guattari devise a useful term to describe the baffled textual screen characteristic of minority writing in its interface with dominant society: "deterritorialization." While they are talking about the strategies devised by Kafka, a Prague Jew whose first language was Czech but who had to write in the language of the majority, German, the term is appropriate for our discussion. By "deterritorialization," they point to a disturbed use of language that foregrounds its surface as a conflicted space. Minority writers, because of their subordinate position, must work in a language that disrupts the social stability of conventional discourse and communication, by setting in opposition "a purely intensive usage of language to all symbolic or even significant or simply signifying usages of it" (61). This recourse to an opaque language is tied to the other two planes of minority writing identified by Deleuze and Guattari: its immediate political implications and its connection to a collective experience.

The act of "deterritorialization" through writing is perhaps a viable method for resisting assimilation, for exploring variations in form that undermine aesthetic norms, for challenging homogenizing political systems, and for articulating subjectivities that emerge from beleaguered communities— even at the risk of incomprehensibility, unreadability, indifference, or outright rejection. The ethical and artistic dilemmas faced by writers of colour are considerable, given the burden of assuming the function of "writer" in various Canadian historical, political, social, and cultural contexts of colonization, marginalization, and discrimination. For Chinese and Japanese Canadians and Natives, these would include the legacy of systemic racism imposed through the historic absence of rights (the right to vote, for instance), discriminatory immigration laws, the extremes of which were the Chinese Head Tax and Exclusion Act, the internment of Japanese Canadians during and after World War II, and the cultural genocide of Native communities. These are issues that cannot simply be wished away, but become an integral part of the responsibility of language, texts, and the theoretical underpinnings of writers and cultural workers of colour.

In short, writers of colour, as minority writers in Canada, cannot escape basic questions about the writing act: for whom do you write? for the majority? or for more localized perspectives? These questions underlie the complicated relationship of the writer to the "reader," that vague unpredictable figure whose own subjectivity is conditioned by a multiplicity of determinants far beyond the intentionality of the text. To problematize the function of readership in current capitalist terms, that is, to transform the process of reading from passive consumption to critical interchange, the process of deterritorialization as a theoretical tool for Asian Canadian writers has to be, at the very least, carried out on two fronts simultaneously: (a) to generate the formal conditions so that the subjectivity of the writer, as a complex weave of internal and external pressures, can emerge in textual practice; and (b) to advance theoretical principles malleable enough to account for the enactment of subjectivities that cannot be contained by codification in mainstream critical discourses. Of course, both fronts implicate each other, though at present the former appears to be running ahead of the latter, at least in Canada.

The new wave of interest in so-called "minority" writing— with both positive and negative implications— is evident in the relative popularity of *Obasan*, and the more recent *Disappearing Moon Cafe* (1990), by Vancouver Chinese Canadian writer SKY Lee, and dramatically so in the production of anthologies. The anthology is, in many ways, a marketable container to present a "variety" of writers from one ethnic or cultural enclave, all at once as it were. In the past couple of years, for instance, there have been two Native anthologies, *All My Relations* (1990) and *Native Literature in English* (1991); *Shakti's Words* (1990), poetry by South Asian Canadian women; *Voices* (1992), writing by African Canadians; and the focus of my closing remarks for this essay, *Many-Mouthed Birds* (1991), poems and stories by Chinese Canadians.

From the perspective of writers of colour who are aligned through a shared history, ancestry, and culture, the anthology as mode of publication can be an empowering process and an opportunity for exchange, as general reading matter but also as educational texts that may penetrate the reading lists of institutions, such as in schools and universities. Nevertheless, the relative absence of theoretical awareness in minority groups has created complex risks of compromise and appropriation by publishers and otherwise well-intentioned editors and critics.

The old truism, "you can't tell a book from its cover," may once have been true, but in this design–obsessed consumerist era, the cover is often a tell-tale sign of power relations, stereotypes, and expectations. The cover of *Many-Mouthed Birds*, the dressing for the anthology, becomes a revealing text of the interface between a minority community and the sociocultural majority. It is the face that strikes the (potential) reader immediately: the exotic "Asian" soft-featured feminized male face, appearing out of the dark enclosure of bamboo leaves. This photo by Chinese Canadian artist Chick Rice is part of a series on Tommy Wong shown in the exhibit, "Yellow Peril Reconsidered"[6] but is here isolated and commodified for this anthology. In this decontextualized condition, the (appropriated) image evokes the familiar western stereotype of the Asian "othered," secretive and mysterious, a sign of "Chineseness"— Edward Said's "orientalism" *à la* Canadian colonialism. Framed by the capitalized territory of the cover, the face is stripped of the self-reflexivity, playfulness, and subtle eroticism of Chick Rice's photo series and becomes, instead, a more one-dimensional eurocentric frame of reference. Here, in an iconized space, "Chineseness" is reproduced as an "inscrutable" pool of silence, one of the "many-mouthed birds," now speaking out, now coming out. The cover invites the reader in to eavesdrop, to become a kind of voyeur— to listen in on the foreign, the effeminate "Asian" of western fantasies. This reaction is reinforced in the blurb explaining the title on the flyleaf and repeated on the back cover: it is an anglicized version of a "Chinese expression used to describe someone who disturbs the peace, who talks out of turn, who is indiscreet," so these writers are the many-mouthed birds "breaking a long and often self-imposed silence." Self-imposed, given the history of discrimination against Chinese Canadians throughout the century? Who is speaking here? I am not denying or downplaying the empowering agenda of the anthology, the cultural objective of its editors to open a venue for writers of Chinese ancestry, but the framing process itself, the anthology as commodity, cannot be ignored as one aspect of the public space within which texts by writers of colour are represented, received, codified, and racialized.

The critical treatment of *Obasan* and the cover of *Many-Mouthed Birds* are reminders of the need for reading approaches that respect and account for the contextual specificities of language, history, and narrative forms in texts by Asian Canadians and other writers of colour. The critical investigation of reader positioning may even be much more critical as their texts attract more attention as "insider" accounts of minority subjectivities. And as the "margins" constituted by centralization and dominancy become viable sites for domestication and normalization, particularly in economic and academic terms, the zone of conflict and transformation may very well become the theoretical spaces of readers, writers and cultural workers of colour— though the relationship is still asymmetrical, since publishers, reviewers, and critics (mostly white) control the conditions of receptivity and interpretation.

The power dynamics which anthologies that group writers of an "identified" ethnicity— the "Chinese Canadians" in the subtitle— have to navigate complicates the positioning of editors. The articulation of editorial decisions can shape the terms of the reception of an anthology as a cultural form, as well as deflect current issues of representation, language, and readership. The introduction, as entrance to the "community" of writers included, takes on added significance for anthologies that will be marked (and marketed) through the signs of ethnicity and "race."

For *Many-Mouthed Birds* the selection policy fails to contradict the implications of "orientalism" on the cover, and instead retreats to aesthetic values that skirt constraints placed on writers of colour: "The sole criterion was well-crafted and honest writing which could surprise, enlighten and entertain an ordinary reader" (1). Who might this "ordinary" reader be— if considered in relation to "many-mouthed birds," a phrase that derives from a Chinese expression that "describes someone who disturbs the peace"? The compromising bridge between the (potential) disruptiveness of the anthology and the commodificatory assumptions of "surprise, enlighten and entertain" misrepresents the texts of writers who resist, even reject, transparent aesthetic norms.

Strategies of deterritorialization in the reappropriation of "English" as the language of dominance and complicity— for instance in Jam. Ismail's "Scared Texts," Laiwan's "The Imperialism of Syntax," Sean Gunn's "And Then Something Went," and Fred Wah's "Elite"— can easily get lost in the absence of a critical foregrounding of writing as textuality. "A few experiment with language and form, while most stick to more traditional modes of narratives and storytelling" (3)— but again, the terminology veers over into the realm of the status quo, i.e., any departure from the norms is seen as "experiment," as if the "wayward" writers will soon return to the "traditional" (whose?) fold. Acts of deterritorialization are neutralized by contextualization within editorial spaces that recirculate idealized standards of canonization. Entering the anthology, white mainstream readers can appropriate the selections without having to read as other than "experiment" the instances of textual critiques of orientalism, exoticization, and cultural colonization.

☐

Today we are moving through a shifting mine-field of terminological cross-dressing and theoretical instabilities. Now more than ever there is an urgency to devise malleable critical methodologies that can adjust themselves to difference and relativity. In the current intellectual climate in which the constructedness of ideas and methodologies has become apparent, the truth-value of statements is open to question, often measured against ideological constraints. Knowledge is no longer the stable end of a process of interrogation and experimentation, but a transitory site, as the late Canadian poet bpNichol said, the "ledge" of what we "know," always subject to alternate directions as the frames keep changing.

I realize that my own comments are subject to the destabilized situation of all positions in these destabilized times. What appears to be a solution today becomes tomorrow's problem. Perhaps, for the

dont try to solve...?

foreseeable future at least, the shaping of cultural theories (I emphasize the plural) to understand the workings of "racialization" in the production of texts must be an on-going negotiation process, in which the terminology and frames applied are open-ended and flexible enough to adjust to exclusions and blind spots when these become visible. Perhaps the critical methodology that is called for at present is one that can articulate difference in such a way that the very notion of "otherness," which western thought has used to centralize "selfness" as source, as hierarchically prior, becomes obsolete as a way of defining people and cultures. What is important for a culture to thrive is a renewed belief in the viability of agency, so that writers from a diversity of subject-positions can develop the conditions in which social justice can be achieved through a language free from the tyranny of hegemonies of all kinds. It may be an impossible end, but the movement towards that "across cultural" end can initiate those heterogenous and indeterminate spaces (potentialities) where writers of colour, including Asian Canadian writers, can negotiate their (non-totalizable) specificities— without looking over their shoulders for the coercive gaze of homogenizing discourses.

NOTES

1. For a useful analysis of Canadian literary criticism and theory in the 1970s and early 1980s, see Barbara Godard, "Structuralism/Post-Structuralism: Language, Reality and Canadian Literature," *Future Indicative: Literary Theory and Canadian Literature*, ed. John Moss.

2. While Canadian literary theorists in academic institutions have been slow to undertake in-depth research on these issues, artists and writers of colour have contested homogenizing ideologies that do not account for the historical legacy of racism, colonization, and white supremacist assumptions. Of a handful of magazines that provide space for protest and dialogue, perhaps the most accessible is the Toronto-based *Fuse*. Marlene Nourbese Philip's collection of essays, *Frontiers*, also takes on the failure of Canadian institutions to face the conjunction of racism and culture behind the policies and practices that deny equality to writers and artists of colour.

3. The conference, "The Appropriate Voice," was organized by the Racial Minority Writers' Committee, at the time an advisory committee to the Writers' Union of Canada. The motion passed on cultural appropriation was subsequently presented to the Annual General Meeting of the Writers' Union. It was accepted, though the term "appropriation" was changed to

"misappropriation" against the opposition of the Racial Minority Writers' Committee, as reported by Val Ross in the *Globe and Mail*, June 8, 1992.

The issue of terminological limitations is far from being resolved for Canadian cultural issues. For instance, the term "racial minority writer," used by writers of colour in the Writers' Union of Canada, sounds outdated because of its implicit origins in the problematic term, "visible minority," a bureaucratic invention now largely rejected by writers and cultural workers of colour as a function of hegemonic discourse. "Racial" itself implies an essentialism that is blind to the historical constructedness of "race" signs in Canada; the term "racialization," as used in this discussion, is an effort to recognize the problematic ideological determination of "race" as an instrument of power. The term "minority," while rejected by many writers and cultural workers of colour for its implied structural subordination and categorization, has been retained for its relative value: that is, despite the global facts of population distributions, in specific Canadian contexts the term reflects the unequal political, social, and cultural status for communities of colour. The term "Asian Canadian" is also tentative and provisional, at least at this moment in Canadian cultural history. Many Canadians of Asian ancestry, if asked, would not relate to the generalization of commonalities implied, and would perhaps react negatively to such an alignment of communities from diverse source countries. Nevertheless, the term has assumed more theoretical importance amongst writers and cultural workers of Asian ancestry as a means of forging alliances necessary to develop a politics of cultural difference. Finally, the term "white" is not intended to erase differences amongst groups with ancestries in Europe or England, but refers to the dominant power system, historically shaping Canadian values and institutions, which has assumed the "racial" superiority and priority of British and European groups to both non-whites and to Natives who suffered the barbarism of colonization and appropriation. As the cultural politics of Canada continues to unfold, no doubt terminology will undergo continuing obsolescence. Like sand castles, the words that look good today will (most likely) be swept away by the tides of interrogation.

4. The term "imagined" is here connected to the term "i mage" as used by Marlene Nourbese Philip in "The Absence of Writing or How I Almost Became a Spy," an introductory commentary to *She Tries Her Tongue, Her Silence Softly Breaks*. Colonized writers for whom "English" is the language of oppression and erasure have to recover denied localisms and specificities through the immediacy of image in the material conditions of memory.

5. Characteristically, Canadian critics foreground this "event" as a moment of transcendence: Naomi, and the novel, too, rises above the politics of internalized racism to achieve a personal peace of mind; see, for instance, Erika Gottlieb's "The Riddle of Concentric Worlds in *Obasan*" and Marilyn Russell Rose's "Politics into Art: Kogawa's *Obasan* and the Rhetoric of Fiction."

6. The catalogue for this exhibit, which featured photo, film, and video work by twenty-five Asian Canadian artists, was published as *Yellow Peril Reconsidered*, ed. Paul Wong.

Sliding the Scale of Elision:
"Race" Constructs / Cultural Praxis

You are better off not knowing how sausages and laws are made.
— Fortune Cookie

One: It's happening only yesterday and today

"Race" under erasure[1]— not in futurity or in a haloed heritage but in present tenseness— becomes itself a floating signifier, stable only apparently in the conformity of reference. Recent interventions in cultural praxis have dislodged its transparency to make visible its historical and current signs of circulation. Lucius Outlaw, echoing other theorists, calls for the exposure of "race thinking" as "a way of conceptualizing and organizing social worlds composed of persons whose differences allow for arranging them into groups that come to be called 'races'" (61), and he proposes critical work that would "challenge the presumptions sedimented in the 'reference schemata' that, when socially shared, become common sense..." (59).[2]

☐

This, then, is a real story. It happened at Pearson International Airport in Toronto. It is told by Makeda Silvera in "Caribbean Chameleon" (from *Her Head a Village*). "She" is not named. "She" is not the teller of the tale but the narration. "Woman in black polka dot pant suit" (28) returns from a visit to Jamaica. "She" is speech, speaking, spoken, moving in a line, in a line-up, crossing the line from body talk into state discourse.

In the passage through the gauntlet of customs, interrogation is the only form that matters. This border zone tolerates no divergences, no irregularities. Speak in the grid of compliance, "safe" (30), pass through.

Speak otherwise, even a miniscule syllable off and the rap trap ties tongue in knots:

> "Purpose?" "Vacation, mam." "Where did you stay?" "Kingston, mam."
> "Did you stay with family?" "No mam, I visit dem, but I stay in a hotel."
> Suspicion. "Hotel?" "Yes mam." "Take off your glasses, please." Officer
> look lady in black polka dot pant suit up and down. (30-31)

Once "she" is gazed as an other, power proceeds to strip "her"— of her rights (though she has, as she *says*, her "'landed papers right here'") and her subject status. The chaoticization of her baggage mimes her own "speaking in tongues," as "Woman in black polka dot pant suit" undergoes linguistic transference into "Black polka dot woman" (31). When a body search is ordered, "she" is pressed into the zone of elision, reduced to mere resistance:

> Black polka dot woman don't wait. Tear off shirt. Tear off jacket. Tear
> off pants. Polka dot woman reach for bra. For drawers. Officer shout
> for Royal Canadian Mounted Police to take mad woman away. "TAKE
> HER AWAY. TAKE HER AWAY." Take this wild savage. Monster.
> Jungle beast. "AWAY. Arrest her for indecent exposure." (32)

The "arrest" brings down the police state, stopping further leakage, further "indecent exposure," through the seams of the event. Ritual banishment then confirms and authorizes the race expectations the "woman in polka dot pant suit" did not, at first, fulfill for the customs officer at the gateway to "Canada." But once "she" is framed by the colonizing discourse of "wild savage," and suitably dehumanized, civilized order (read here "whiteness" as measure) is restored.

The miscodes of elision, then, disperse a semiotics of static and the criss-cross of duplicities on the surfaces of race constructs. On the other hand, the power these constructs have to mutate, in the light of exposure, ensures the recirculation of dominant relations. Such odds make the project of anti-racism all the more formidable and open to neutralization and containment. The encounter (as in "Caribbean Chameleon") is not unlike the dream landscape suddenly rendered arational by site-specific quicksand, the linguistic body drawn into the collapsing folds of liquid white-out. Where, under erasure, is the line to resist disappearance?

□

This, then, is a social construction. This is the narrative as "Neil Bissoondath" who masquerades in the folds of *Saturday Night*— "don't call me ethnic"— saying "i" has transcended race yet speaks as one whose authority derives from his "colour." The resurrected body on the cover identifies "multiculturalism" as an infection that produces "the ethnic deracinated and costumed" (19) who then transforms into the divisive social force embodied in the racialized other. "To be 'racialized,'" says Bissoondath, tying the term to "Miki"— labelled "Canadian of Japanese descent" by a supposedly beyond race and ethnicity perceiver— "is to have acquired a racial vision of life" (18). The logic of association mimes the state discourse used to justify the internment of persons "of Japanese race" in the 1940s.[3]

"Racialization," as used by Miki, applies to the imposition of race constructs and hierarchies on marked and demarked "groups" whose members come to signify divergence from the normative body inscribed by whiteness. The subject racialized is identified by systemic categorizes that winnow the body, according privilege to those glossed with dominance and privation to those digressed to subordination.

In reworking the term to re-racialize writers of colour, Bissoondath would have *his* readers believe that racialization is not a social script but an identity formation wilfully assumed— and this willy-nilly recasts the racialized into the racist. Such illogic, through which the victim becomes the victimizer, is a historical model of blame very familiar to those with not-white bodies in Canadian social topographies. But what is finally more telling of the nation's media machine is not Bissoondath's words— it is his own marked body and the privileges it is given for speaking the discourse of whiteness.[4] Long before the *Saturday Night* feature face, Dionne Brand had pinpointed the more pervasive neo-colonial strategy at work: "In producing a Neil Bissoondath to denounce the cultural appropriation critique, the white cultural establishment produces a dark face to dismiss and discredit all the other dark faces and simultaneously to confirm and reinscribe that colonial representation which is essential to racial domination" ("Who Can Speak for Whom?" 19).

□

In the title story of Silvera's *Her Head a Village*, the unnamed narrator, a writer, struggles with an essay, "Writing as a Dangerous Profession," while her head is filled with conflicting voices of a "noisy village" all pulling her in contrary directions. The story rejects the autonomous self of western humanism and instead spatializes the narrator's imagination as the site of variable and conflicting subject positions as "Black woman writer" (12). The textual seams she exposes begin to reconfigure a language in which discourses of racialization are revealed as the medium of social and political power. This move acknowledges the limits of representation, while calling for a cultural praxis that can work through the alien-national effects of "racial formation"— a term adopted by Michael Omi and Howard Winant to identify "the process by which social, economic and political [and cultural] forces determine the content and importance of racial categories, and by which they are in turn shaped by racial meanings" (*Racial Formation* 61).

Two: A caveat for this "i"

When the "i" is inscribed in this sentence, what are the signs of race? In an interview with Sneja Gunew in *The Post-Colonial Critic*, Gayatri

Spivak says that "the question 'Who should speak?' is less crucial than 'Who will listen?'" (59)— and in that shift displaces the weight already straining the back of the speaker and locates responsibility in those who decode the signs. If the economy of race governs the rules of reception, and if subjects are spoken by discourses even as they speak through them, how do the dynamics of power and the making of identity operate in the contextual field of a text performed, as this one is? Does the signifying body remain the veil of race constructs, or can an interventionist tactic of writing the body enable a transformative act of listening?

Homi Bhabha talks about the encounter with "identity" as a disruption, and when it "occurs at the point at which something exceeds the frame of the image, it eludes the eye, evacuates the self as site of identity and autonomy and— most important— leaves a resistant trace, a stain of the subject, a sign of resistance" (*The Location of Culture* 49). The racialized subject in performance enacts such limits and in the effects of dispersal cannot take shelter in the so-called "reasonable" academic model of exchange. In each syntactic turn, even in the vehicular language of information, the racialized seams of social, cultural and political formations produce the "i" as a conditioned pronoun reference. So Chantal Mouffe writes in *The Return of the Political*:

...we are in fact always multiple and contradictory subjects, inhabitants of a diversity of communities (as many, really, as the social relations in which we participate and the subject positions they define), constructed by a variety of discourses, and precariously and temporarily sutured at the intersection of those subject positions. (20-21)

When *this* "i" addresses race elision, in which subject formation (of many "multiple and contradictory") will it be listened to, if such listening occurs in the first place? Media constructions have identified "him" as a "writer of colour," as a member of a group called "Japanese

Canadian," as a "Canadian of Japanese ancestry," as an "academic," an "editor," a "cultural activist," even a "trouble-maker." Given space to speak here, in addressing a "you," is this "i" then a given or is this space determined by the proliferation of race signs on the borders of what even now gets told, seen, and heard?

Three: Wither goeth CanCrit?

The institutionalization of CanLit with its twin CanCrit— since the nationalist zealotry of the 1960s— rather than articulating, has left unexamined the cultural conditions conducive to race elision. The "normally" benign rhetoric of "national identity" has worked to cover over the nation-building role of an exclusionary "identity" in the neo-colonial shadows of cultural sovereignty. The ethnocentricity of the quest to possess colonized space, operating through a masking of motive and power, has been disguised in the compulsive will to reify the authority of one's own nation as a sign of liberation. In a critique of this "displaced form of nationalism," Robert Lecker foregrounds the self-serving— that is, insular and unreflexive— production of literary criticism that established, in a period of only twenty years, a canon-forming industry serving as "an expression of national self-consciousness" ("Canonization" 658).

"We do not know why the Canadian canon includes certain texts and excludes others" (659), Lecker argues— but speaking as he does *within* his institutional boundaries, he can only point the finger of blame, not advocate methodological strategies to explode the Anglo-European identity politics that imprints itself through a process of differing at the expense of "its" racialized others. In response to Frank Davey's charge that he has failed to interrogate difference, Lecker admits to his own "split emotion" on the consequences of his "inquiry into value" (the subtitle of his essay) that he promotes.[5] If nationalist CanLit (a "security blanket") is destroyed, the "orthodox fantasy of the peaceable kingdom" ("Critical Response II" 683) will also be de-

ROY MIKI

stroyed. This "split" in Lecker is less personal than symptomatic of a strategic displacement that simultaneously critiques the institution and protects its territory. Lecker may appear to destabilize boundaries in calling on his colleagues to recognize (citing Louis Montrose) "'the textual construction of critics who are themselves historical subjects'" ("Canonization" 661), but in rationalizing that the "split" in himself "has nothing to do with intellectual validity or sophistication or consistency" ("Critical Response II" 683), he retreats to the already constituted chambers of the institution's cultural authority. In other words, the terminological normalizations that scaffold Lecker's discourse remain intact— in a taken-for-granted position. Terms like "canon," "value," "literary history," "national," and the most telling of all, "Canadian," may allow for gestures towards those "differences" outside, but they function to prevent them from infiltrating the rhetorical borders of the inquiry.[6] What would happen, for example, if the term "Canadian" were dispersed into all the lines of alterity that, in actuality, striate the social body?

The predictable recourse to the unproblematized "we" in the concluding section of Lecker's essay forestalls this question, drawing the discourse into alignment with the originating narrative of cultural sovereignty. CanLit, like the "Canadian" nation, is a formation that cannot be separated from the cultural territorialization of space that accompanies the colonization process. This line of descent echoes D.G. Jones' astounding declaration at the outset of *Butterfly on Rock* that the land is "ours" because "our westward expansion is complete" (3), so that, in national cultural terms, "we" have also "arrived at a point where we recognize... that we are the land's" (3). Such an apparently affirmative nativization (the underbelly of nationalism) displaces, while neutralizing, the violent appropriation of First Nations lands and cultures.[7]

The messianic-like declaration of ownership, though, betrays an "ambivalence" (to draw on Homi Bhabha's analysis of "nation" narration) that seeks to be exorcized by assertions of "identity," assertions of "value," assertions that CanLit does indeed exist. The academic labour that went into the three-volume *Literary History of Canada* (1965), with its famous "Conclusion" by Northrop Frye, was less a descriptive task and more the making of a teleological history that narrated CanLit into existence.[8] It is in this context, moreover, that Canadian nationalists (e.g., prominently by Margaret Atwood in *Survival* and Dennis Lee in "Cadence, Country, Silence") adopted the language of victimization to place "Canadian" cultural identity in opposition to its external enemies, American and British imperialisms. This triadic model justified a reductive "Canadianness"— a cultural lineage linked to an essentialized British past— that elided the relations of dominance inside the country, what has been called "internal colonialism."[9] The internal structures of dominance include a racialization process in which non-white subjects in the Canadian state are subordinated as "others" who inhabit a realm of shadows, of chaotic darkness, of "non-persons" (see Marcia Crosby, "Construction of the Imaginary Indian" 288).[10] If the assumption is that critics, academics, and theorists are social subjects whose actions are necessarily enmeshed with dominant values, then the products of their research and writing must signify in terms of omissions, containments, and displacements.

Even critical work that proposes itself as the cutting edge may be unable to extricate itself from the historical determinants of its institutional setting. One example (of mid-to-late 1980s criticism) is *Future Indicative: Literary Theory and Canadian Literature* (1987), the proceedings of an academic gathering hailed by its editor, John Moss, as "prophetic," the next fold in the "open future" of criticism following the "exhausted condition" of "thematic criticism" (1).[11] The announcement of this radical departure— this movement beyond "thematic"— is nonetheless contained within the familiar walls of the CanLit institution. Despite the fine essays presented by a number of the most accomplished critical theorists in Canada, including essays that address questions of difference,[12] the readers who make their way through the collection find few signs that "Canadian" signifies much more than a diversity of approaches to "Canadian literature," a term that is itself not dismembered. *Future Indicative* may be a welcome relief from the totalizing and homogenizing agenda of nationalist thematic criticism, but critical race consciousness is still parked in the boundary zones both outside and inside the limits of its discourse. When signs of difference and contradiction do appear, the conference context and critical framing— which is to say, the institution of CanCrit that governs inclusions and exclusions— neutralize potential disruptions to the projected social and cultural spaces in the texts.

For this reason Moss' praise for the theoretical audacity represented in the collection is misleading, as evident, for instance, in a statement such as the following:

> They have been deconstructing the box in which we have tried to contain our culture; not peering over the garrison walls but walking right through them. Suddenly, people working from a literary base which includes *Wacousta* and Carman along with Wordsworth and Arnold are bringing critical theory from Paris and Oxford and New Haven to bear, from their perspectives in Vancouver or Fredericton or, yes, even Ottawa, on literary experience of their own country. (3)

In the assumption of national maturation, of liberation from colonialism, of an internationalist literary context, and of a cosmopolitanism, the term "Canadian" continues to function as a Derridean transcendental signified, and "flourishing diversity" (1) has more to do with the individual points of view of the speakers than to the cultural condition of Canada. The ambivalences cutting across the institutional history of nation-based criticism are absorbed by a) concluding that "future" work will have to find solutions for exclusions— think here of the racialized "Canadians" who are not represented in the collection; or b) difference is addressed in the attention paid to gender (Godard and Neuman), "the image of the indigene" (Goldie), ethnocentrism (Murray), and ethnicity (Loriggio)— think here of the term race that

makes possible "our heritage" (93) as derived from white, patriarchic, Anglo-European, and imperialist/colonialist legacies. For all
the implications of change, the critical mapping remains the representation of the national space: there are no writers and critics from
First Nations communities and communities of colour in the
volume.[13]

Future Indicative, as a textual performance, discloses the power of
literary discourse to establish and arbitrate norms, stances, and perspectives in the production of paradigms for framing cultural processes. In
the face of contradictions and contestations that threaten to unravel
institutional borderlines, establishment discourse can manoeuvre terminology that reinscribes relations of internal dominance. In "'Circling
the Downspout of Empire,'" for instance, Linda Hutcheon displaces
the immediacy of race issues in contemporary cultural politics by
differentiating the "postmodern" from the "post-colonial" in what can
be read as a strategic manner:

> The current post-structuralist/postmodern challenges to the coherent,
> autonomous self or subject have to be put on hold in feminist and
> post-colonial discourses, for these must work first to assert and affirm
> a denied or alienated subjectivity: those radical postmodern challenges
> are in many ways the luxury of the dominant order, which can afford
> to challenge what it securely possesses. (70-71)[14]

The critical logic of Hutcheon's statement, while apparently
"making sense" of the dividing line between postmodernism and
post-colonialism— which is why it sounds the note of clarity— is
symptomatic of the pattern in Canadian criticism to establish a binary
model that relegates those subject to subordination and alterity to the
margin and simultaneously bestows priority and founding status on the
centre. In the evolutionary model presented, the "postmodern," as
what comes first, becomes an extension of the "dominant order." In
a Canadian context this "order" stands in for the Anglo-European

(white male) norms that designate certain writers to be "coherent, autonomous" subjects, while those then framed as the excluded "others," i.e., feminists and post-colonials (read here, non-white, immigrant), "must work *first* to assert and affirm a denied or alienated subjectivity" (emphasis added). These poor souls are still struggling with their "alienated subjectivity," so cannot yet enter the "luxury of the dominant order" where the "autonomous self" can be challenged— because the postmodernist has a "self" that is "securely possesse[d]," as securely as the land has been possessed by the nation. By separating the dominant order (postmodernism) from the dominated (post-colonialism), Hutcheon maintains the hierarchic social order that situates the racialized under the sign of those "others" who are still struggling to enter the dominant order (where the postmodernist already resides). This terminology depends on the static and containing model of "centre-margin" (dominant-subordinate) as a means of eliding the instrumental power of racialized assumptions in critical discourse.

Such an effacement, on the other hand, accounts for the very contradiction that exposes the seams of a "beyond" where cultural production is instrumental for those who cannot claim "secure" representation in dominant institutions.

Four: But what about *Obasan*?

Obasan, Joy Kogawa's first novel, was born into an enviable milieu of glowing reviews which immediately attached the seal of authority and authenticity to its narration of Japanese Canadian internment. The approval was followed by a succession of critical articles, as Canadian academics circled its textual body with interpretive strategies that penetrated its apparent foreignness: on the one hand, by decoding its "Japanese" values and "Japanese Canadian" identity; and on the other hand, by aligning its textual strategies to contemporary critical values reified by academic critics, for instance, its problematization of genres, its stylistic or "poetic" density, and the individualization of its main character, Naomi Kato, a third generation Japanese Canadian.[15]

But whose interest does literary theory and criticism serve? Is the acclaim of *Obasan* a sign that "Japanese Canadians" have transcended racialization, and that they can be conceptualized as normalized "Canadians"? Are formerly ethnocentric institutions, such as CanLit, being radically transformed by the inclusion of a racialized text? Is the critical attention heaped on *Obasan* a blessing in disguise? Or if, as Omi and Winant remind us, the "meaning and salience of race are forever being reconstituted in the present" ("On the Theoretical Concept of Race" 7), is such institutionalization a contemporary recirculation? Can this be a factor in the absence of race awareness in the critical frameworks that have evaluated *Obasan* as a CanLit novel? And if, following on Lawrence Grossberg, a cultural text such as *Obasan* is approached as "a place at which a multiplicity of forces (determinations and effects) are articulated" (90), what are the politics of representation implied by its valorization? Such questions raise obfuscations that call for a consideration of race variables in the reception and institutionalization of texts.

The disruption of a non-reflexive model of reading brings into play a contextual reading of *Obasan* that exposes a "multiciplicity of forces," including internalizations connected to complex patterns of complicity, substitution, and containment. The reader's subject position, for instance, would implicate such terms as "race," gender, class, and institutional affiliations. The non-white writer's subject position, in turn, would implicate effects of racialization, oppression, education, cultural conditioning, response to social expectations of genre and history. The representation of the subjects, "Japanese Canadians," would operate within social, historical, and politics limits, not just in the reader but in the writer as well, and the terms of representation would necessarily incorporate historical precedents in the community, in government documents, in institutionalized studies, and in the visual and print media. The institutional frameworks that establish boundaries of significance would be investigated as ideological determinants of race assumptions, and this would raise the question of a coalescence of complicities between textual strategies and the canonizing agenda of nationalist-oriented institutions.

One site of *Obasan*'s textual space that exacerbates the coherence of narrative form— and deflects the seams of race in the interpretive process— has operated under erasure. Readings have circled so intently the central character, Naomi, and her portrayal— accepted, even if provisionally, as an autobiographical pointer to author Joy Kogawa— that authorial positioning has not received serious critical attention.[16] Representations, though, as Linda Alcoff says in "The Problem of Speaking for Others," conflate the act of speaking for (i.e., standing in for absent subjects) and speaking about. In the case of *Obasan*, non-Japanese Canadian (mainly academic) readers have essentialized the author "Joy Kogawa," as a typical Japanese Canadian who experienced internment and whose representation (in both senses) of Japanese Canadians must be authentic. Such transparent "realism," however, imposes homogeneity on the racialized subject and denies knowledge of the perceptual limits of "Kogawa the writer" whose imagination participates in the invention of a "Japanese Canadian" subject positioning. It ignores the often multifaceted, indeterminate, and even duplicitous zones in texts that are constrained by racialized systems of power.

The limits of representation become visible in *Obasan*, as the first-person narrative of Naomi is spliced by the barely visible hand of the author who shapes the narrative through perspectival immersion in a reconstructed history/memory, but who also stands beside the narrative to construct a text that responds to the internalized pressure of racialization. Authorial interventions are most apparent in textual sites that harbour a consciousness external to Naomi's personal memories, which is to say a consciousness functioning beyond Naomi's bounded range of knowledge, awareness, and understanding. At least five such sites— more may be isolated by indirection or implication—

foreground themselves through heightened textual density and doubleness in the narrative: the biblical citation used as an epigraph to open
the text; the document signed by three white men that closes the text;
the prose poem preceding the beginning of Naomi's story, in which
"silence" has "no reply" (iv); the passage of descent marking the
uprooting from the west coast, dated 1942, as the communal "we"
form first appears and is said to "disappear into the future undemanding
as dew" (112); and the "Canada" passage, near the climax of the
narrative, in which the "we" form re-appears, this time embodying
the nation, as "Japanese Canadians"— once "aliens" in their own
country— are born in the landscape: "Oh Canada, whether it is
admitted or not, we come from you we come from you. From the
same soil, the slugs and slime and bogs and twigs and roots" (226).
Removed from the narrative frames of Naomi's first-person quest,
Japanese Canadians in these sites are identified as silenced, bereft of
authority, disappeared, assimilated— in other words, as an erased
collective that has lost the agency of self-representation.

It is this thematic that accommodates the ambivalent significance
of the opening and closing of *Obasan*. The epigraph, for instance, when
re-read in terms of representational contingencies, is far more conflicted than at first appearance. Indeed, the implications of its doubled
textual signs destabilize the pervasive use of biblical allusions and
references, including the symbolic overlay of exodus to narrativize
Japanese Canadian internment as ritual banishment, wandering, and
eventual salvation. The citation, lineated to resemble a found poem,
comes from the Book of Revelations:

> To him that overcometh
> will I give to eat
> of the hidden manna
> and will give him
> a white stone

and in the stone

a new name written...

Within a conventional literary treatment of reference, the epigraph can be read— and has been read— as a premonition that the narrative conflict of *Obasan* will be resolved. The implication is that the protagonist, Naomi Kato, will emerge with a new identity after she has made her descent into her repressed history and memory. When read as a reaction to racialization, the same biblical frame reverses into a doubled discourse of white supremacy and reveals itself as a mechanism (as Christianity was used in colonization) of enforced assimilation. The "othered" racial "object" undergoes translation into whiteness; her former subject identity, already under erasure by the racism of the past, is abandoned for a new name written on "white stone."

This biblical text finds its symmetrical counterpart in the document that closes *Obasan*, the excerpt from a brief submitted by the Cooperative Committee on Japanese Canadians, a group of white liberals who spoke for— in the absence of— Japanese Canadians on the federal government's unjust deportation proposal. The excerpt opposes the deportation of "Japanese Canadians" on the basis of their obvious innocence. While such a document, again in the common sense of reference, demonstrates that not all Canadians were brutally indifferent to the violation of citizenship rights, it also closes the novel with Japanese Canadians framed as the "other" with no voice and language, and who therefore have to be spoken for by white males. The rhetoric of their letter, its use of liberal terminology, mimics— albeit for other purposes— the same rhetoric adopted to justify the dispossession of Japanese Canadians. The writers, in fact, point to the destruction of the community and assimilation as evidence that they *no longer* pose a security threat to Canada. There is no outrage at the victimization made possible by racist legislation and policies. The system, in other words, remains intact. The discourse of dominance— in contrast to

Naomi's gentle aesthetic moment of recovery and healing at the coulee— still controls the positioning of those violated by the state machinery of racialization.

It is this forking into dichotomous paths of resolution, reinforced by the textually flat, hence effect of mundanity, of the found text/brief, that enables the crescendo of Naomi's personal "salvation" within the aesthetic agenda of the novel. Once the material conditions of an actual community have been placed under narrative erasure, and with the language of politics reduced to a supplement, non-Japanese Canadian readers are prompted to identify with Naomi— which is to say, assume her subject position— without having to negotiate the race codes that constitute the semiotic field of their relationship. The fullness of the aesthetic moment domesticates the foreignness of "ethnicity," "race," and "subject-position" and allows access to a transcendent position that reinscribes the liberal humanist values of national (read here white anglocentric) culture.

Obasan, then, can be read as a "Canadian" story of an individual who achieves self presence, and therefore liberation from racialization, through aesthetic transcendence. Understandably, from this perspective, as attractive as Aunt Emily may appear because of her incessant discourse on racism, injustice, citizenship, and democracy, her subject position is futile: "All of Aunt Emily's words, all her papers, the telegrams and petitions, are like scratchings in the barnyard, the evidence of much activity" (189) but finally leading nowhere. Seeking political redress for the internment, Aunt Emily is represented as trapped in her discourse and thereby prevented from developing an interior life, as Naomi does. The novel instructs readers that the only means of resolving the past is through personal transformation— a point that is driven home in its final aesthetic moment that begins as Naomi dons Aunt Emily's coat (246), in effect silencing her endless political chatter.

In *Post-National Arguments: The Politics of the Anglophone-Canadian Novel Since 1967*, Frank Davey challenges the depoliticization of

literature by nationalist readers who "aestheticize literature by conceal-
ing its participation in the social and conflictual processes that produce
culture" (17). Novelists, on the other hand, construct protagonists who
"seek the shelter of individual salvation" (253), who "place the source
and responsibility for social interaction outside the social arena" (253),
or who "withdraw from politics" (255). Both end up endorsing the
"classical liberal model" of the individual who must make it on her
own, or who must "console herself with visions of transcendence"
(262). *Obasan*, one of the sixteen novels discussed, falls into this
"anglophone" pattern by rejecting the political (as embodied in Aunt
Emily) in favour of a "universal nature" (108) as the totalizing source
of meaning— "much like that of Morag's mysterious river [which] is
made to appear to cancel out all the social injustices of *The Diviners*"
(108). The comparison with Laurence is apropos, given the nationalist
strategies evident in *Obasan*, but even Davey homogenizes *Obasan* by
not considering the politics of difference that marks its textuality in the
"race" constructs that operate in CanLit to limit its production and
reception.

Naomi's recovery of a "universal nature" that transcends the
specificity of injustice needs to be read as an effect of internalization.
Indeed, the very presence of an author who narrates the Japanese
Canadian community as disappeared implies a strategy of bridging—
not between two separate "cultures"— but two interlocking racialized
sites: that of the other and of the norm, whiteness. Here, the atomic
blast in Nagasaki functions not only to resolve Naomi's narrative quest
for knowledge but also to recontextualize Japanese Canadian internment in relation to an event of such horrific proportions that it flattens
its enormity. On the scale of human suffering, in other words, the
"Japanese Canadian" examples cannot compare to the devastation
caused by the atomic bomb. From this narrative perspective, the bomb,
as a textual element, serves simultaneously to relativize and universalize
the particularity of Japanese Canadian internment, and it is this doubled
recontextualization that deflects the political ramifications of its site-

specific "Canadian" conditions. Moreover, in the logic of the Judeo-Christan symbology that gives coherence to the narrative, the bomb fills in for that apocalyptic moment, hinted at in the biblical epigraph, when Naomi's old racialized identity will undergo translation in a new name written on "white stone."

That translation, and its primacy as a textual construct, thus performs the personal redemption of history achieved through narrative. As Japanese Canadian internment is transformed through this lens, race comes under erasure to allow for a depoliticization process in which the power of the victimizer, the Grand Inquisitor, who is both Old Man Gower (the child abuser) and the Canadian government, is internalized by the victim. "Am I her accuser?" (228) Naomi asks herself, assuming the burden of being her mother's Grand Inquisitor. This misplacement of blame, on the one hand, elides the materiality of history, but on the other, valorizes the humanist allegory of suffering as a "universal" condition. Japanese Canadian internment loses its phenomenological edges and takes on the exegetical role of the exemplum. In the descent passage already mentioned, the intervening authorial presence speaks through a biblical allusion that frames the expulsion of Japanese Canadians from the west coast as a moral tale: "We are the man in the Gospel of John, born into the world for the sake of the light. We are sent to Siloam, the pool called 'Sent.' We are sent to the sending, that we may bring sight" (111). The livestock buildings used to confine Japanese Canadians at Hastings Park in Vancouver, also called the "Pool," are read as the biblical Siloam where the blind man in the Gospel of St. John receives sight again. As an exemplum, Japanese Canadian suffering brings sight to readers of *Obasan*.

It is this moral intent that has formed the crux of what might be described as an interpretive complicity, perhaps explaining why *Obasan* has been the one novel of colour that has been situated so canonically in the institutional halls of CanLit. Playing on this exegetical cross-road of critical potential, the cover's blurb— in the Penguin edition—

invites nation-minded readers of this "moving novel" to remember "a time and a suffering *we* have tried to forget" (emphasis added). As Scott Toguri McFarlane also confirms in his critical reading of the cover itself, the implication is that *Obasan*— the text of Japanese Canadian internment— belongs to this country.[17] That collective "we," which of course acts to exclude subjects identified as "Japanese Canadian," is the operative term for methodologies of institutional readings that consistently fail to account for issues of appropriation and misrepresentation. The critical traffic, at least in a Canadian context, has been mainly a one-way affair: the critic as objective (read here "professional") reader extracting meaning from the text without reflecting on the politics of such interpretation. The blindness to subject position— a blindness that has been endemic to CanCrit— allows the reader from the majority white "we" to inhabit the text, see through the third-generation eyes of Naomi, and reconstruct patterns of resolution for the "suffering we have tried to forget." From this vantage point *Obasan* can become an object of knowledge as a Canadianized text that teaches "us" about racism in "our" past. This pedagogical legitimation expells the ambivalences of race in the nation's forms and serves to compensate through proof that "we" have learned from the past. "'It was a terrible business what we did to *our* Japanese'" (emphasis added; 225), reflects Mr. Barker, the white patriarch of the farm that contained the racialized chicken shed that housed Naomi and her family. Two decades later, the past in which he benefited from Japanese Canadian suffering has been absolved in the nation's memory. Perhaps in a similar way the hierarchic model of readership ("our" *Obasan*) re-enacts the internment process through which "Japanese Canadians"— once branded the "enemy alien" within— are assimilated by the gaze of institutional possession.

As a field of multiple determinants, the text of *Obasan* both constructs and is contructed by critical approaches that open pathways of least resistance for the majority "we" whose own subject positions are linked to the nation-state powers responsible for victimizing

Canadians of Japanese ancestry. One can argue, then, that *Obasan* was negotiating an entrance to majority culture at a time racialized writers were under pressure— both internally and externally— to present their so-called "minority" subjectivity in dominant aesthetic, linguistic, and narrative forms. How might readers have responded to the opacity of the Japanese language had translation not been so smoothly inserted in the narrative? What would have been the effect of the absence of biblical references which anchor Japanese Canadian experience in Judeo-Christian myths and allusions? What would be the narrative consequence had Naomi not framed her memory under the signs of British imperialism— but had been more critical of their influence on her self identity? These questions remain in the realm of speculation to encourage theorization that acknowledges the labour and risk already undertaken by writers such as Kogawa, and that also assists in understanding complicity as a limit to textual production. In the meantime, *Obasan* remains— and will remain— a key text in the on-going struggle to resist misrepresentations in institutional incorporations of "raced" texts.

Five: Re-Siting Writing thru Race

This weekend we've gotten a glimpse, the tip of the iceberg.
— Lillian Allen, Press Conference for "Writing thru Race," July 3, 1994, Vancouver

For a brief period, February to May 1994, the traces of race proliferated and came to visibility around a writers' conference when enrollment was limited to "First Nations writers and writers of colour." The speckled bird of media, "Writing thru Race" even infiltrated the House of Commons where, in a posture of white outrage, Reform MP Jan Brown called the conference policy "racist" and demanded the removal of federal loonies. In a posture of response, Minister of Canadian Heritage, Michel Dupuy, announced his *personal* decision—

perhaps as himself a cultural activist— to deny support of $22,500 already approved. The event was saved from the dustbin of discarded tropes through a last minute fundraising campaign.[18] In the midst of the verbal spectacle, the institutional silence was systemic. Cultural and literary specialists remained in their garrisons as the "voice" of media isolated writers of colour with the markings of race spectres that spooked the ideological undercurrents of a white Canada. The elision of race in CanLit guaranteed that a conference bringing together writers of colour would be vulturized and canned by the media in the common-sense terms circulating in everyday Canadian life.

The domino effect by which "Writing thru Race" was framed can be tracked to Robert Fulford's appropriation of a report published in the newsletter of the Writers' Union of Canada, to which he had access as a member.[19] But instead of responding to the membership, he capitalized on his privilege by making the report the focus of a *Globe and Mail* column, "George Orwell, Call Your Office" (March 30, 1994), labelling the conference "apartheid" in what he termed the "no-whites rule"— with "rule" a reference to conference policy, not to power, though that may have been intended. The article ignited fellow columnist Michael Valpy. In his "A Nasty Serving of Cultural Apartheid" (April 8, 1994), Valpy transforms Fulford into a cultural hero, as he too echoes "apartheid," then goes one step further to read "Writing thru Race" as the harbinger of a social "cancer" that threatens "Canadian cultural identity." In Valpy's sociopsychic space, there are shades of the demons in the dreams of "white men and women" in colonial BC who were haunted by visions of being "daily over-run by hordes of Chinese laborers" (words of "Amor do Cosmos to the Electors of Victoria District, June 20, 1882," cited by Patricia Roy in *A White Man's Province* [37]). Read here, for Chinese labourers, writers of colour, and the shadows begin to flutter.

After an editorial ("Excluding Whites") in the *Toronto Star*, April 5, condemning the conference for its policy, a critical turn occurred, so notes Sourayan Mookerjea in his reconstruction of media reaction, as "the controversy switched circuits and moved from being something to editorialize about to something to report on" ("Some Special Times" 118).[20] The first report, from Canadian Press, appeared on April 7 (titled "Conference Stirs Controversy" in the *Vancouver Sun*) and functioned to identify— not the purpose and details of the conference— but the media's treatment of the conference as a "controversy." The only story was the "non-whites only policy" (echo of Fulford's "no-whites rule") and the interrogation of funding agencies. In other words, the issue of "white exclusion" took front and centre as the power of whiteness represented by public funders— which included at its apex the Minister of Canadian Heritage— was evoked to threaten writers of colour with retaliation. The naming of the conference as a "controversy," then, established the binary narrative of a conflict: innocent whites excluded on the basis of *their* race versus self-centred writers of colour using "taxpayer" funds to segregate themselves. The assumption, of course, is that the cardboard cut-out of nationhood, the "taxpayer," is white.

On April 16, when Bronwyn Drainie entered the fray with her column, "Controversial Writers' Meeting Is Both Meet and Right," editorials had appeared in the *Globe and Mail*, the *Toronto Star*, and the *Vancouver Sun*, more reports had reinforced the conference as a "controversy," and many letters "for" and "against" had appeared in newspapers. Drainie criticized fellow columnists, Fulford and Valpy, for their "apocalpytic doom and gloom," and pointed to the "all-white-male editorial board" of the *Globe and Mail* in saying she had "no problem, in a democratic society, with groups meeting behind closed doors to share their frustrations and map out their campaigns." Drainie's intervention— supposedly in support of the policy— in effect slotted itself into the narrative terrain that had already been ploughed by the media: the white majority on one side, the "we" which included Drainie; writers of colour as a minority group on the other, the "they" who are feared by whites and who fear whites.

Race had threaded its way through the seams to restabilize the social and cultural model of a white centre with groups of non-whites on the margins whose writers struggle to gain entrance to the centre. The discourse of racial difference, of otherness, had covered over the specificity of the conference itself and the contemporary manifestations of race that had surfaced in reactions to it.[21]

By June, the conference had been so racialized by the media in terms of dominant representations that the "controversy" was ripe enough to be easily plucked for politicization by the moral forces of the white/right, as it was by Jan Brown in the House of Commons.[22] Dupuy's compromised response confirmed the race cover-up that would inevitably lead him to deny funding. Dupuy, as quoted in the press, rationalized that he did not oppose "groups" (read here non-whites homogenized in the media) from meeting together (read here freedom of assembly ensured by the Charter of Rights)— but he did not accept the "principle of discrimination" (read here "no-whites rule"). As the Minister of Canadian Heritage, Dupuy found himself peering down from his seat of power into the border zones of race in this country, and he clearly acted to reproduce the discourse of white rule. Declaring himself opposed to discrimination, he then went ahead and discriminated on the basis of race codes inscribed in the ideology of *his* nation.[23] The historical and contemporary contexts of systemic exclusion, dominance, and white privilege were placed under erasure in the discourse of white moral outrage that substituted for his white body. When the manifestations of his subject position appeared on the front page of the *Vancouver Sun*, the now signified "controversy" had entered the sphere of national news, and by then all the signs of race had been encoded for mass consumption in the headline, "Feds Won't Fund Writers' Workshop That Bars Whites" (Peter O'Neill, June 9, 1994). Indeed, "Writing thru Race" had been read by dominant systems of representation as an event not worthy of public support.[24]

But, of course, another text was written in the seams.

The framing of "Writing thru Race" as having its origins in "white exclusion"— the media plot construction— was the initial act of territorialization that, first, misplaced the specificity of an event that was to address the internalization of racism in writing and, then, re-centred its challenge to mainstream values on the turf of whiteness as the boundary being violated. The conversion of "white" from a norm into an identity-formation made possible the claim, even by those such as Fulford who were supposed to be colour-blind, that "white" is a "colour," an excluded sign, hence the victim of racism. And the guilty perpetrators? Of course, those "writers of colour," the monstrous outgrowth of multicultural policy, whose monolithic aim is to destroy the Anglo-European way of life. It was this demonization of the other that drew a circle around whiteness as the domain of power and concealed the role of the racialization process in maintaining systemic racism.[25]

In this contemporary instance, though, the concealment was only apparent. The disruption of the public sphere and the hyperbolic drive to own "white" as a "colour" exposed the anxieties permeating the white mainstream. Dionne Brand, in her talk at "Writing thru Race," pointed to the "real panic" emanating from the white "intellectual elite" (i.e., Fulford et al): "It now hears other opinions and experiences of the people of colour in the country who challenge its definitions of what the country is and what it looks like. And that panic you can also see in the everyday social life of the country" ("Notes" 13).

That panic lit up the colonized switchboard of normative cultural values that are constituted through the otherization of "non-whites" in its midst. Gayatri Spivak distinguishes between "questions of identity and voice" in cultural struggles, with their risk of collapse into self-defense, and the project of "clearing space... to create a perspective" ("Bonding in Difference" 278-9). "Writing thru Race" adopted the term "of colour"— problematic though it is *relative to* "whiteness"— to foreground in more provisional ways than state bureaucratic terminology ("racial minority" or "visible minority") the actuality of everyday lives marked by race hierarchies. As an anti-racist tactic, "of colour" was to be a means to construct a space and time— even a transitory institution— to enable the interaction of subject positions, histories, and knowledges that have been conditioned by racialization. "Of colour," then, was to act as a pretext for the shift in current cultural praxis away from the conflation of ethnicity and race in multicultural ideology.[26] For example, in the identity politics of the 1970s and 1980s, race lines were mapped onto group formations that isolated— and often divided— communities of colour from one another. Ironically, Fulford has a point in arguing that multiculturalism has fostered separate enclaves in which ethnic and race constructs bled into one another. What he fails to question, though, is the complicity that has linked his liberal pluralism to the discourse of multiculturalism. As Scott McFarlane argues in what is, to date, the most thorough analysis of the race politics unleashed by the conference, it is a discourse through which non-whites and First Nations people "are figured outside... as, for example, immigrants or nonpersons who become 'Canadian' through their relationship to whiteness, as opposed to 'the land'" ("The Haunt of Race" 22).

The Multiculturalism Act (1988) can be read as the space of the "other" for the liberalism enshrined in the Charter of Rights and Freedoms. In the inscription of the terms "race" and "racial" as essentialized signs in a national social text, people of colour, or "non-whites," are produced as ethnic and racial identities that differ from the constitutional base. The relativization of culture in what gets called "the cultural and racial diversity of Canadian society" (Canada, *Multiculturalism Act* 13) removes its forms from the political sphere, laying the foundation, as Edward Said writes in *Culture and Imperialism*, for a "radical falsification": "Culture is exonerated of any entanglements with power, representations are considered only as apolitical images to be parsed and construed as so many grammars of exchange, and the divorce of the present from the past is assumed to be complete" (57). The past, then, becomes an apolitical "heritage," a term given official status by the new Department of Canadian Heritage, the space that now subsumes federal multiculturalism and determines which cultural events are to be supported by public funds. Dupuy's actions, in other words, signified the overt political manipulation of the cultural sphere in the interests of state-sanctioned representations of Canadian life.

The divorce of culture from politics in state multiculturalism— a divorce that finds its counterpart in CanCrit— has meant that "Canadian" culture could continue to represent Anglo-European ethnocentricity. It is no wonder, then, that despite multiculturalism as official state policy, dominant literary institutions— for example, English Departments in Canada— bear only faint token effects of its influence. Indeed, as the nesting place for the other, Canadian multiculturalism has proven to be an efficient means of engineering internal inequities in ways that have protected white neo-colonialist cultural representations. It is in this ideological warp that the undoing of multiculturalism is tied directly to the perceived decline of liberal values lamented by Fulford, Michael Valpy, and other malcontents. The two crises, then, are symptomatic of a collapsed cultural system that cannot represent the everyday life of the country.

☐

The malleability of systemic race constructs poses serious challenges to those who undertake anti-racist work through cultural and literary production. The stabilization of positions through theory, criticism, and pedagogy is always open to complicity and cooptation. Terminology is a shifting field of duplicity and temptation. Subject positions move through contradictions that are often labyrinthine in their effects. Lillian Allen reminds us that "awareness and education," the older eurocentric goals of anti-racist work, are inadequate markers for real change: "There are two significant litmus tests for anti-racism work: meaningful change and critical mass. When does what we do make an actual difference and how much do we need to do to ensure this change?" (50)

The hyperbolic reaction to "Writing thru Race," along with the deathly silence from academia, would suggest that the cultural transformation necessary to render obsolete the technologies of race remains in the future tense. Under erasure, race has to be continually brought to visibility as a construct that never stands still, or if it does stand still, then its nets will continue to snare the body. Cultural praxis— in this "meantime" that becomes "our" historical condition— becomes itself a performance of the political which opens what Homi Bhabha calls "a space of translation: a place of hybridity, figuratively speaking, where the construction of a political object that is new, *neither the one nor the other*, properly alienates our political expectations, and changes, as it must, the very forms of our recognition of the moment of politics" (*Location of Culture* 25). More than ever, textual production becomes a survival tactic in the construction of the imaginary that enacts the actual in our lives. "It is in the realm of imaginary writing that relationships other than those authoritatively prescribed come to be" (Alfred Arteaga 33). Dionne Brand said as much at the conference when she advised writers "to guard against only writing about our encounter with 'whiteness,' or exoticizing our experiences for 'white consumption'" (15). The more productive necessity, at this moment, is to "write the interiority of our real lives in detail, in minutiae" (15). That much, at least, "Writing thru Race" brought to crisis.

Listen, then, for a moment to Jam. Ismail, a poet whose cultural praxis generates the text of a theoretical engagement that looks to future possibilities, future cultural formations. Listen as her imagined figure, "young ban yen," puns a way through exploding race constructs in a flurry of sound, syntax, and intellect:

> ratio quality   young ban yen had been thought
> italian in kathmandu, filipina in hong
> kong, eurasian in kyoto, japanese in anchorage, dismal in
> london england, hindu in edmonton, generic oriental in
> calgary, western canadian in ottawa, anglophone in

montreal, metis in jasper, eskimo at hudson's bay
department store, vietnamese in chinatown, tibetan in
vancouver, commie at the u.s. border.

on the whole very asian. (128)

NOTES

I would like to thank Kirsten Emiko McAllister, Scott Toguri McFarlane, and Charmaine Perkins for sharing many of the race issues that are part of this paper. I have been encouraged by their comments, friendship, and scholarship.

1. "Race," in quotations, is understood throughout this essay and the essays that follow as a construct, but to avoid typographical clutter I have removed the quotations and ask the reader to imagine them present in every use of the term. The phrase "under erasure," borrowed from Jacques Derrida, is here extended to evoke race signs beneath the surface of erasure— in what perhaps can be understood as the realm of the negative.

2. Aside from such collections as *Anatomy of Racism* (ed. David Theo Goldberg), *The Bounds of Race* (ed. Dominick Lacapra), *"Race," Writing, and Difference* (ed. Henry Louis Gates, Jr.), and *Race Identity and Representation in Education* (ed. Cameron McCarthy and Warren Crichlow), the rethinking of race is evident in numerous publications. Significant for this essay are Homi Bhabha's *The Locations of Culture*, Trinh T. Minh-ha's *When the Moon Waxes Red*, Edward Said's *Culture and Imperialism*, and Gayatri Spivak's *The Postcolonial Critic* and *Outside the Teaching Machine*. Work on race theory in relation to cultural production in Canada has lagged, but important publications include Marlene Nourbese Philip's *Frontiers*, *Returning the Gaze*, edited by Himani Bannerji, and articles in *Fuse*, *Border/Lines*, *Harbour*, *West Coast Line*, *Parallélogramme*, and *Fireweed*.

3. Bissoondath perhaps takes the term "racialization" from a report on the "Writing thru Race" conference, "A Mid-Stream Report," by Roy Miki, which was published in the *Newsletter of the Writers' Union of Canada*; or he is drawing from Robert Fulford's attack on the conference based on the same report; see his "George Orwell, Call Your Office," *Globe and Mail* March 30, 1994.

4. It is not surprising that Robert Fulford, in a follow-up column to his attack on the "Writing thru Race" conference, endorses Bissoondath as the legitimate voice in the condemnation of multiculturalism. "I share Bissoondath's view that, in racial matters, Canadian is plunging blindly down the wrong road, heading toward a place we don't want to be. The Vancouver conference is worth debating because it's a minor symptom of a major problem" ("Down the Garden Path of Multiculturalism," *Globe and Mail* June 9, 1994).

5. Robert Lecker's essay, which was published in *Critical Inquiry* and likely intended for an American academic readership, is critiqued by Frank Davey in the same issue. Lecker's response to Davey is also included. I agree with Davey that Lecker's model of "CanLit" is too homogenous and bounded,

given the heterogeneity of the cultural field, and given too the contestations within "Canadian" literature and criticism (680-81).

6. In what reads as a follow-up to the issues raised in "The Canonization of Canadian Literature," Lecker, in "Privacy, Publicity, and the Discourse of Canadian Criticism," historicizes what he calls the "privatization" of CanCrit that led to the formation of a professional group of specialists who have lost contact with the public realm. Again, however, Lecker situates himself as operating only within the confines of that "privatization" and makes no attempt to address the actual cultural conflicts that have erupted all across Canada in the past decade. The divorce of the academic sphere from contemporary cultural praxis, particularly that of minority writers and artists, has brought into focus a conspiracy of silence that implicates mainstream CanCrit in a neocolonailist perspective. The situation, fortunately, is not as monolithic as it once was, as more critics and theorists deconstruct the institution both from within and without. The most vital critiques in recent years have come from racialized writers and artists, for instance, Dionne Brand, Marlene Nourbese Philip, Ashok Mathur, Himani Bannerji, Richard Fung, and Marie Annharte Baker, whose works necessarily position themselves in the midst of struggle and contestation.

7. First Nations writers have spoken against the appropriation of "Indian" identity and culture, often provoking emotional defenses by white mainstream writers who claim immunity on the basis of western liberal notions of freedom. But as Richard Fung argues in "Working through Cultural Appropriation," "The critique of cultural appropriation is... first and foremost a strategy to redress historically established inequities by raising questions about who controls and benefits from cultural resources" (18). Lenore Keeshig-Tobias, among a number of First Nations writers, has written compellingly on the devastating effects of cultural appropriation from First Nations positioning; see, for instance, her "Stop Stealing Native Stories"; see also Jeannette Armstrong's "The Disempowerment of First North American Native Peoples and Empowerment through Their Writing"; Loretta Todd's "Notes on Appropriation"; Lee Maracle's "The 'Post-Colonial' Imagination"; Richard Hill's "One Part Per Million: White Appropriation and Native Voices"; Marie Annharte Baker's "Dis Mischief: Give It Back Before I Remember I Gave It Away"; and Janisse Browning's "Self-Determination and Cultural Appropriation."

8. I am thinking here of Said's comment that "the ruling elites of Europe felt the clear need to project their power backward in time, giving it a history and legitimacy that only tradition and longevity could impart" (Culture and Imperialism 16). In the Canadian colonial narrative, the lands conquered are projected as embodying monstrous amoral forces that the administrative, military, and cultural power of "civilization" had to tame and control. "Survival," then, became the term to displace the estrangement of the European humanist colonizer, transferring his own emptiness onto the body of a founding metaphor, "the land." Read in this light, George Grant's description of colonization as the "meeting of the alien and yet conquerable land with English-speaking Protestants" (19) shares the anxiety of exposure that underlies the colonialist obsession to take possession of "the land."

9. The phrase, used by Julia Emberley in Thresholds of Difference, comes from Paul Tennant; see Emberley for a discussion of its application to First Nations issues.

10. Crosby says that the federal government through the Indian Act not only produced the homogenizing legal term "Indian" which divided First Nations people into "status Indians" (those on reserves under the jurisdiction of the Department of Indian Affairs) and "non-status" (those not on reserves), but also identified "Indians" as "non-persons." As a result, "The laws pertaining to the many nations contained within the large geographical area now called Canada address an imaginary singular Indian" (288).

11. This publication collects the papers and talks presented at a conference held at the University of Ottawa, April 25 to 27, 1986.

12. Barbara Godard, for instance, raises a concern for writing by "minorities"— "women, natives and immigrants" (44)— and she comments that "reading deconstructively in Canada is ultimately a political practice" (46). Francesco Loriggio inserts the material existence of "ethnic" texts into what has been, for him, the homogenous space of mainstream literature. Heather Murray critiques the totalizing discourse of nationalist thematic criticism, its determination to construct coherence by subordinating difference to sameness, and proposes discourse analysis to read for "contradiction" in the "discursive organization of Canadian literature and literary study" (80). Murray admits to "residual essentialism and considerable ethnocentrism" in her own work— but looks to a new theorization that would assist in a cultural understanding of "who is included and who excluded, who speaks and who is spoken for" (81). Terry Goldie endorses a semiotic approach for his interest in "the image of the indigene," a construct in the texts of "Canadian" imperialism and colonialism that projects the doubled "fear and temptation" of the "native" in Canada. The methodology, for him, enables the possibility of contributing to the liberation of First Nations people and may even be "an agent of native sovereignty" (92).

These gestures of bumping against the walls of CanCrit, while directed toward the future, nevertheless subscribe to a progressivist model of already institutionalized authority. The intent to expand boundaries retains the stability of a nationalist centre— "Canadian" remains unproblematized— which, in turn, allows for a recognition of differences not accounted for in previous critical methods (primarily thematic criticism), but without actually shifting its power base.

13. I acknowledge that my own critique could be seen as itself reductive because the conference itself was not intended to address the problems of race that are the focus of my attention. Nevertheless, the identification of obvious absences, such as the absence of critics and writers of colour, points to a more systemic absence in CanCrit. The race silence, then, may serve as a means of maintaining unity in diversity, a liberal ideal that would certainly have been challenged through the insertion of race issues into the conference.

14. The term "post-colonial" is variously defined depending on the contexts of its use and purpose. For a critique of Linda Hutcheon's containment of the post-colonial in Canada, which comments on her "'Circling the Downspout of Empire'" and its companion essay, "'The Canadian Mosaic: A Melting Pot on Ice,'" both in *Splitting Images*, see Diana Brydon's "The White Inuit Speaks." See also the essays collected in *Colonial Discourse and Post-Colonial Theory* (ed. Patrick Williams and Laura Chrisman) for analyses of the critical contexts through which the term has been represented.

15. Since its publication in 1981 *Obasan* has received sustained critical attention, beginning with many positive reviews of its stylistic qualities and social relevance, and continuing with numerous critical articles which examine the novel from a range of perspectives. The history of the critical reception, or what is more accurately described as the institutionalization of *Obasan*, falls well outside the limits of this note (it warrants detailed critical analysis); the general pattern of the articles, though, points toward three broad institutional contexts, somewhat in chronological order: a) *Obasan* as a "Canadian" novel, with Naomi as a "Japanese Canadian" subject whose memory is the product of Canada's mistreatment of her Japanese Canadian community; b) *Obasan* as an "Asian North American" novel that is assumed to be part of the body of literature studied in Asian American studies; c) *Obasan* as a text that embodies certain theoretical concerns (e.g., feminist, postmodern, and post-colonial) becoming popular in academic studies from the late 1980s on. In the "Canadian" context conditioned by the "nation" as norm in Canadian literature studies, much attention has been placed on the character of Naomi, as an individual, in what might be called salvational aesthetic terms (see, for example, Erika Gottlieb, Mason Harris, Lynne A. Magnusson, Marilyn Russell Rose and Gary Willis): that is, critics address to what extent the central character Naomi, a contemporary "Japanese Canadian," resolves her conflicted relationship to the past. In Asian American critical circles, on the other hand, it is Naomi's (usually gendered) "asian identity" that is foregrounded, so that notions of recovery, retrieval, and reconnections with repressed sources of cultural and psychic energy become important points of entry to the novel (see, for instance, Kong-Kok Cheung, Cheng Lok Chua, Gayle K. Fujita, and Shirley Geok-Lin Lim). The now canonic status of *Obasan* in Asian American literature courses, however, has resulted in the erasure of the difference that "nationalisms" make; in an act of institutional appropriation by US academics, the site-specific formation of the Japanese Canadian subject (as one effect, say, of the Canadian-based War Measures Act which allowed for more severe violations in Canada) tends to become another version of the "Asian American" example. More theoretical approaches (see, for instance, Donald C. Goellnicht and Manina Jones) have raised questions of representation, historiography, and textuality which help to redress the absence of attention to the novel as a textual formation, evident particularly in the "thematic" methodology of most Canadian academics. With the exception of Scott McFarlane, in "Covering *Obasan* and the Narrative of Internment," the critical history has been lax in examining *Obasan*'s problematic relationship with representational frames which work to contain the effects of racialization generated by its fictive constructs. My own critical approach seeks to question the function of objectivity in mainstream critical articles, specifically the unquestioned assumption that *Obasan* represents (in the sense of "speaking for" or "standing in for") Japanese Canadians. This critical blindness has helped forestall readings that examine the novel as a limited framing of "Japanese Canadian," a term which is inseparable from codes of racialization delimiting the authority of racialized texts and readers alike. I would also like to acknowledge a growing body of criticism developing around *Obasan* by Japanese readers (see, for instance, Yuko Fujimoto and Ayako Sato) who offer new insider-outsider perspectives on the "Japanese" elements fictionalized in the narrative.

This awkwardly lengthy note— which could be much longer— is not meant in any way to delegitimize any of the articles on *Obasan*, but I hope encourages readers to account for the relations of institutional power implicit in critical constructions of *Obasan*.

16. The exception to this rule is the recent reading of *Obasan* by Frank Davey in *Post-National Arguments*. Davey identifies the work of what he terms the "author constructor" who is evident at the beginning in the epigraph, author's note, and the prose passage, and at the end in the choice of the document signed by members of the Cooperative Committee on Japanese Canadians.

17. Through a comparison of the covers of *Obasan*— the Lester & Orpen Dennys first edition (1981) and the more familiar Penguin edition (1983)— Scott Toguri McFarlane offers an excellent discussion of the social construction of Joy Kogawa's novel as a re-internment of the Japanese Canadian subject; see his article, "Covering *Obasan* and the Narrative of Internment."

18. For reports on the conference from the perspective of participants, see the articles by Gerry Shikatani, Monika Kin Gagnon and Scott Toguri McFarlane, Cecil Foster, Cyril Dabydeen, and Afua Cooper.

19. In his column, "George Orwell, Call Your Office," Robert Fulford focused on my progress report, "A Mid-Stream Report," to the Writers' Union of Canada, as the Chair of their Racial Minority Writers' Committee; the committee was given the responsibility for establishing a Conference Committee in Vancouver, which was to include many non-union writers of colour, to organize "Writing thru Race."

20. Mookerjea's essay was first presented as a paper at the conference.

21. In 1992, when the Racial Minority Writers' Committee was organizing the first gathering of First Nations writers and writers of colour, "The Appropriate Voice," held in Ontario in May 1992, the issue of cultural appropriation— with all the accompanying signs of race— flared up in the media and stirred up defensive, and often hyperbolic, responses from self-identified "white" writers. Prominent writer Timothy Findley, for instance, trivialized the issue by saying, "...if I want to write in the voice of the tea cozy sitting in front of me, believe me, I'm not going to ask for its permission" (quoted in Lynda Hurst, "Can(not!) lit," *Toronto Star*, April 11, 1992, and cited by Richard Fung in "Working through Cultural Appropriation)."

22. Then Calgary MP Jan Brown, for instance, condemned the conference as "racist" and was instrumental in having the federal funds withdrawn, but later when donations came in, she said she supported it as an initiative of private citizens. "It seems," as Scott McFarlane writes in his account of the politics surrounding the conference, "she doesn't mind 'racist' conferences as long as they are privately funded" ("Haunt of Race" 30). Special thanks to Ashok Mathur for keeping track of Brown's political machinations and for sending this news from Calgary.

23. When Dupuy wrote to the Writers' Union, a long time after the event, he said he supported the Writers' Union anti-racism work but he did not support the conference because he is against all forms of "discrimination." What precisely did he mean by "discrimination"? Was he not "discriminating" when he judged that the conference did not deserve the funds that had been approved by his office?

Dupuy's intellectual collapse elicited vocal opposition. In the weeks following his decision, many writers, artists and cultural workers, artist-run associations, cultural and labour organizations rallied to save the conference. They wrote letters and donated badly needed funds. In the wave of support were two petitions urging Minister Dupuy to reinstate the grant. The participants of a Japanese Canadian conference on the arts in Toronto pointed to the way the conference had been misrepresented: "Media constructions of the conference have avoided contextualizing the event and have served to further the views of mainstream gatekeepers and arbiters of 'Canadian culture.' Their rush to denounce the conference reveals the high stakes involved in any discussion about 'race' and racialization that challenges the *exclusive* power, authority and entitlement of white Anglo English Canada to control the processes used to define literature in this country." Delegates at the "Crossing Frontiers" conference in Ottawa— a conference sponsored by the Department of Canadian Heritage!— referred to principles of human rights affirmed by the United Nations and the Canadian Charter of Rights when they declared that "...the Writing thru Race conference is a significant historic event moving forward the long standing debates on race, representation, cultural voice and racism for the *entire* writing and publication community of Canada."

24. As for the conference itself, in one brief weekend— including Canada Day— at the Coast Hotel in the heart of Vancouver's West End, 180 First Nations writers and writers of colour from all across the country came together in what was the largest gathering of its kind. Energy levels were high, and the air of the conference site was abuzz with rich helpings of language spillage. Total immersion was the only workable strategy— a full weekend, day and night, of talk, talk, and more talk, punctuated by spontaneous sessions all over the hotel and in scattered restaurants in the neighbourhood. Conversations expanded long into the night, during walks along the beach and in the more cramped space of the conference hospitality suite.

The atmosphere was carnivalesque— initially dazzling with all the writers commingling— yet there were currents of urgency and purpose: in a country as vast as ours, with writers spread out far and wide, the conference had taken on massive weight for having to pack so much into so little time. It was a mere weekend, after all.

The program included concurrent panel talks, small group writing workshops, plenaries, and evening literary events. There were numerous thought-provoking sessions— on First Nations storytelling, the politics of editing anthologies and magazines, writing from a position of "mixed race," the positioning of "mother tongue" for writers working in so-called non-official languages, the use of literary and cultural theory, strategies for accessing mainstream cultural institutions and granting agencies, and storytelling for children. The highlight had to be the evening readings open to the public. On Thursday, Friday, and Saturday, some 400 listeners each night were captivated by a collage of stories, styles, genres, performances, and voices by over forty writers attending the conference. Saturday night featured tributes to two senior writers who had died that year, Roy Kiyooka and Sam Selvon.

The Sunday morning plenary session concluding the conference began with a resolution addressed to Minister Dupuy. In a motion passed unanimously the delegates asked him to recognize that his decision not to support the conference was "ill-considered and precipitous" and urged him to "actively fund and support initiatives such as the Writing thru Race Conference, toward the total elimination of racism in Canada." Then followed a discussion of recommendations that would help resolve the cultural constraints facing First Nations writers and writers of colour. In the limited time available, many were offered, prominent among them:

— lobby to get copyright protection for oral storytellers, particularly from First Nations communities, whose stories have been appropriated by non-native writers and then published as a written text

— work to ensure equal access to government grants for writers who do not write in either of the two "official" languages

— establish regular national festivals of readings, performances, and events that celebrate achievements of First Nations writers and writers of colour

— form coalitions in local communities to continue the work begun at the conference

— approach a cross-section of Canadian cultural and literary magazines to request space to feature First Nations writers and writers of colour

— create a newsletter to disseminate information of new publications and forthcoming events relevant to anti-racism work in the literary arts

— set up a mentor system by which established First Nations writers and writers of colour can provide assistance to younger writers

— organize a national conference, similar to "Writing thru Race," every three years

— develop marketing strategies to distribute books in First Nations communities and communities of colour

— foster closer ties by bringing in First Nations writers and writers of colour to local literary events

— produce a national database of First Nations writers and writers of colour

— establish an editorial advisory committee to seek out ten manuscripts per year from First Nations writers and writers of colour, and approach ten publishers to publish them with the assistance of committee members

25. The one exception was a mild piece in the Saturday book section of the *Vancouver Sun*, by Marke Andrews, "Racism Charges Color a Conference on Race."

For the record, only one newspaper editorial looked upon the public hysteria over "Writing thru Race" as a positive sign for contemporary writing. The *Vancouver Sun*, in "Victim-Writers Meeting the Stuff of Great Art," defended government funding for the event: "If anything, the conference... strengthens the writers' case that they deserve public support, since they are demonstrably performing their proper task of wrestling with new and hazardous ideas and then writing the rest of us about their experiences."

26. Up until recently, "race" has stood in for "non-white," though it has now become common to hear, in the untheorized corridors of social formations, the term appropriated by those positioned as normative to construct "white = race." "Colour," a term often used for "race," has been adopted by those marked by racialization, not to identify, but to acknowledge the wider nets of "race" formation in Canada. Kwame Dawes, for instance, defends the use of "people of colour" to articulate the shared "experience of oppression and

disenfranchisement at the hands of white society" (7), and he uses "First
Nations people" to foreground "the relevant and pressing nature of
oppression and abuse that is distinctly and undeniably Canadian— that of its
relationship with the First Nations of this geographical area" (7). Such
terminology, which Dawes admits is an "artificial construct" (7), serves a
specific purpose of mobilization and coalition-building at a specific moment in
the cultural struggle against racism.

"What's a racialized text like you doing in a place like this?" Reforming Boundaries, Negotiating Borders in English and CanLit Studies

Columbus did lack

    cultural awareness

    equity

    affirmative action

    political correctness

— Marie Annharte Baker, *Coyote Columbus Cafe* 14

The question posed some years before by Trinh T. Minh-ha— "how can one re-create without re-circulating domination?" (*When the Moon* 15)— can be recycled here to ask: how can one re-form institutional boundaries without re-inscribing existing relations of power? The question takes on urgency for writers, theorists and cultural workers who cross over into the often fraught academic confines of English and CanLit studies to theorize "racialization" (aka "colour"[1])— those processes by which race signs are encoded and disseminated— only to encounter elaborate unspoken codes of defensiveness, denial, and the presumption of "innocence." Academic removal, while itself an extension of everyday public spheres, is also conducive to the assumption that critical methodologies, applied in the service of knowledge, are free of vested interests and therefore not accountable to quotidian social issues. How could academics who worry over minute— and often rarefied— textual analyses of literary texts harbour any of those motives associated with ethnocentrism, oppression, and cultural appropriation? The narrow scope of the question— its defensiveness aside— has helped cordon off self-reflexive questioning of the critical transactions that authorize the academic control and production of cultural representations.

Such transactions are far from innocent reader responses and call for critical interventions that can articulate the relations of power embedded in the "moment of infiltration or insertion" (Gayatri Spivak's phrase).[2] The lack of sustained theoretical disturbance in CanLit and English studies concerning the institutionalization of racialized texts perhaps bespeaks the capacity of liberal thought to cover over its own transgressionary practices. In the presence of this lack, it is then a matter of some urgency to inquire why, in recent years, such texts as Joy Kogawa's *Obasan*, SKY Lee's *Disappearing Moon Cafe*, Marie Annharte Baker's *Being on the Moon*, M. Nourbese Philip's *Looking for Livingstone*, and Dionne Brand's *No Language Is Neutral* are now taking on institutional re-dressing (pun intended).

The entrance of a select number of such texts into an academic sphere saturated for so long by anglo-dominant standards sets in motion a complex of variables which (drawing on the "field" model proposed by Pierre Bourdieu in *Language and Symbolic Power*) would include but not be limited to the intersection of textual production, the products of that production, and all the conflicting interests establishing the parameters of reception and valorization. No single critical I/eye can survey in its totality the intricate and layered networks of multiple interferences that delimit the (apparently) unencumbered act of reading a racialized text. Nevertheless, the inability to account for all the variables operative in the moment of reading— of history, for instance, and subjectivity, gender, class, social relations, identity constructs (both subjectively claimed and imposed)— does not exonerate the normalizing notion that institutionalization ensures a critical place of recognition.

In such a place, the issue of representational schemata and values cannot be isolated from such interlocking grids as specializations, period divisions, nationalisms, eurocentric critical biases inflected in "professional" publication outlets (e.g., journals, books, conferences). This would include the circumscribed locations of CanLit, still largely narrated through the historical projectile of (white) Anglo-European "settler" culture. In substance and methodology, much of what has become an academic industry has been enabled by a segregationist agenda of a "specialization" supplemental to a privileged British-derived canon. This depoliticization of CanLit— now only an echo of the potential threat it posed to British literature in its inaugural phase— would help ensure the continuation of the colonialist legacy: until the late 1970s and 1980s when its nationalist configuration was opposed, then exceeded, largely through creative, critical and community-based work by writers, artists, and cultural theorists of colour, who were for the most part identified with social movements outside the university's jurisdiction.

Current anti-racist critical scholarship is indebted to the legacy of this activism. The transition to the regulatory processes of institutionalization, however, enacts a discontinuity separating (in Sourayan Mookerjea's terms) "political agency" from "institutional agency," the former "a matter of a collective *praxis*" (*Crisis and Catachresis* 2) aligned with social movements, and the latter affiliated with the corporatization of knowledge which is premised on modes of competition and individualization. Political efficacy in the university, then, is constrained by various academic and administrative procedures that neutralize, or otherwise devalue, critiques of racism, sexism, classism, and ethnocentrism within the system. The perils of oppositional or resistance scholarship have become even more compelling in the wake of neoconservative reactions to the influx of "difference"[3] as a perceived threat to "business-as-usual" forms of knowledge production. A climate of real (and not imagined) hostility has arisen towards "minority" voices that press for social transformation and inclusiveness.

The editors of *Beyond Political Correctness: Toward the Inclusive University* (Stephen Richer and Lorna Weir) date the entrance of neoconservative "PC" discourse "into North American homes beginning in October 1990" (3) with its infiltration of Canada's institutional spaces in the years following. The one advantage— or compensation for this Canadianization of a US-constructed crisis— is the fact that "PC" unveils a defensiveness which bears out the destabilization of the status quo. Whether US-style "PC" fostered the articulation of what was latent, or actually caused the reaction, the Canadian version of "PC" also recirculates the familiar face of otherization. In the hollowed out consciousness of "PC" discourse, spectral figures of race come to be euphemized as "different," "marginal," "immigrant," "visible minority," and they are disavowed as subjects of knowledge by recourse to a one-dimensional binary structure: the upholders of what "goes without saying" become the "defenders" of traditional cultural values and those challenging disciplinary boundaries become the "destroyers" who are also the enemies of "academic freedom." At the structural core of the PC-constructed conflict is the literary equivalent of a moral allegory— "defenders" versus "destroyers"— which functions to displace (or invert) critical and theoretical interrogations of power relations inside the institution. This simplistic but mobilizing narrative, according to Victor Shea in *Beyond Political Correctness*, "is inscribed in PC discourse as the opposition between disinterested standards ('our' cultural heritage) and ideological interests ('their' attacks on the culture of dead white European males)" (98).

When the allegory materializes in a rupture of process and responsibility, the (normally) subdued administration of academic life is thrown into a tail-spin of reaction, rationalization, and postures of outrage. It is interesting to note, for instance, that the McEwen Report on the Political Science Department at the University of British Columbia— which caused such neoconservative uproar— was itself a long-delayed response to allegations of structural racism and sexism in a document submitted by a group of graduate students two years before. Only when one student, identified as a female graduate student "of colour," threatened to take legal action, was a decision made to retain an outside consultant to assess the crisis.

Closer to home base, in the English Department at Simon Fraser University, a similar crisis of legitimation arose in a graduate course offered with the question-begging title, "Women of Colour/Colourful Women in Commonwealth Literature." The reference to "women of colour" and the course texts implied a post-colonial focus for research and discussion, but conflicts soon arose when graduate students whose knowledge included "race," gender, and post-colonial theory attempted to situate that knowledge in discussions. Instead of enriching the course, their contributions were reframed as signs of racialization according to the familiar binarization: on one side of the colour line, the "white" students, and on the other, the students of "colour" who could be identified as proponents of a "political agenda" intended to destroy the authority of "white male professors." The professorial withdrawal from the course led to its breakdown which, in turn, prompted departmental authorities to fulfill the contractual obligation of the course by allowing it to continue through the supervision of other faculty.

Despite calls for a departmental review, no action was taken other than the formation of a committee to facilitate dialogues on race and "gender" issues in literary studies. The committee never took action and, in the passage of bureaucratic time and memory, collapsed into obsolescence. The lack of an official investigation into this instance of racialization inaugurated an era of silence in a strained social arena, as some faculty members were quick to designate the crisis as PC-related and the students "of colour" (now homogenized as a "group") as radicals requiring discipline. One faculty memo circulated on departmental e-mail characterized the students as engaging in calculated disruption— on unacknowledged evidence since there was no formal inquiry— and evoked a neoconservative use of the term "academic freedom" to name and narrate the crisis, assign blame, and recommend disciplinary retaliation. In this representation the students are marked as motivated by the "intention to intervene" through "disruption," and the professor is identified as the one harassed because of, among a number of categories, his "sex" (i.e., as a male) and race (i.e., as white). The more critical issue of racialization is absent in this politics of blame.

A month later, the attack on the students had spread outside the department through an e-mail message directed to Simon Fraser

University faculty, only this time the shorthand "PC" made its appearance. In this narration, by then only remotely based on a knowledge of the course, the faculty member from another department writes:

> A current example of "P-C" ideology is the notion that the writings of authors who are black or female can not, and indeed, should not be taught by a white male professor. Last semester a group of "P-C" (my label, not theirs) grad students in the English Dept. disrupted a course for just that reason. The unfortunate professor was so harassed by them that he gave up teaching the course.

In this pseudo-moral tale, the graduate students are divested of individuality to become members of a "PC" group, whereas the professor-as-individual is seen as a victim. Translated in these reductive terms, the effects of racialization are subsumed by an abstract category— "P-C" ideology— that misrepresents the specificity of the course crisis. The power to pave over the dispute by simply assigning blame to a "group" whose "race" identity is simultaneously constructed in the tale bespeaks the (largely) uncontested privilege of institutionalized norms of whiteness.

In her essay, "Anymore Colourful and We'd Have to Censor It," Charmaine Perkins, a graduate student in the course, explains the consequences of racialization for those students of colour perceived as disrupters— and not as "active, present, intervening, intellectual subjects." She points to the subordination and exclusion visited on them for speaking out on race issues in academic spheres:

> Knowing we will be held responsible for the ways in which we are racialized, what is otherwise known as "calling it" on ourselves, we risk the very careers that we are there to pursue. We have yet to be included or welcomed as intellectual in these institutions. In this way,

we continue to be anomalies and exceptions, especially in graduate
studies. (25)

□

How, then, is a racialized text
like you doing in a place like this?

as Charlie Chan said to his dutiful no. I son "beware of the white
rascals— particularly their investigative modes and their ordinances."
—Roy Kiyooka, *December / February 1987, 1988*

The "racial formation" model of influential theorists Michael Omi and
Howard Winant situates the term "race" at the constitutive nexus of
social, cultural and political processes. Its normative role in the historical
trajectory of colonization and the subordination of those classified as
not-white[4] has meant that racism needs to be conceptualized as (to
quote Glenn Jordan and Chris Weedon in *Cultural Politics*) "a cultural
and institutional phenomenon, not fundamentally a matter of individual psychology, not of 'racists' and 'prejudiced individuals.' It is deeply
ingrained within the dominant social structures and signification
systems of contemporary Western societies" (253).[5]

In the institutionalization of race discourses, and here the university
is implicated, as Stephanie Wildman and Adrienne Davis argue in
"Language and Silence," "...privilege manifests itself and operates in a
manner shaped by the power relationship from which it results. White
privilege derives from the system of white supremacy" (576). In such
a system, texts as well as bodies, both encoded in relation to whiteness
as given, take on visibility in the same signifiers that disguise the
boundaries determining its power relations. The after-effects of the
graduate course crisis made this process evident.

The body signified as not-white is then marked by the racialized
contexts of audience and representation. It awakens in the space of

whiteness as a sign moving along the corridors, generating strained language rituals, and socialized in a terminological screen wherein "race difference" functions to pre-scribe gaps that silence and are silent. The body of colour, in the currency of blame politics, is clothed in signs of negativity, mistrusted, and distanced because of its subjectivity. Himani Bannerji in "Re: turning the Gaze" speaks of the tenuous border tensions of theorizing race in the university as a woman of colour who is both professor and text, both a knowledge producer and a gendered body written over by racialized signs. She articulates a splitting apart, a dissociation between the private and public, as the effects of knowledge become the property of others— "my public 'me,'" she writes, "remains frozen in the public space where she was called forth by the occasion while I take the subway and go home..." (221).

The invisibility of racialization sets up a pattern of contradictions and constraints for the handful of graduate students and faculty of colour whose research and pedagogy involve the application of race theory to the study of literary texts. Since no courses exist for such work, they often have to incorporate it in existing courses, or to offer it, as a unique event, in a special topics course. In the process, they often come to be identified as a zone of so-called "issue-oriented" scholarship, its boundary becoming the social equivalent of ghettoization. The language of racialization gets drawn around what Bannerji calls the "body in a space" (222), the body of colour in the university, in that space as a field of already pre-scribed mediations.

The scarcity of non-white academics engaged in anti-racist scholarship, especially so in literary studies, contrasts tellingly with the abundance of creative and theoretical work by writers, artists, and community-based activists of colour. Indeed, much of the opposition to the exclusionary effects of English and CanLit studies has come from this constituency external to the university— in critiques and texts transported by various indeterminate routes across institutional borders from social and cultural movements enmeshed in daily resistance to racism. The recent coalescence of activism, academic conservatism,

and the politics of representation, which has gone hand in (contradictory) hand with the institutional management of "diversity," has given
way to an escalating cultural capital for texts of colour and for academic
studies of such texts. Strange though the mixture may be, it is in this
conflicted scene that various liberal gestures, such as "sympathy,"
"empathy," and "opening space for non-white writers," need to be
addressed.

One danger may be the phenomenon that Ashok Mathur calls the
"rhetoric of approval," in which there is "an appearance of radical
change without any actual commitment to such change on a systemic
level" (2). Discussions of racism, sexism, and cultural chauvinism are
politely tolerated in a climate that leaves unspoken the outsider status
of those constructed as "minorities" (read here people of colour) and
covers over the paucity of non-white faculty undertaking anti-racist
scholarship and pedagogy. The well-intentioned but uncritical work
of white academics "amazed" Bannerji, and continues to amaze,
because of its failure to acknowledge "that the exclusion of non-white
people was not accidental, [and] that the social organization of Canada
actually expressed itself in the social organization/relations of the
academic world and general production of knowledge as well" ("Re:
Turning" 234).

In her analysis of representations of "amerasian occupation babies," Kyo Maclear writes of the "narrative of border transgression and
re-consolidation" (24) and posits the danger of white researchers who
purport to cross the race line to assume the perspectival specificity of
those othered. They may appear to do so in the guise of discourse—
but only in disguise when they still retain their position of privilege in
the production of knowledge based on their textual sojourn. In the
transaction, a boundary may be re-formed with the "othered" now
contained and identified as an "object" of (academic) systems of
identification otherwise known as objectivity and legitimation. Is it
possible, then, to conceptualize the inclusion of texts of colour in
institutions so that such containment can be averted? When such texts

are resurrected in the spaces of whiteness, what do they speak, to whom do they speak, and how do they get spoken for? Can whiteness unthink and thereby undo its privileges?

The site of contact between readers positioned in a sliding scale of "race," class, gender determinants and racialized texts remains a largely unconceptualized area of contemporary criticism, more so in CanLit.[6] When it has received attention, the problem has been reduced to issues of critical appropriation, insider-outsider knowledge and experience, and tokenism— in other words, the problem itself has been neutralized through a binaristic framework of assumed social and race hierarchies: "dominant" versus "subordinate," "mainstream" versus "marginal," and "white" versus "non-white."[7] Beyond the static of binarism, or in its nomadic interstices, at the fluid interface between the reader-subject and text-production, the contractual event of reading sets into play a field of discourses of which the personalized moment of so-called consciousness is one effect. The representational limits of the multiple— and multiplying— social, cultural, political, linguistic, historical, and institutional configurations that intercept the capacity of the reading subject and the evaluation of texts call for theoretical work that can articulate what texts do, what is done to texts, and the implications for anti-racist practices.

What, for instance, are the principles that can determine whether the representation of the contact zone— no matter how benign or sympathetic the discourse used— resists racism or reproduces its signs? What are the criteria to measure whether the institutionalization of a racialized text is an oppositional move or a process of containment and control? What are the means of developing transformative critical methodologies within those academic boundaries that restrict the application of critical race theory to exclusionary literary histories? What are the strategies for theorizing the consequences of complicity as a condition of academic discourse? How can the recognition of complicity assist in the transformation of the university into a more "inclusive" site of knowledge production?[8]

□

Where, then, is a racialized text
like you in a place like this?

The world is not a flat white world in which I lie buried underneath.
— Lee Maracle, *Telling It* (166)

Certain reformulations of the "post-colonial" for Canadian academics can pose certain critical dangers to texts by writers designated as outside the given culture. One recent publication, for instance, may be symptomatic of a (new) invisibility in which the (old) centralist borders of CanLit— neo-colonialist and white— are reconfigured to positivize the negativity of racialized texts. "English Canada's Postcolonial Complexities," by Donna Bennett, appears in the 20th anniversary issue of *Essays on Canadian Writing*, an academic journal whose history is itself consonant with the evolution of CanCrit. Strategically or not, the "post-colonial" claimed by Bennett is identified with the colonial history of white settler groups— which then marks a terminological boundary that externalizes the specific histories which have been "otherized" by colonial discourses. This "post-colonial" extends the familiar narrative of nation-formation that assigns "origin"— in the critic's "English Canada"— to imperial Britain, and in this way, affiliates itself with the anglocentric cultural model of Northrop Frye, Margaret Atwood, D.G. Jones, et al. The indifference to the signs of race allows for the displacement of First Nations positioning through the process of colonial indigenization— a process memorialized in John Newlove's "The Pride," a poem in which the "land" is possessed by the "colonists" through the "spirit" of dead "Indians":

...in
our breath, in our
ears, in our mouths,

in our bodies entire, in our minds, until
at last
we become them. (385-6)

This reification of "indigeneity," a constitutive moment for white settler CanLit, simultaneously— and this is its danger— erases memory of the appropriation of First Nations' spirit and culture and justifies the colonialist "resistance" to its imperialist past as the basis for a national ("native") literature. Bennett rationalizes the narrative of conquest by recourse to the "common" connection to an originating ground:

This resistance could be assumed to be present whether the colonists were indigenes, on whom a colonial rule had been imposed, or settlers, who had brought the structures of empire with them, because it would arise from the bond with the land that superseded the claims of, and the ties to, the imperial country. (198-99)

The veiling of historical violations (i.e., the brutalization of First Nations communities through confiscation of lands and cultural genocide) and the reidentification of the colonizer as "native" to the "land" enables the homogenizing model of CanLit that functions only *in relation to* the founding discourse of anglocentricity— and this, in turn, enables the recuperation of a teleological literary history that valorizes the present as the outcome of signposts already embedded in the initiating moment of colonization.

When Bennett turns to the problematics of difference, the unwritten agenda of her model is manifest in the continuing otherization of writers who are framed as having been silent (read here a code for "non-white"). I quote a lengthy passage as one example of a new form of exclusion within the institution— a sober warning that visibility is no guarantee that racialized texts can perform liberatory effects on readers:

Canada's multiculturalism policy, as well as enabling newly arrived immigrants to maintain external cultural ties, has encouraged the literary expression of those groups who have maintained separate ethnic identities although their ancestors arrived in Canada before mid-century, Canadians whose cultures have long been present, though relatively silent. Books from these groups are also rapidly entering the Canadian canon: novels such as Joy Kogawa's *Obasan* (1980 [sic]), about the World War II displacement of Japanese Canadians, and Sky Lee's 1990 reconstruction of four generations of life in Vancouver's Chinatown, *Disappearing Moon Cafe*, are now frequently taught in surveys of English-Canadian fiction and written about in critical journals. In contrast to narratives by non-British immigrants, theirs is a kind of ethnic writing that focuses on the post-colonial condition of belonging to two cultures *within* the same country— that is, on what it means to identity oneself both as Canadian and as a person from a culture that exists as a de facto colony, a marginal group that is no longer as closely related to the mother country as it would appear to be to outsiders, or even as it might claim. (191)

Several unspoken assumptions in this critical argument implicate a reactionary mode housed in the discourse of white settler literature as the norm. In the gaps of this discourse are the ghosts of an ethnocentric CanLit institution dispelled in codes that evade the history of racialization. The term "multiculturalism," for instance, allows for the construction of "groups" (read here "other" than those of British and European origin) who are assigned free will in maintaining "separate ethnic identities." Such individualization in the guise of ethnicity, which accords with liberal notions of choice, displaces the technology of race discourse so necessary for the whiteness bound into the prior term "Canada." Moreover, the historical demarcation, "before mid-century," does not signify— though it appears to— as an empirically derived "fact" but as a line that evokes the influx of non-whites (the "newly arrived immigrants"), and more especially

"Asians," after mid-century. Or at least the examples given, and the absence of concern for historical specificity, imply as much. There is no indication that Chinese Canadian history dates back to the 1850s and Japanese Canadian history to the 1870s, and while being "present" is noted, the phrase "relatively silent" strikes the chord of dominant relations. Silent for whom? And how silent? The identification of lack leads to the conclusion that "[b]ooks from these groups"— now the "group" writes the book, not an "individual" writer— are "rapidly entering the Canadian canon." What is this "Canadian canon" if not the literature valorized by institutions, such as English Departments? The verb "entering" assumes both the existence and the stability of this undefined but obviously central space. Indeed, the adoption of naturalized terminology depends on codes of racialization that operate under erasure but which assure academic readers that social and cultural hierarchies and priorities are observed— even while the two novels mentioned are seen as having "entered" the customs house of canonical CanLit. But to draw on a distinction made by Marie Annharte Baker in *Coyote Columbus Cafe* (48-49): are they tokenized or totemized? Notice that the novels, described only briefly, are not approached in terms of aesthetic form— the prevalent CanLit index of cultural value— but for the transparency of the referential, confirming the assumption that the signs "Joy Kogawa" and "Sky Lee" are products of "groupness," a term that situates them, not as reified "individuals," but as members of a binarized and not-white mass.

The conclusion to this framing reconfirms this process of otherization by appropriating the familiar model of "two cultures": "theirs" versus "ours." For the authorial signs "Joy Kogawa" and "Sky Lee," then, the term given priority as "Canadian" represents one "culture," homogenous and autonomous, and their "other" identity derives from a "culture that exists as a de facto colony." Who is the authority speaking here? On what grounds are persons of "Japanese" or "Chinese" origins members of a "colony"? On what evidence does the writer make judgements on a subjective relationship to the "mother country"? And how are we to read the final qualification, "or even as it might claim"? The element of mistrust, even the suggestion of a false authenticity, creeps into the discussion, as if the writer senses the possibility of deception. Are there shades here of the "yellow peril" discourse that continues to persist in contemporary recontainments of the sign "Asian" in Canadian cultural politics?

I have dwelt on this one passage to suggest the need for critical readings of critical statements that respond to the new visibility of racialized texts. Here the re-formation under the auspices of a "Canadian post-colonialism" appears to reproduce the nationalist (white) centre as an expanded space that (now) contains non-white texts— but does so through the very racialization that formerly excluded them.

□

Much more can be said on this critical issue, and much more needs to be said, but for now, to suggest the future work that needs to be done, let me invoke Rey Chow's sobering admission: "The weight of old ideologies being reinforced over and over again is immense" (*Writing Diaspora* 17).

Unreflective liberal gestures toward "cultural" and "post-colonial" studies— while an encouraging shift in weighty neoconservative environments— can all too easily become a vehicle for disciplinary management, in fact stabilizing existing structures by confining critiques of race discourses to curricular sites and protecting the institutional boundaries from the threat of transformation. To resist the threat of neutralization, race theory needs to be de-ghettoized through research and pedagogical practices that confront the privileged body of whiteness in dominant cultural and literary representations. It is only when such privilege is made visible that the reading subject can begin to assume responsibility for undoing systems of complicity that control and maintain hierarchies of power. Anti-racist work, as Wildman and Davis point out, needs to recognize the "companionship between domination that accompanies subordination and privilege that accompanies discrimination" (577).

The years ahead, in all likelihood, may witness the intensification of the neoconservative backlash against those constructed as "minorities" (read here women of colour, non-white writers and graduate students), bringing with it modes of demonization and charges of "politicization," "reverse racism," and the like, which reassert the privilege of whiteness. It may be that the buzz term "academic freedom" already heralds an era of more open academic warfare between liberalism and social justice. "Academic freedom" for whom and at whose expense? The contestation over terminology spills onto the institutional stage where the s word o pens the p age on the alpha bet a wave to unsettle the h alls of h ired learning.

According to the authors of "Academic Freedom *Is* the Inclusive University" in *Beyond Political Correctness*, "The opposition to the pursuit of the academic imperative of intellectual inquiry, examination, and re-envisioning reveals that there is a considerable gap between the *precept* and the actual *practice* of academic freedom in the academy" (121). Between the precept and the practice is perhaps to be found that gap in knowledge formations where critical race theory can begin to transform institutional visibility. Reading the recently published first novel by Calgary writer Suzette Mayr, *Moon Honey*, I am drawn to the influx of race signs in Carmen's perceptual field. Through the lens of ideological spectravision, once metamorphosed from a "white" into a "brown girl" (23), she sees the material traces of what whiteness had erased:

> She used to like antique stores back when she was a white girl, now she walks into antique and collectibles stores and all she sees are images of brown people eating watermelons, gobbling fried chicken drumsticks. Tacky representations of Chinese people with pointy hats and bowls of rice. She's been fitted out with some kind of radar over the past year.... (169)

Well, radar may be the answer. Not Columbus who lacked "political correctness," not Charlie Chan who had his "dutiful no. 1 son," and certainly not the "flat white world in which I lie buried underneath."

□

SUPPLEMENT
Race Research:
A Ten Point Primer

1. To enter English (and CanLit) studies is to cross over into the bounded institutional discourse of requirements, specializations, required reading lists, qualifying exams where the invisibility of race coexists with the quotidian pressures to align one's critical methodology and research with dominant literary values. Even the construction of radicality will depend less on the efficacy of performance and more on its service to disciplinary unity and coherence. The economic and career implications of accommodation, reinforced as they are by faculty endorsement and established professional networks, all work to discourage theoretical research that seeks to transform the institutional norms that sustain the privilege accorded to standards and expectations.

2. In the midst of such constraints, research and writing that aligns itself with efforts to make the university more accountable as an anti-racist site of learning and knowledge production has to surmount the stasis of reaction and adopt critical and pedagogical tactics that make racialized effects visible.

3. Liberal humanist gestures of using racialized texts and subject matter for expansionist purposes may offer the appearance of "inclusion," and may for this reason alleviate the so-called "guilt" of privilege, but these

(still) need to be read either as the ownership of the constructed "other" or as defensive mechanisms that counter the spectre of social disorder.

4. Even the disciplinary frames offered by "cultural" and "post-colonial" studies, while not to be denied, may present further closures— in fact stabilizing the critical industry by confining critiques of neo-colonialism and ethnocentricity to curricular concerns and thereby protecting the institutional boundaries from the threat of change.

5. Race research needs to be de-ghettoized through critical theory and pedagogical practices that expose the social dominance of "whiteness" as the measure of value-laden cultural and literary representations, and in CanLit as the medium in which the national body has been shaped and identified.

6. Here, too, binaristic models of racialized dualities— dualities that were the necessary ingredients for a colonizing model of literary history and cultural origins— have to achieve the status of obsolescence. Only then can the reading subject in institutional locations begin to assume responsibility for codes of racialization that continue to generate the institutional effects through which "not-white" subjects stand in for alterity and "difference."

7. The language codes of "sympathy," "intention," "guilt," and "white identity," i.e., the interwoven paraphernalia through which "whiteness" is personalized outside the political contexts of reception and representation, need to be re-read as part of the lexicon of racialized norms.

8. Knowledge production has to be continually deconstructed in terms of its limits, and to whatever extent possible— a daunting task in the face of the powerful corporatization of the knowledge industry— oppositional and resistance research has to connect with social groups

and movements. The depriviieging of university-sanctioned discourses brings into play knowledge formed in the daily lives of those engaged in social struggles. Here involvement needs to be participatory rather than the mere application of academic modes of abstraction to serve the ends of institutional validation and individual proprietorship.

9. The possibility of an "inclusive university" depends not only on the inclusion of racialized texts and writers on the curriculum, but calls for the expertise of academics of colour in a critical mass sufficient to transform literary studies into a vital mode of social and cultural critique.

10. The work being done by graduate students, the product of the theoretical shifts evident in the past 15 years, harbours the possibility of radical change through a new political awareness of the productive nature of power and the consequent recognition that public space is not a homogenous and stable entity but is created as a praxis. Such a praxis would reject models of domination and attempt to work through the signs of racialization that continue to shadow "our" (in this site-specific context) social relations.

NOTES

Graduate students with whom I've had the pleasant opportunity to work have given me hope that the future need not simply reproduce the past. For conversation and support on race issues, I would like to thank, at SFU, Scott McFarlane, Charmaine Perkins, Glen Lowry, and Karlyn Koh. An earlier draft of this essay was given as an address for "RE / forming Borders / Bodies/ Boundaries," a conference organized by graduate students in the English Department, University of Calgary, March 1996. A chapbook series published by The Production House, a project of graduate students in the English Department, Simon Fraser University, was launched at this gathering. The series, "The Space of Race in a Class," consists of three chapbooks: Mookerjea's "Crisis and Catachresis," Perkin's "Anymore Colourful and We'd Have to Censor It," Mathur's "Rhetoric of Approval," and a visual work by Melinda Mollineaux, "Cleave: a bookmark."

1. "Colour," as used here, is taken as provisional, not referential; its insertion rests on a tentative intent, relative to this moment in social and cultural history,

not to occlude the not-white as mere absence. What is not-white marks the
constituting negative of social spaces in which "whiteness" is normative, hence
not visible as such. In such conditions, whatever terminology is attached to the
"racial" will be limited by an overly determined though semantically
disarticulated field of references. Troublesome as it may be in the current
politics of positioning, the term "colour" still retains a strategic use— namely
as recognition of those bodies which signify the not-white in the social
production of whiteness. "Colour" then offers a less restrictive linguistic space
calling into appearance a spectrum of bodies that are racially codified—
beyond more benign signs of ethnicity and culture— including (especially in
Canada) those who subjectively have identified themselves as "mixed." It may
be useful to be reminded of Stuart Hall's comment, in "New Ethnicities," that
the term "black," used to signify non-whites in England, was adopted, not as a
form of homogenization, but as a political gesture: "Politically, this is the
moment when the term 'black' was coined as a way of referencing the
common experience of racism and marginalization in Britain and came to
provide the organizing category of a new politics of resistance, amongst
groups and communities with, in fact, very different histories, traditions and
ethnic identities... Culturally, this analysis formulated itself in terms of a critique
of the way blacks were positioned as the unspoken and invisible 'other' of
predominantly white aesthetic and cultural discourses" (252). Here in Canada,
dominant cultural institutions, in particular English Departments, have yet to
account for the role played by race discourses in the formation of its
institutional spaces. As long as the institutional conditions which elide race
determinants continue, "colour" will serve as a functional interventionist term
to expose and resist these conditions— and the phrase, "writers of colour,"
can signal the hierarchically structured domain of cultural politics inscribed by
norms of whiteness. Adequate scholarship on the microspaces of racialization
in acts of the imagination remains lacunal in critical theory.

For another comment on the term "colour," see the notes to "Sliding the
Scales of Elision" above.

2. The critical problems inherent in the institutionalization of racialized texts
has received more attention in the US, as evident for instance in *The Ethnic
Canon*, edited by David Palumbo-Liu, where the term "ethnic" (less
threatening) stands in for "raced." Invoking Spivak's phrase to address the
incorporation process, Palumbo-Liu argues that "...certain 'texts' deemed
worthy of representing the 'ethnic experience' [in Canadian contexts these
would be 'race experience'] are set forth, yet the critical and pedagogical
discourses that convey these texts into the classroom and present them to
students and readers in general may very well mimic and reproduce the
ideological underpinnings of the dominant canon, adding 'material' to it after a
necessary hermeneutic operation elides contradiction and smooths over the
rough grain of history and politics, that is, those very things that have
constructed the 'ethnic' in the United States" (2).

3. The term remains in scare quotes here to recognize its doubled and hence
slippery semantics: as both a sign of heterogeneous social and culture relations
and an ideological construct that imposes identities on bodies (raced,
gendered, and ethnicized).

4. The legal history of the term "white" in the constitution of the US and its

power to disenfranchise and racialize the not-white is the focus of Ian F. Haney López's essay, "White by Law."

5. As a function of social formations, race and "racialization" are constitutive in relation to the construction of difference, alterity, and otherness. All too often in untheorized academic contexts, they are conceptualized as extensions of pathological conditions of aberrance and psychological disturbance in subjects, not as a vehicle for producing hegemony. The application of "racism" as pathological to the study of literary texts then leads to the disappearance of racialization as an enabling term in institutional readings of writers and texts of colour. The challenge, then, is to begin to read academic discourse as itself a constituting medium of dominant modes of managing identities.

6. See Michael Awkward's *Negotiating Difference* for an analysis of "race and reading" in the context of African American texts.

7. I use the term "non-white" to retain the normativity ascribed to "whiteness" as, in fact, the pole against which non-whiteness (or colour) is constructed.

8. Only a diehard essentialist would argue that readers and critics who have a transparent relation to codes of whiteness are incapable of comprehending racialized texts, but only the "colour blind" would refuse to recognize that critical negotiations involving such texts are not conditioned by "whiteness" as a sign of privilege, priority, and institutional stability. Gestures of inclusion by those positioned as whites, then, while not to be discouraged, cannot remain transparent to individual intent and the dangers of critical strategies that re-invisibilize (often below the level of conscious choice) the effects of race constructs. For example, when a racialized text is drawn into institutional contexts and the institutional conditions of reception come into play, the same text which enacts the site-specific production of racialized positioning, when re-situated in the language of dominant knowledge-based discourses, transforms into an object of a disciplinary framework, and hence marked as a sign of alterity or difference. Re-identified in this way, the text comes to be read in terms of what Sabina Sawhney calls the "exhibition of differences" (210), an object of knowledge rather than the effect of subjectivity. Even the often evoked confessional, "I write from the position of an anti-racist white male/female academic," does not necessarily ameliorate the binarist hierarchies maintained by the fiction of academic neutrality. Instead of undermining the privileging of whiteness, the declaration of such positioning may actually maintain the racializing discourse through which the text gains institutional representation.

Unclassified Subjects:
Question Marking "Japanese Canadian"
Identity

I feel like a burglar as I read, breaking into a private house only to discover
it's my childhood house filled with corners and rooms I've never seen.
—Joy Kogawa, *Obasan* 79

The journal journey tilts tight-fisted through the gutter of the book,
avoiding a place to start— or end. Maps don't have beginnings, just
edges. Some frayed and hazy margin of possibility, absence, gap.
—Fred Wah, *Diamond Grill* 1

'lineage' must have something
to do with these precipitous rock ledges—
this serpent river follows
—Roy Kiyooka, *Wheels*, in *Pacific Windows* 140

The name is at once the setting of a boundary, and also the repeated
inculcation of a norm.
—Judith Butler, *Bodies That Matter* 8

I

I am an imaginal "i" dawdling at the corner of Logan and Sherbrooke,
central Winnipeg, circa 1952.[1] The location is itself only a point in the
spatial dimensions of what might be identified as a neighbourhood,
"Logan Neighbourhood" in the common parlance of the time. The
"i" may be reading a Mickey Mouse comic book just outside the
site-specific drug store, the "Rexall," oblivious to a professionalized
language of lack, deprivation, and social welfare that could have framed
the corner as the scene of class abjection. For the "i" that urban zone
is wrapped in the still invisible immediacy of what might be called a

totalizing ideolect— the historic port of entry for some 1200 scattered JCs in the late 1940s and the field of contingencies which spoke the "i" into a social designation as itself a qualified designation, a "Japanese Canadian"[2] subject. Neither the one nor the other, but constituted by a gap. Spoken, then, by the unspoken, or sentenced by a frame— "Japanese Canadian"— which is not recoverable as an etymological retrieval.

Memory— never the less— intercepts this "i" and I later move to reinscribe the geography of childhood, circa 1960. This time a differently positioned "i" is inside the institutional bus of a field trip, safely ensconced in the ethnographic allegory of knowledge production. The status of "undergraduate student" subject allowed for, even released, the perspectival pivot that translated the cornered "i" into a social aberration— the sign of waywardness, of displacement, of circumscription. As imagined locations, the terms "inside" and "outside" confused the origins and ends of positioning. In the bus, traversing the sites of memory, the patterns of coherence and rationality assumed the mantle of knowledge power.

Did the allegory make "us" real? Or is the real the absence both constituted and disguised by its border lines? Such questions which could have brought the institutionalized "i" to crisis, were not— or could not— be articulated. The mapping of the known in the so-called "imperial eyes" of the knower, guided by the pedagogical authority of the translator / professor, was not made manifest as such. It follows that the "i" on the corner— surveyed as the lone "Japanese Canadian" subject— may not have existed then either. Only memory (now) can foretell.

□

In a compelling critique of the "anthropological situation" as a paradigm for modes of representation dependent on asymmetric relations of power, Rey Chow discusses the ethnographic limits of productions on "subjects" who function as "objects" in knowledge

formations legitimized by institutional normalization. In her analysis
of conflicts over the portrayal of "China" in recent Chinese films—
specifically, the "nativist" attack on film-makers who ostensibly reproduce the exoticism constructed in the West's eyes— she exposes the
now "classical" anthropological endorsement of the "inequality inherent to the binary structure of observor / observed" in approaching "the
West's 'others'" ("Film as Ethnography" 177). The transparency of
such an assumption underscores the role of bias in all knowledge
production on subordinated identities. The cost of mis-representation
intensifies for those inflected by signs of racialization— dramatically so
within a nation-state discourse in which "Japanese Canadian" became
a classified subject. For such a restricted identity the micro-spaces of
subjectivity come to be marked by privileged regimes of representation— so that the task of oppositional representation must not fall
into the trap of simply reversing the binary structure.

Is it then possible to adopt a critical strategy that interrupts the
structure by inhabiting the dominant representations, not as external
frames of reference, but as internalized artifacts— artifacts that can be
re-inscribed? The production of this "new ethnography," as envisioned by Chow, "is possible only when we turn our attention to the
subjective origins of ethnography as it is practiced by those who were
previously ethnographized and who have, in the post-colonial age,
taken up the active task of ethnographizing their own cultures" (180).
Elaborating on the attention to visuality this methodological shift
requires, she proposes the phrase, "to-be-looked-at-ness" (180), to
signify the condition of being objectified as informing the creative acts
of artists aligned to groups colonized in hierarchically structured social
and political formations. This condition explodes the "realism" of
institutionalized knowledge such as documentaries where the hierarchic binary of the observor / observed is maintained, and instead allows
for cultural forms in which the represented produce themselves
through the co-ordinates that have set the historical contours of their
identities.

The question of identity, or more (in)appropriately, the question marking identity is, on the one hand, so seemingly contained in the legalized documentation of birth certificates, familial naming, and lineage. On the other hand, amidst the currents of unravelling positions in the proliferation of "posts"— post-nationalism, post-colonialism, postmodernism, post-feminism— it becomes a perilous trace of the fantastic as the real. It is the "'lineage'" tracked by the late JC poet Roy Kiyooka in his journal / journey through the imagined "Japan" of his own "Japanese Canadian" eyes, the stark vistas opened by the "pre-cipitous rock ledges— / this serpent river follows" in the text *Wheels*, as the "i" is disoriented in the place of the other— "an intransitive noun at best" (*October's Piebald Skies*, in *Pacific Windows* 280), as Kiyooka writes.

For the imaginal "i" on the Winnipeg street corner, the figure of its "other" framed by the bus window would have been witnessed as a passing figure, unnamed, but pointing toward upward social mobility. The transportation from the familiar back lanes, secret hideaways, the punctual wail of diesels, the backside of billboards, the linguistic heteroglossia, the layered histories of displacements[3]— none of this disrupted, invaded, infiltrated the discursive borders of the view from the bus.

2

In a re-reading of the term "Japanese Canadian" from the vantage of research, writing, critical reflection, and activism, the historical fissures covered over in nation-formation would return as internalized inscriptions and suspicions. The hauntings in the contradictory language of "nation," "place," and "race" shaped the matrix of that "private house" in Joy Kogawa's *Obasan* which, burglarized, disclosed itself as one's own "childhood house filled with corners and room I've never seen" (79). Re-reading as an act of breaking and entering, though, required that the term acquire opacity and semantic instability. For the generation undergoing the negativity of social marking, identity formation was either a transparency drifting across plateaus of unchangeable social relations (say *Japanese* Canadian), or a site of desire to move beyond "Japanese race" (say Japanese *Canadian*). Either and/or both trajectories sought affiliation, hence incorporation, into the nation-state. JC writer Muriel Kitagawa recalled her allegorical English class in New Westminster, the first capital of BC, in the early part of this century in "Anglo-conformist" Canada.[4] Segregated by racialization, her subjectivity inflected by her outsider status, "English" stood for the language, culture, and power of the Anglo-nation family— a social identity that she longed to attain. "By the time I got to my third year my marks in English were higher than the others in my class, and the Principal even carried around my exam paper to show to other teachers that a little Jap girl took the best marks... in English, mind you!" (22)

In English, mind you— so the addition of "Canadian" to the designated identity, "Jap" or "Japanese," became part of that imagined nation for Canadian-born JCs like Muriel Kitagawa. The same held true for most of the 23,000 who, in the early months of 1942, were classified as persons "of the Japanese race," re-named "enemy alien," and expelled from their west coast homes. As Kitagawa's memory spells out, the discursive terrain for this identification process had been prepared long before 1942. Indeed, when the first JCs entered colonial Canadian territories— the grandparents of the "i" among them— the regulatory lexicon of "yellow peril" was there to greet them as "Japs," "asiatics," and "orientals."[5] The demonization of the "asian" body, a white supremacist projective field of anxieties and animosities, evoked the forces of mis-rule threatening to "mongrelize" the white body of "civilization."

In what is now a largely buried interventionist moment, October 19, 1900, Tomekichi (Tomey) Homma, a naturalized "British subject," decided to challenge the discourse of the Provincial Election Act, Section 8: "No Chinaman, Japanese, or Indian shall have his named placed on the Register of Voters for any Electoral District, or be entitled to vote at any election." Although "Japanese" was defined as "any person of the Japanese race, naturalized or not," Homma proposed to re-read, in the language of citizenship, the identity which disenfranchised him. In effect, when Homma appeared before the city clerk to insist that his name be placed on the voters' list, he performed a disidentification (Judith Butler's term in *Bodies That Matter* 219). Disavowing himself as "of the Japanese race," he re-invented this "other" self as an "insider," a colonial "British subject."

In an un-naturalized response, Judge McColl of the BC Supreme Court sided with Homma. "The residence within the province," he ruled, "of large numbers of persons, *British subjects in name* [italics added], but doomed to perpetual exclusion from any part in the passage of legislation effecting their property or civil rights would surely not be to the advantage of Canada and might even become a source of national danger" (cited in Adachi 54). The decision was even upheld by the Supreme Court of Canada— but Homma and the JC immigrant community that he represented would have their hopes shattered in BC's appeal to the imperial centre in London. There the Privy Council, the final authority for colonial Canada, restored the legitimacy of "race" as the basis of disenfranchisement— despite naturalization— citing British precedent. "From the time of William III down to Queen Victoria," the Lordships reasoned, "no naturalization was permitted which did not exclude the alien naturalized from sitting in Parliament or in the Privy Council" (see Privy Council). The legitimacy of a policy of exclusion based on "race" was considered "not a topic which their Lordships are entitled to consider."[6] The Victoria *Colonist* celebrated Homma's defeat, a tangible confirmation that racialization and democracy are compatible in a white colonial nation:

> We are relieved from the possibility of having polling booths swamped by a horde of Orientals who are totally unfitted either by custom or education to exercise the ballot, and whose voting would completely demoralize politics... They have not the remotest idea of what a

democratic and representative government is, and are quite incapable
of taking part in it. (Cited in Adachi 54)

☐

The legalized discourse of race threaded its way through the first fifty
years of this century to ratify the scripting of immigration laws to
protect and defend "white Canada forever" (Peter Ward's title for a
study of racism in BC). One notorious example— still an unresolved
contemporary issue— remains the infamous "head tax" imposed on
"Chinese" subjects whose labour was expendable once the nationalist
epic, the construction of the railway, was completed. In the words of
Dr. Joseph Adolphe Chapleau, the man who introduced the 1885 Act
to Restrict and Regulate Chinese Immigration: "Is it not a natural and
well-founded desire of British subjects, of the white population of the
Dominion, who come from either British or other European States
and settle in this country, that their country should be inhabited by a
vigorous, energetic and white race of people?" (Cited in Anderson
57). The tax began at $50 in 1885, but rose to $100 in 1890, escalating
to $500 in 1907, only to be followed, in 1923, with the Chinese
Immigration Act, in reality an "exclusion" act cutting off immigration
from China.[7] The act, according to Kay Anderson, gave "the category
'Chinese' an administrative existence and a reality in Canadian official
life that did not need to acknowledge the criteria immigrants from
China might have used to define themselves and each other" (57-58).

　　Writers and artists from racialized minorities with multigenera-
tional histories have grown up without ever being able to claim the
term "Canadian" without the burden of the supplement. Fred Wah
in *Diamond Grill* narrates the familiar ritual of identification in the early
post-war classrooms:

When I was in elementary school we had to fill out a form at the
beginning of each year. The first couple of years I was really confused.

The problem was the blank after Racial Origin. I thought, well, this is
Canada, I'll put down Canadian. But the teacher said no Freddy, you're
Chinese, your racial origin is Chinese, that's what your father is. Canadian
isn't a racial identity. (53)[8]

3

The white patrol belt crossed the chest, over the shoulder, wrapped
around the waist, and clicked closed with a silver buckle. The wearer
was then vested with the awesome power— for a child in any case—
to control traffic flow. Incorporation into the troop itself projected the
aura of entry into the geography of authority— a distanced positioning
from the racialized and internalized geography of the "i" as merely "of
the Japanese race." The transaction or exchange of identities, in this
sense, replayed an initiation into Foucault's productive field of power,
with the subjective "i" re-formed as a disseminating extension of
stabilizing social rules that maintain public order. So far so good.

What haunted the otherwise lacklustre instance of socialization
was the persistent memory of expulsion, wordless, with only the close
up stern features of the white-haired principal, Mrs. Lang. Her slap
performed the divestment of the belt before all the patrols. Over time,
or in its palimpsestic wake, the memory was supplanted by the logic
of analogy, mirroring the family's— not the I's own— expulsion from
the home place in Haney, BC, in the Fraser Valley. Why the
substitution occurred went without saying, until one moment of
archival immersion in the National Archives of Canada, the same
scene— wide angled— brought into the frame that imaginal "i"
looking high up at the national flag, the British Union Jack. Slapped
for not saluting on command. How had the iconography of contexts
entered the subject unannounced? Why did that posture of resistance
materialize? But, then, could it even be called resistance?

□

The body dressed in the social and cultural signs of stigmata, in childhood more so, has little control over the unspoken undertones it elicits— "membership in a racial minority can be considered neither self-induced... nor alterable" ("Words that Wound" 159), as Richard Delgado says. Or in the words of the young Canadian poet, Hiromi Goto, in "The Body Politic": "That which you carry with you at all times and / cannot be removed like a costume or eaten like a five course dinner" (218). On the other hand, as Goto's poetic text dis-plays, the formation of a subjectivity that interacts with the racialization of the body is never necessarily passive in its relations with the mediating boundaries of language. The codes of outsiderness with its negativity— of the "not-so"— incorporated in the imagination become the medium in which the "i" is produced in consciousness. Processes of internalization in the always shifting fields of race signs often escape detection— or if not escape, cannot be decoded in the normative lexicon of social relations that structure unequal distributions of power, privilege, and resources.

In 1942, all such subtleties were abandoned when the state-con-·trolled possessive phrase, "of the Japanese race," was legalized in a barrage of orders-in-council scripted by administrative fiat under the powers of the (made-in-Canada) War Measures Act.[9] The erasure of "the citizen" as that "individual"[10] so sacred to liberal democracy (an irony not lost on the JCs dispossessed) meant the abrogation of rights, protections, and even responsibilities— until early 1945, for instance, the "Japanese Canadian" subject could not demonstrate loyalty through service in the armed forces. Racialization, in other words, designated the "Jap" within the nation as a body whose movements had to be documented, policed, and contained through state repre-sentation. How else could so many thousands of "citizens" be rounded up, incarcerated, dispossessed, interned in prisoner-of-war camps, deported, and dispersed— all through legal actions that circumvented parliamentary and judicial accountability? Once coded as raced, the "Japanese Canadian" subject was rendered invisible— i.e., visible only in unilateral terms as a figure "of" administrative mechanisms and discursive fixations. The federal cabinet minister most influential in the mass explusion of JCs from the west coast acted in full awareness that politicians could seize the moment to their own advantage. In a memo (dated June 5, 1943), now housed in the National Archives of Canada, Ian Mackenzie assured his colleague, Norman McLarty, of the ease by which properties could be confiscated: "...we should not be deterred by any representations by Japanese [sic]. Any action we take under the War Measures Act cannot be challenged in the courts" (Cited in Sunahara, *The Politics of Racism* 109).

The JCs caught in the proliferating network of orders-in-council were powerless to unsay their representation as the classified body that had to be displaced for the sake of social order. It was this relentless pressure of painful constraints on consciousness which, in turn, found transformation in an internalized complex of disturbed and seemingly irresolvable conflicts. For the "Japanese Canadian" subject who yearned to be seen as "Canadian," where would the boundary line between complicity and co-operation lie? Is resistance, no matter how unjust the government policies, proof of disloyalty? Or is it a defense of democratic principles? Is compliance a capitulation to race discourse, and so a perpetuation of racism? Or is it an effort to contribute to Canada's war efforts?[11]

The danger of attempts to speak back to administrative policy was brought home with a vengeance in the case of the most vocal JC resistance movement, the Nisei Mass Evacuation Group— the N-M-E for short. (Is this an instance of linguistic subterfuge, or a prophetic pun left for another generation to decode?) These were mostly younger nisei from outside the urban Vancouver centre who "protested," through traditional democratic means, the unnecessary break-up of families, clearly a punitive policy that had nothing to do with military security. In an articulate emotional appeal to the BC Security Commission, the civilian body established in early March 1942 to engineer the mass uprooting, they refused the government's term "race" and insisted on naming themselves "citizens." They supported "co-operation" but would obey orders to leave only when the government treated them as law-abiding "Canadians." "When we say 'NO' at this point," they stated, "we request you to remember that we are British subjects by birth, that we are no less loyal to Canada than any other Canadian... and that we are willing to accept suspension of our civil rights" (cited in Miki and Kobayashi 37). In retaliation, the BC Security Commission, quickly acting in tandem with the RCMP and the Department of Justice, simply scripted another policy for these so-called "trouble-makers" (the RCMP's term)— indefinite "detention" at the "pleasure of the Minister of Justice." Over 600 men associated with the NME were incarcerated behind barbed wire in prisoner-of-war camps in Ontario, without trial, many for the duration of the war.[12]

The containment of resistance and protest ensured the administrative "solution" to the so-called "Japanese problem" in BC. Early in 1945, when the US Constitution finally allowed interned Japanese Americans to return to the coast, the Canadian government, acting under the War Measures Act, could pass another set of policies to re-invent the "Japanese Canadian" subject once again. With the war all but over, further justification was needed for permanent expulsion from the BC coast— the subtext of the government's actions from the outset of uprooting. Enter the narrative of what JCs have termed "the second uprooting."

□

Unlike Japanese Americans, JCs had to pay for their own internment through the liquidation of their assets by the Custodian of Enemy Property. By 1945, with their financial resources all but depleted, the government seized the political opportunity to obstruct their return to the coast. Written notices for two policies, "repatriation" and "disper-

sal," were posted simultaneously: either go to Japan, even the Canadian-born— who, of course, could not, at least according to linguistic
and legal conventions, be "repatriated"; or move away from BC, "east
of the Rockies," in the phrasing of the policy. Cast in the bureaucratic
vocabulary of resolving what was reinforced, in the national media, as
"the Japanese problem," the terms "repatriation" and "dispersal"
assumed transparency as normalized solutions. The public sphere had
already been prepared to expect some disciplinary measures for the
"Japanese" bodies in its midst. After all, were they not uprooted
because they constituted a threat to social order? Why else would the
government take such extreme measures? The cloaked readings of
governmental motivation explain why politicians in the House of
Commons failed to question the subtext of the double-edged "repatriation" / "dispersal" policies. In political statements carefully choreo-
graphed by administrative speech writers, government officials insisted
that the "Japanese" exercised freedom of choice. But then why, with
the war over, was it illegal to remain in BC?

Only the "Japanese Canadian" subject, it appeared, could ask this
question. The ideological drift of the white majority, including the
most sympathetic among them, followed the pattern set out by the
government's discourse and assented to so-called "resettlement" and
"assimilation." The logic of "race" had already produced a narrative
for the "Japanese Canadian" body: those who would go to Japan—
despite a whole complex of reasons that made the question of "choice"
a misrepresentation— were "disloyal" to Canada; those who complied
by moving "east of the Rockies" were "loyal" subjects. The JCs
reading the dispersal notice, in their heightened state of consciousness,
were not mistaken by language that made a mockery of the liberal
term "choice": "Failure to accept employment east of the Rockies
may be regarded at a later date as lack of co-operation with the
Canadian government in carrying out its policy of dispersal."[13]

□

The process of forced assimilation, following on forced uprooting, had profound and long-term effects on JCs, beginning in a post-war period of administrative declassification. All the intimate personal, social, religious, cultural, and economic relations making up the sites of JC experience for the previous fifty years had been violently dismantled— almost in a flash— by government decree. Blanket homogenization as no more than "of the Japanese race" had, in a sense, rendered them stateless. This massification, conjoined with the loss of economic sustenance, reduced them to an undifferentiated pool of labour— grist for the Canadian economy. In the aftermath of war, this declassified subject— no longer the "enemy alien"— underwent a "rehabilitation" program designed and administered by the Canadian Department of Labour under its "Japanese resettlement program." The enactment of this re-incarnation of racialized social policy depended on the co-operation and complicity, not only of "Japanese Canadians," but of white liberal Canadians as well. Most came from organizations with Christian affiliations, and often with members who saw the rehabilitation of JCs as an extension of missionary work. The government, for its part, sought out such organizations to promote its dispersal operations. One example among a plethora of documents in the National Archives of Canada is a call issued by the Department of Labour, Japanese Division, for Canadians to assist in the "Farm Placement Plan" for "Japanese Canadian Families" (dated 1945). The notice explains that some 23,500 "people of Japanese ancestry" (the term "race" is no longer in use) were removed from the west coast for "reasons of military necessity." Those who remain in "relocation centres" in BC are currently "available for employment." This government program enlists the support of church groups through the "Church Sponsored Placement Plan" of the National Interchurch Advisory Committee on Resettlement of Japanese Canadians. Now more clearly identified as

"Japanese Canadians"— hence loyal subjects— these displaced persons can fill labour shortages anywhere in Canada (outside of BC, of course). As the directive says, "The [sponsoring] Group would continue to sponsor the family until it becomes firmly established and its members able to take their places as *normal Canadians* in the community" (emphasis added).

The term "subjectivation," as Judith Butler says, commenting on Foucault's analysis of power, is paradoxical in that it "denotes the becoming of the subject, but also the process of subjection: one inhabits the figure of autonomy only through becoming subjected to a power, a subjection which implies a radical dependency" ("Subjection, Resistance" 229). In the remaking of the racialized subject, the once uprooted and dispossessed "person of Japanese race" was administratively allowed to be redesignated as "Japanese *Canadian*," an identity formation sanctioned by the state that inscribed the racialized "Japanese" as the subordinating limit of "Canadian." This reproduction of "Japanese race" in the more benign face of "Japanese Canadian"— the preferential term of those identified as such— coincided with their desire as "outsiders" to enter the nation's family as "Canadian." The gaps and contradictions, temporarily covered over, turned inward, and even the darker reaches of memory could be translated into the seduction of progress: what some, only half ironically, would even call a "blessing in disguise." The myth of acceptance— the apparent disappearance of a racialized identity— helped to disguise the disjuncture, the betrayal, the violation of social justice.

☐

The "Japanese Canadian" subjects who would be remade in the image of "normal Canadians" would indeed fit in well, and in a short period of time "they" would take their place in the public sphere as the "model minority." On April 1, 1949, the last of the restrictions would be lifted and voting rights followed. Upward social mobility would also become possible when professions like law, pharmacy, and accountancy were finally open.

The "rehabilitation" process that accompanied resettlement brought with it a prolonged period of social silence, and the so-called "evacuation," the government euphemism that also "named" the event for JCs, itself settled into "the past." Social invisibility set the boundaries for a subjectivity positioned on the precarious edge of nation-state identity— as the model (still racialized) minority, more "Canadian" than the norm, and as "Japanese Canadian," the victim of injustices that had never been "acknowledged." The language of "redress" intercepted the unspoken gaps maintaining that edge, and like an underground river seeking its own outlet, impelled the means to re-imagine— in public form— the specific and multiple memories of the mass expulsion (not "evacuation").[14]

For a group whose voices and subjectivity had remained outside the nation's narratives, however, the entry into the mainstream political arena was a tentative and provisional process of "negotiations" with the tongue-tied ghosts of an internalized history. As a unifying term, "redress" hinged those spaces of memory to the daily tumult of archival research, social activism, community empowerment, and media interventions. In the process "Japanese Canadian" subjectivity would undergo its most radical reinscription since the 1940s. Only this time— three decades later— the reinscription would be enacted through the mobilization of the subject.[15]

4

It was the morning of September 22, 1988. A handful of JCs from Ottawa with members of the Negotiation Team, myself included, were lined up outside the door leading to the House of Commons gallery for "special guests." We were about to witness the official statement— the language of which we had negotiated. Conservative Prime Minister Brian Mulroney was to announce a redress agreement reached with the National Association of Japanese Canadians to resolve the wartime internment. The government aide who arranged our entrance in the dark hallway advised us that protocol prohibited "guests" from standing or applauding. No matter what, remain seated in silence, he said.

As we took our designated places, to the left and right of us the seats were empty. The whole gallery was almost empty but for a handful of JCs on the opposite side who were "spectators," not "guests." We looked down on the politicians, and given the momentous air of the occasion, the perspective was eerie: MPs (Members of Parliament) were seated together, appearing scrunched with so many empty seats to their left and right (though the TV cameras framed only those in attendance, as we saw later on the national news, presenting the illusion of fullness). The Prime Minister rose, paused as he glanced up at the "guest" gallery, and began his own prepared speech: "Mr. Speaker, nearly half a century ago, in the crisis of wartime, the Government of Canada wrongfully incarcerated, seized the property, and disenfranchised thousands of citizens of Japanese ancestry..." (Miki and Kobayashi 143) and already the moment was diffused in the overlapping angles of memory.[16]

The parliamentary acknowledgement of the "citizen" in "Japanese Canadian" is evidence that identity formations are never fixed and determinate, but can be re-configured through transformational processes. In part, the silence of "Japanese Canadians" was not simply a matter of erasure, or even negation. While the narrative of self-imposed "speechlessness" was evoked as an explanation for the lack of "redress" in the past, it is equally the case that such a positioning was not "called for" within the boundaries of an assimilated minority. "Redress," the word, functioned as a conceptual rupture that initiated as well as necessitated what was a massive subjective act of remembering to remember. As a discursive provision, "redress" displaced the earlier horizon of a contained identity. It thereby constructed a "beyond"— an imagined future— as the frame for the making of "community memory," itself a term that provided the cohesiveness and enclosure needed to reinvent the "Japanese Canadian" subject as a "Canadian" whose "rights and freedoms" were "abrogated" "during and after World War II" by "racist policies," adopting the language that narrated the "case for redress" (National Association of Japanese Canadians 24).

When the Prime Minister finished, he was given a standing ovation by all the MPs, a sign that all three political parties, the Conservative government, the Liberal and New Democratic parties, were locked into their own rare moment of solidarity. We too— was it spontaneously?— rose and clapped, and as quickly as we exchanged glances, the moment had already become the past.

Except for a brief moment when the New Democratic Party leader, Ed Broadbent, visibly moved, said his former spouse was nisei, and then read a brief passage from Joy Kogawa's *Obasan,* there was the manifest absence of JC voices. "Japanese Canadians" were re-presented through the handful of subjects in the guest gallery above the politicians, but the official discourse was managed by the translation of "Canadian of Japanese ancestry" from surviving "victim" to exemplary "citizen." In this moment of closure, the narrative of JCs was re-written by the political system as a national story of resolution. No longer the outsider wronged by the state, the "Japanese Canadian" subject is redressed— in metaphoric terms, dressed anew— in the garment of reconciliation and resolution— in the garment of citizenship. In the process, the nation to which this redressed subject belongs is redeemed.

The gain, then, signifies the loss of the "wounded attachment"— to use Wendy Brown's phrase[17]— to the unredressed identity. The loss functions as both a stabilizing resolution to an identity now "past" and the harbinger of an as yet unknown identity formation. The absence of JC subjectivity, of Chow's "being-looked-at-ness," other than the unspeaking reified bodies in the gallery, cast a shadow over the language, and was not ameliorated by the JCs in the gallery who— after being told not to— stood and applauded the acknowledgement.

What was it we stood and applauded on that historic day? The irruption of this question had already rendered unstable the "Japanese Canadian" identity that was written into Hansard that day.

5

The loss, or demise, of any given subject formation ensures that identity not become a residence but a performance of multiple and often contradictory positionings. In spatial terms, this performative translates as a border zone, what cultural theorists and others have approached as the "in-between" (Trinh T. Minh-ha, *When the Moon Waxes Red* 21) or the "interstitial perspective" (Homi Bhabha, *The Location of Culture* 3). In theoretical terms, it brings to crisis those knowledge formations that contain the objects of their attention by normalizing limits, absences, exclusions. In creative terms, it enacts a textual field open to the radical mediation of language's power to sentence the producing subject. In cultural and political terms, it transforms the effects of domination into critical methods responsive to "identity" as site-specific, hence always subject to strategic transformations and mutations.[18]

Positioning, then, is a spatio-temporal condition governed by boundaries that are structural extensions of such discursive formations as history, race, gender, and class.[19] These boundaries would prove (finally) to be tyrannical and inflexible were they only "that at which something stops," to borrow from Homi Bhabha's use of Heidegger, but also and much more generatively "that from which *something begins its presencing*" (*Location of Culture* 1). This distinction forestalls the closure implicit in subject positioning by opening up the imaginal "beyond"— where both a past "i" and future "i" perform a calling?— which operates, not as a transcendent removal of the subject from materiality and the mortal, but as the borderline where the subject, as an event of intersections, assumes multiple social, political, and cultural position-ings.[20] The term "identity," then, unravels as centred to become a collage of distribution points in the power dynamics that narrate the inclusions and exclusions of the naming process. This destabilization, while often applauded as liberatory, does not— as if by fiat— displace the effects of racialization. In more material terms, the resistance capacity of a minoritized subjectivity not to be absorbed by these effects is thwarted by internalized contradictions that are so normalized they rarely reach the state of conscious articulation and subjectivity. "If you win, you lose" ("An Acoustic Journey" 5), so Trinh T. Minh-ha cites Henry Louis Gates, situating the difficulty of detecting the co-optation of "raced" bodies. The potential for any given minority identity formation— "Japanese Canadian" for instance— to empower the subject is always in danger of the subject being taken hostage, "reproducing thereby the confine-and-conquer pattern of dominance dear to the classic imperial quest" ("An Acoustic Journey" 7). The challenge, then, is to engage a poetics which takes on the burden of social struggle and still attends to creative acts which begin (not merely end) at the boundary lines.

Gayatri Spivak addresses the profound complications posed by creative and critical methodologies that attempt to encounter and represent subjectivity— and I would add, even the subjectivity we take to be our own.[21] Such engagements, in relation to what she calls "ethical singularity," must be reciprocal, involving both "responsibility and accountability," and bounded by the impossibility of identification with each other:

For a collective struggle *supplemented* by the impossibility of full ethical engagement— not in the rationalist sense of "doing the right thing," but in this more familiar sense of the impossibility of "love" in the one-on-one way for each human being— the future is always around the corner; there is no victory, but only victories that are also warnings. ("Translator's Preface" 270)

NOTES

I. In adopting the linguistic convention of the "I" (capitalized) to signify the subjectivity of the writer produced by the text— in contrast to the imaginal (lower case) "i" evoked in the text— I do so with the assumption that the enunciated "I," stable as it may appear in this articulation, is tied to historical processes, and therefore simultaneously presences and situates itself in a network of collective signs, some of which I can perform, but a vast array of which is governed by indeterminate fields of reception. Two questions then become apropos: Am "I" the subject of the sentence? Or am "i" sentenced by its historicity? Judith Butler, in *Bodies That Matter*, writes: "Where there is an 'I' who utters or speaks and thereby produces an effect in discourse, there is first a discourse which precedes and enables that 'I' and forms in language the constraining trajectory of its will" (225). The "subject" is constrained by the discursive limit that "precedes and conditions" its formation (225), though the limit is never static and inflexible but always "subject to" reinscriptions that disturb and transfigure the social relations of power. Such is, thankfully, the malleability of the acts of writing and reading.

2. In this essay I approach the term "Japanese Canadian" as a bounded identity formation but also recognize that for those who identify themselves as such the term cannot be completely denaturalized. To avoid cumbersome qualifying phrases for each instance of use, I have adopted "JC" for subjective affiliations. The two letters are intended to signify both acceptance of common usage for JC subjects and awareness of the terminological limits— part of the broader language limits— marking questions of identity in our time.

3. Displacement was once a term of abjection in the early post-war years of Canadian nationalism, heard, for instance, in the stigmata of "DP," a common shorthand for "Displaced Person" in the Winnipeg of my childhood. Recently, the term has been re-appropriated in postmodern and post-colonial strategies to signify the condition of destabilized or pluralized identities that reflect contemporary life— no longer a term of derision, but often a sign of liberation. The concern with "displacement" is evident in numerous recent publications by cultural and literary theorists: see, for instance, *Displacements*, edited by Angelika Bammer; *Displacement, Diaspora, and Geographies of Identity*, edited by Smadar Lavie and Ted Swedenburg; *Rethinking Borders*, edited by John C. Welchman; Homi Bhabha's *The Location of Culture*; and Trinh T. Minh-ha's *When the Moon Waxes Red*.

4. The phrase has been used to designate the overall dominance of white "Anglo-Saxon" values in the social and cultural history of Canada. See Audrey Kobayashi 221.

5. Kirsten Emiko McAllister, writing on Ruby Truly's "With Our Own Eyes: A Trip to Lemon Creek," a video on JCs returning to sites of internment in the BC interior, points out that elements of "yellow peril" discourse continue to inform eurocentric cultural perceptions of "Asian"-identified bodies— and this has prompted Asian Canadian artists, such as Truly, to create artistic forms that resist and deconstruct the reproduction of that discursive history. As an early example of "yellow peril" discourse, McAllister cites a passage from the *Victoria Times*, August 16, 1907, positioning itself against "unrestricted immigration of 'Orientals'" because "they" would become "a vast alien colony, exclusive, inscrutable, unassimilative, bound together in a secret offensive and

defensive organization, with fewer wants and a lower standard of living than their neighbours, maintaining intact their peculiar customs and characteristics, morals, and ideals of home and family life, with neither the wish nor the capacity to amalgamate with or even conform to the civilization upon which they have intruded, and gradually, by the mere pressure of numbers, undermining the very foundations of the white man's well-being" (68; also cited in Adachi 78).

6. For an informative discussion of the inconsistent and racialized history of legal discourse around the term "race" in the United States, see *Critical Race Theory*, edited by Richard Delgado.

7. Kay Anderson's *Vancouver's Chinatown*, a study of the discursive history of the "Chinese" subject, is exceptional for its account of racialization and the development of Canada into a nation-state built on white British and European norms. "The decision to restrict Chinese entry to Canada," she writes, "cannot be conceptualized simply as a reactive one, in which politicians blindly acted out the role of representing white interests. Insofar as politicians attempted to legitimize their control over the social order, they actively wielded and dramatized their calling, in part to secure votes, but also to build a national unit in the image of a European society. In that sense, the state-society relationship was reciprocal in the making of a culturally based hegemony" (140). For Chinese Canadians, the date July 1— Dominion Day in white-based Canada— would henceforth be identified as Humiliation Day.

The campaign to redress those "Chinese Canadian" subjects who were forced to pay the head tax was mounted during the 1980s by the Chinese Canadian National Council. Soon after the Japanese Canadian Redress Agreement of September 1988, federal representatives promised— but failed to take action— to resolve this historical claim. Finally in December 1994, after a prolonged period of political silence on the issue, then Secretary of State for Multiculturalism, Sheila Finestone, announced that the government had decided to deny redress, citing as a reason the liberal principle of being "just in our own time," which in effect elided the historical injustices that shaped the privileges accorded the ruling powers of the present (see article by Kim Bolan). For the redress brief issued by the Chinese Canadian National Council, see "It Is Only Fair! Redress for the Head Tax and Chinese Exclusion Act."

8. For a discussion of how "racism and sexism were and continue to be an integral part of the way things are done in Canadian society" (57), see Roxana Ng's "Racism, Sexism, and Nation Building." Ng approaches "racism" and "sexism" as relational terms in "systems of domination and subordination that have developed over time as taken-for-granted societal features" (51) and examines, as one specific example, how "Indian" as a constructed race category— the product of colonial relations of power— functioned in shaping the Canadian nation.

9. For an informative treatment of the abuse of the War Measures Act in Canadian history, including the mass uprooting of Japanese Canadians, see Ann Sunahara's "The Abuse of Emergency Law in Canada: Is It Inevitable?"

10. The implications of this liberal reification of the "individual" as the basic unit of social formation has multifaceted ramifications for the positioning of those who are signified as "not-white" in Canadian public spheres. It is a marking that has to be read in relation to racialization as a fundamental component of

Canadian nation-state identity. The very triadic structure of its constitutional framework performs the dominant hierarchies: "official" culture as the domain of the "founding" groups, the English and French, the Multiculturalism Act for those external to that hypostasized origin, and the Indian Act for those whose territories and cultures were invaded and appropriated in the violence of colonization. "Race" has been the crux of the enabling discourse, shifting with specific historic conditions (for instance, Ukrainian Canadians were once considered not-white), but always in the service of drawing the invisible lines that have situated whiteness as the normative ground of identity.

11. These questions only brush the surface of the deeper consequences of ambivalence which await further research. Where, for instance, are the psychoanalytic boundaries to measure the deprivation of memory sites, the violent loss of social infrastructures constituting identity formations, and the residual effects of self-denial, ostracization and dominance?

12. For more detailed information on the Nisei Mass Evacuation Group, see Adachi and Sunahara.

13. Prime Minister Mackenize King attempted to justify the government's dispersal policy in the House of Commons on August 4, 1944. In the official nation's narrative, "Japanese" created "racial hostility" because of their visibility on the BC coast. The mass uprooting, dispossession, and stripping of rights was a move necessitated by the "problem" they created by living in close proximity to one another. Now displaced, for their own protection, they needed to be dispersed so that they could no longer "create feelings of racial hostility" (King's speech is cited in Adachi 431-33). Not one member of the all-white Parliament asked the obviously relevant question: What does the "Japanese Canadian" subject think? Representation was a one-way street.

14. For the Canadian-born nisei, especially those who desired "incorporation" into white Canada, the term "Japanese" became a barrier to overcome. In thought, gesture, and most importantly language (the "English" of dominant whiteness), they were attracted to the prospect of finally being able to identify themselves as members of the "Canadian" nation-family. That gesture, though, required a distancing from their "Japanese" ancestry, from that cultural and linguistic matrix of values, represented most materially in the lives of their first generation parents, the issei. This shift explains why many nisei, when uprooted and reconstructed into a "model minority" by government decree (i.e., the assimilationist agenda underlying the dispersal policy), bought into the government's narrative that living in close proximity caused racism to flare up in white Canadians. Better then to disperse— to become invisible. It is this notion that yielded "blessing in disguise," a phrase used by some JCs "to say" the uprooting and dispossession was beneficial because it led to incorporation in dominant white society. For an earlier discussion of the complexity of this internalization process, see nisei historian Ken Adachi's final chapter in *The Enemy That Never Was*, "'A Blessing in Disguise?'"

15. Contexts are crucial here. "Redress" as a term is part of the social cauldron of the 1970s, a period marked by the emergence of identity politics, in which the ideology of assimilation was subsumed by a new buzz word, "multiculturalism." In its language-scape the former qualifying term "Japanese" became a social value, no longer the sign of "enemy alien," and consciousness of civil rights brought critical awareness to the legacy of racism. The notion of minority rights led to the resignification of hyphenated ethnicities, so that "Japanese Canadian" could be reconceived as a historical identity calling for

reclamation as a "Canadian" narrative. The notion of the nation as homogenous— that is, as the enclave of WASPness— was deconstructed in a flurry of pluralization. These contextual sites for making sense of "redress" are beyond the bounds of his essay and would easily require another essay or more.

16. The official acknowledgement of redress is reproduced in Miki and Kobayashi 7.

17. In her critique of identity formations, Wendy Brown warns against the potentially self-destructive consequences of identities constructed in states of resentment. Such identities cannot perform the disidentifications necessary for social transformations that restore agency to the subject.

18. Here I am reminded of Chantal Mouffe's notion of a "social agent" whose identity is constituted by an "ensemble" of intersecting and contradictory subject positions that never achieve the cohesion of a totality. "The 'identity' of such a multiple and contradictory subject," she writes, "is therefore always contingent and precarious, temporarily fixed at the intersection of those subject positions and dependent on specific forms of identification. This plurality, however, does not involve the 'coexistence,' one by one, of a plurality of subject positions but the constant subversion and overdetermination of one by the others, which makes possible the generation of 'totalizing effects' within a field characterized by open and determinate frontiers" ("Democratic Politics" 33-34).

19. For a development of this argument, see Liz Bondi, "Locating Identity Politics": "Post-structuralism has relied strongly on spatial terms of reference, and the reconceptualization of identity politics I have drawn out effectively spatializes our understanding of familiar categories of identity like class, nationality, ethnicity, gender and so on. Rather than being irreducible essences, these categories become positions we assume or are assigned to..." (97).

20. Charles Merewether adopts Frantz Fanon's phrase, "zone of marked instability," to describe the context in which new forms are able to emerge. Here identity is not linearly tied to an originating point in the past— the fixity of abstract nostalgia— but is always in process and thereby marked by relations of power. Merewether renames this shifting configuration as a "borderline in the sense that it is always a sequence of trans-positions, always engaged as a performative moment of translation" (101). Translation then becomes the continual movement across the territorial divisions which signify the contestations manifest in the public sphere.

21. In cultural politics the notion of subjectivity has been obscured by the normalization of the "subjective" as somehow owned by the subject who experiences. The perils of "self" appropriation— analogous to the issue of cultural appropriation— have not been sufficiently examined, for instance in autobiographical works or any work dependent on authorial life conditions. The assumption that the "personal" is owned by the subject is itself an idealization that replays the autonomous "self" of liberal humanism. The psychoanalytics of identity constructs, however, would suggest that the "self" can be appropriated in modes of representation that reproduce systems of repression, racialization, and invisibilization. Here Judith Butler's comments on subject formation are apropos: "What is refused or repudiated in the formation of the subject continues to determine that subject. What remains outside this subject, set outside by the act of foreclosure which founds the

subject, persists as a kind of defining negativity. The subject is, as a result, never coherent and never self-identical precisely because it is founded and, indeed, continually refounded, through a set of defining foreclosures and repressions that constitute the discontinuity and incompletion of the subject" (*Bodies That Matter* 190).

Can I See Your ID?:
Writing in the Race Codes That Bind

Judith Butler, from *Excitable Speech* : "Language sustains the body not by bringing it into being and feeding it in a literal way; rather, it is by being interpellated within the terms of language that a certain social existence of the body first becomes possible" (5).

For example:
dirty jap
are you a jap?
the japs are coming
a jap is a jap
no japs from the rockies to the seas
jap oranges

or nip:
short for nipponese
slant for "hamburger" (winnipeg, c1950s)
slang for intercourse south of the 49th

qualification:
this entry manifests
the site-specific memory
of a finite subject and
cannot be transposed
without disrupting the
cross draft of nation

□

Disavowal as a dominant— and dominating— reaction towards

the race codes that bind needs to be recognized as a lynch-pin for social productions of the body. The fantasy of liberal individuation is belied by the regulatory shorthand of not-so-white designated identities declassified through signs of gender, class, and race. The big three— the triumvirate enabling a "Canadian" nation— together mark out the territory of what gets represented and what then displaces the unrepresented. A sleight-of-hand is always operative in the wings of the theatre. This is a country that asks its citizenry in polls whether "non-white immigrants should not be allowed into Canada" and then prides itself on its "tolerance." The question of the question never becomes the news, only the poll results. It's still a "white man's country," the poll does not say.

In this site-specific context of an unread but (potionate?) language of mute signs, "Can I see your ID?" inhabits the potency of a language that names but which is itself un-read. Take this "i's" Vancouver, for instance, where a discursive trajectory can easily invoke a lexicon that spells "asian" as "gang." The scene could very well be the interior of Eric Bontogon's visual text, "Black Night." On a vacant but textualized street. The car pulled over. The body interrogated. "Yellow Peril," the sound track, draws on archival reserves. Ripple effects in the voices translating the race codes that bind:

> Do you have a record?
> No officer, I only have C.D.'s.

"I" (capitalized) missed that reading— "I" missed that boat— "I" miffed that FOB code. A close shave. A brush with the law. Still, the lower case "i" wonders what it was that gave it away? Why the punch-line was unheard as an ironization of the verbal transaction. Was it the "brown skin, / black hair"? The "almond shaped eyes"? Yellow Peril whispers, "You just happened to be in the right place / at the wrong time" (199).

□

Poet and artist Roy Kiyooka, whose death in 1994 at 67 left an awesome silence, was often dumbfounded by the machinations of a state lingo that bound his Canuck born and bred body. See him age 15, already an eager beaver artist absorbing the heteroglossic inner city streets of a working class lean 1930s Calgary. Overnight, the wake of Pearl Harbor, and he crosses the borderline, from Canuck to "enemy alien." The "jap" incarnate. Say goodbye to the WASP dream of an invisible language. Later, in his mid-1930s, Kiyooka composed the serial text, *Kyoto Airs* (1964), his first book of poems. By then his "english" had become what he called "inglish"— a lower case "i" functioning as both noun and slanted participle. It was the heyday of Canadian cultural nationalism. Kiyooka's performances— his "inging" in the "uncouth vernacular" (*Pacific Windows* 278) of displacement— found few ears outside the proper "english" saturating the white anglo-dominant cultural nomenclature of his life and times. "It's as though you found yourself, despite yourself, having to do everything the most difficult way imaginable because you had to explore the whole terrain before you got a purchase on it," was the way he remembered his beginnings as a not-so-white Canadian poet in the early 1960s (Miki, "Interview" 61). Kiyooka's movement through that "whole terrain" exemplifies the necessary deterritorialization of his personal and social contract with the "english" of his upbringing.

It is a writing strategy, though, that needs to be read alongside the internalization of the race codes that bind in the social and historical basin of 1940s Canada. Those were formative years in the language of racialization which would subsequently mark the contours of the social imaginary. So Kiyooka recounts that period when he inhabited an "enemy alien" body: "In and through all the ideological strife we avidly attended via the local paper and the radio a small 'i' felt as if a punitive fist kept clenching and unclenching behind my back but each time I turned to catch it flexing it would disappear into the unlit corners of our small log house" ("Dear Lucy Fumi" 125). The "log house" was the Opal, Alberta, farmhouse that the Kiyooka family moved into after being forced out of their Calgary home.

□

The "asian" inside "canadian" has a long and painful history, marked as it is by the spectral evidence of voices gone awry, of intentions distorted, of subjects maligned and excluded. The colonial legacy manifested the "not-white" body as a sign of the monstrous "asiatic," then later as a deviancy to be assimilated, and more recently as a variance that is scripted as the "multicultural." The disciplinary naming of the not-so-white body as a "visible minority"— Canada's contribution to the bureaucritization of race— maintains the normative value of whiteness. Sticks and stones may break my bones, but words can turn me in. Listen to Fred Wah, who grew up in small-town Nelson, BC: "Until Mary McNutter calls me a Chink I'm not one... I'm stunned. I've never thought about it. After that I start to listen, and watch. Some people are different. You can see it. Or hear it" (98). It's that old "yellow peril blues" tuning its fork again.

□

On stage, or as staged, "Can I see your ID?" is a question that signifies in excess of pull over, do you have a record? Not so much the covering over, or even the cover up, but the spillage of the social unconscious. In the muteness of sign language, race codes glow in the dark. I am speaking here of "Canadian" infections.

□

The writer whose subjectivity is read into or out of the nation-state sanctioning of "difference" encounters a min[e]d field— as in mind, mine, mined— fraught with linguistic duplicities. Think here of the classic unclassified portrait of the artist as a raced body. What can critical readers make of the minute diversions and accommodations made in the linguistic transactions of the forming writer? How are the codes that bind inflected? What syntactic rivulets map the imagination of one whose desire awakens to the very words that name its body as "visible" and "minor"? Where does the writer who misreads or mistakes the norms turn for reception? What happens to static? Where are the institutional terms for writers whose subjectivities rehearse the social unconscious? Of course, all of these kinds of questions can be tossed to the wind. After all, what about the more pressing problems of authority, access, and audience, i.e., economic and cultural capital?

□

History teaches that efforts to sustain critiques of race codes can turn back on themselves to yield anxiety, complicity, and the bottom line of guilt. This may explain why, amongst racialized writers, discomforting issues of language, stance, and form are ignored, skirted, even disavowed— even as the shadows lengthen over their texts. By calling attention to race codes, do they not recirculate racialization? If they deviate from the formal expectations of dominant aesthetic values, won't they simply ghettoize themselves all over again? Isn't it their responsibility to make their subjectivities accessible?

It is perhaps instructive, at this point, to retrieve what Erica Hunt a few years back says about the pitfalls of shaping an oppositional poetics: "The languages used to preserve domination are complex and sometimes contradictory. Much of how they operate to anesthetize desire and resistance is invisible; they are wedded to our common sense; they are formulaic without being intrusive, entirely natural— 'no marks on the body at all'" (199). Dominant literary discourses— which include, for example, genre conventions, language and style, authorial positioning, narrative modes, aesthetic regulations— circumscribe the boundaries of knowledge and desire, so that its writer-subjects, to use Hunt's words, "are simultaneously bearers of the codes of containment" (199-200). In the micro-spaces of this language of containment, the race codes that bind function as systemic points of transmission. The "raced i" that is textualized, whether manifestly by content or latently by assumption, assumes social form in institutional representations. First you see it, now you don't. "No marks on the body at all." The colour-blind reader paradoxically can only see things in black and white.

□

To be in a state of doubt and uncertainty, suspending for the moment that irritable reaching after fact and reason, the racialized writer— if one chooses to recognize such a condition— is introduced to a proliferating series of questions which, in their restlessness, threaten to disrupt the liberal discourse of rights and the individual. The translation of disturbance into the static of the supplement moves the frame back into focus, as if to say:

> the burden of racism
> is a gift of liberal democracy
>
> thank you kindly for
> that identitarian rush
> but please don't moan as
> the door shuts behind you
>
> what was it they said?
> i can no longer remember.

Instead, the "i" listens to Hiromi Goto in "The Body Politic":

I can never unzip my skin
and step into another.
I am happy with my colour until someone points
out it clashes with my costume. (220)

◻

So was multiculturalism simply a dress code?

Not really, listen closely:

The Canadian take on "multiculturalism" needs to be read as a contradictory zone of vested interests, made more so by the engineering role played by the federal administration. While its more benign public face has supported cultural "diversity" and "pluralism," the company it keeps with hierarchically structured relations of "difference" exposes a subtext of racialization.

In other words, as a top-down term "multiculturalism" has been deployed strategically by policy makers to project a political and cultural history built on "tolerance" and "inclusiveness." For those who have internalized the networks of racialization, this narrative remains a fantasy that deflects the colonial history of white supremacist power. Critical theorist and activist Himani Bannerji has commented in a recent interview that "... there is a state within a state in Canada. The liberal democratic Canadian state enshrines within itself a colonial state." This condition is concretized both in Canada's continuing failure to settle its colonial debts to First Nations people and in its "multiculturalism" policy which Bannerji describes as "management through racialization" ("Multiculturalism is..." 9).

◻

I would like to agree with Trinh T. Minh-ha who, in a recent essay, calls for an end to the assumption that the "other" (aka "alien") is somehow external to cultural regimes, and as such be invited into the dominant house of customs. The assumption of host/guest relations relies on the fiction that the geography of the public sphere is transparent to insider/outsider boundaries. The staticity of that binary— and its endurance in the race codes that bind— has rendered unconscious the violence of the colonial project in which the incorporation of the "alien" has been a founding gesture of nation-state identity. "The named 'other,'" Trinh T. Minh-ha writes, "is never to be found merely over there and outside oneself, for it is always over here, between Us, within Our discourse, that the 'other' becomes a nameable reality" ("An Acoustic Journey" 1). If the "other" is always already inside, then the term "alien" can be re-read as a misidentification that exposes the historically rooted race codes circulating in "difference"-producing cultural and political discourses.

Coming into language in Canadian contexts, here, is full of perils. To speak of "race" and "whiteness" is to conjure the backlash of disavowal— a defensiveness that can be fierce in its toleration and appropriative in its desire to absorb. It is here, as well, in this conflicted public space, that the most resistant and tenacious cultural work has emerged. I am thinking of those (strategically described as the not-white) minority writers who have consciously worked to make visible the race codes that bind— and who, by so doing, have opened up the possibility of cultural texts moving "beyond" the reproduction of dominant expectations of aesthetic correctness towards a proprioceptive reflexiveness for racialization.

The temptation of the racialized— a further effect of internalization— is to get bound up a "wounded attachment," (see Wendy Brown), an identity forged in the pain of subordination and which thereafter functions only as an extension of anger and resentment. While such identities are understandable, as enclosures they can only perpetuate (in negatives) the race codes that bind. In the face of such an impasse— the writer's certain dead-end where language loses its edge— Homi Bhabha perhaps offers the salutary prospect of a reconceptualization. He contends, for instance, in "Postcolonial Authority and Postmodern Guilt," that the "disjunctive, fragmented, displaced agency of those who have suffered the sentence of history— subjugation, domination, diaspora, displacement— forces one to think outside the certainty of the sententious." I take it he points to the "sentence" as a technology that organizes identities, including racialized ones, according to regulatory schemata and laws that maintain given relations of power. "It is from the affective experience of social marginality that we must conceive of a political strategy of empowerment and articulation," he says, "a strategy outside the liberatory rhetoric of idealism and beyond the sovereign subject that haunts the 'civil' sentence of the law" (56).

□

Writing "through" the race codes that bind— as both material condition and the desire for the future "beyond"— proposes the productive tension of a reflexivity that enables the performance of a "here and there." This is a doubling which repels the static of binarism and yields a dispersal of frames— textualized sites in which the racialized subject negotiates the construction of representations that do not simply rescript the deformation or even the liberal privileging of so-called "marginalized" positioning.

□

On the other hand, the unravelling scripts of nation-states on the cusp of that ubiquitous word "globalization" are being played out, as if fatefully, in the mediascapes that "our" public lives have become. "Canadian" identity has lately been reduced to the hollowed out sound of "unity" in a bereft political language fed by an economic hunger for globalization. As the commodification of culture escalates, Canadian politicians, still for the most part white males, now take crash courses to polish their "asian" accents and body language. They no longer return to their British and European roots, but seek to befriend "Yellow Peril," dine on noodles and rice, and have their photos taken in famous "asian" sites (e.g., in Korea at the DM zone). These representatives of the liberal west— fifty years after Hiroshima— have no problem overlooking racism, genocide, and the abrogation of rights, as long as global capitalization is served. The influx of "asian" capital, goods, and populations into the urban core of Canadian cities (more so on the west coast) is rapidly transforming the scripting of "asian" in what is still a white man's country.

For those of us raised and formed in Canada during the nation-state era of the race codes that bind, economic "asianization" has brought in its wake cultural destabilizations which are radically altering the conditions of visibility and invisibility. How these changes will reconfigure the lexicon of current cultural politics— and thus the mutations of racialization— waits to be seen.

□

For me, the trope of "migrancy" suggests a malleable holding position in a cultural immediacy where "centrist" terms such as nation-states, identity politics, multiculturalism and even cross-culturalism can no longer frame— which is to say name— the zones of the "marginal." Cultural theorists and writers have, of course, pointed to "migrancy" as a dominant fact of the 20th century. The application of the term to cultural production, I would hope, in no way diminishes the suffering caused by violent global displacements— but rather emphasizes the pervasive effects the movement beyond and across national boundaries has had in the nooks and crannies of our everyday lives.

Young Vancouver-based visual artist Melinda Mollineaux, for instance, has recently spoken in an interview about the centrality of a "migrant sensibility" for her familial history of crossings, between countries, but also between "island spaces" and "mainlands" (see Bell). Mollineaux's subjectivity is informed by her Caribbean lineage and her experience of racialization in England and Canada. The localities—the "islands" and "mainlands"— that constitute the boundaries of her identity are not separate and self-enclosed spaces which contradict one another, but exist for her as a reciprocity that situates the finite subject's specificities (language, lineage, history, etc.) in social relations guided by a recognition of limits.

A poetics of migrancy would reject the discourse of "differences" construed in a normative system of power hierarchies, i.e., the "different" as always and only what "deviates." On the other hand, it would necessarily be attentive to the effects of racialization as often a trauma of painful displacement between a "here" and "there," a "near" and "far," a "familiar" and "foreign." Displacement calls for a language to enunciate the radical non-telelogical shiftings that perform the present tense or the tense present "we" are in. Demetrio Yocum writes that "...the uprooted subject— moving through the uncertain paths of the world— negotiates and articulates in the poetic text the dramatic experience of a precarious condition." While this text will call forth "a world of memory and nostalgia" that prompts the writer to rewrite "the dramatic conditions of alterity," it also offers "a way of seeking another sense of 'home' on the borderline between belonging and exclusion" (222). The figure of migrancy comes into appearance at the intersection of textual sites where an ethical limit allows for the co-existence of subjectivities not arranged according the "same" and the "different." Here, at this intersection (this siteline?) the race codes that bind can be re-read as a staging of norms which are rejected through the efficacy of poetic texts refusing the law of the sentence.

BIBLIOGRAPHY

Adachi, Ken. *The Enemy That Never Was: A History of the Japanese Canadians*. Toronto: McClelland and Stewart, 1976.

Alcoff, Linda. "The Problem of Speaking for Others." *Cultural Critique* 20 (1991-92): 5-32.

Allen, Lillian. "Transforming the Cultural Fortress: Setting the Agenda for Anti-Racism Work in Culture." *Parallélogramme* 19.3 (1993-94): 48-59.

Anderson, Kay J. *Vancouver's Chinatown: Racial Discourse in Canada, 1875-1980*. Montreal: McGill-Queen's University Press, 1991.

Andrews, Marke. "Racism Charges Color a Conference on Race." *Vancouver Sun* June 11, 1994.

Anzaldúa, Gloria. "Haciendo caras, una entrada." *Making Face, Making Soul: Creative and Critical Perspectives by Feminists of Color*. San Francisco: Aunt Lute Books, 1990. xv-xxviii.

Armstrong, Jeannette, "The Disempowerment of First North American Native Peoples and Empowerment through Their Writing." *An Anthology of Canadian Native Literature in English*. Ed. Daniel David Moses and Terry Goldie. Toronto: Oxford University Press, 1992. 207-11.

Arteaga, Alfred. "An Other Tongue." *An Other Tongue: Nation and Ethnicity in the Linguistic Borderlands*. Ed. Alfred Arteaga. Durham and London: Duke University Press, 1994. 9-33.

Atwood, Margaret. *Survival: A Thematic Guide to Canadian Literature*. Toronto: House of Anansi, 1972.

Avison, Margaret. "Snow." *Winter Sun / The Dumbfounding: Poems 1940-66*. Toronto: McClelland & Stewart, 1982. 27.

Awkward, Michael. *Negotiating Difference: Race, Gender, and the Politics of Positionality*. Chicago: University of Chicago Press, 1995.

Baker, Marie Annharte. "Dis Mischief: Give It Back Before I Remember I Gave It Away." *Colour. An Issue*. Ed. Roy Miki and Fred Wah. *West Coast Line* 28.1-2, Nos. 13-14 (Spring-Fall 1994): 204-13.

_____. *Coyote Columbus Cafe*. Winnipeg: Moonprint Press, 1994.

Bakhtin, Mikhail. *The Dialogic Imagination*. Ed. Michael Holquist. Trans. Caryl Emerson and Michael Holquist. Austin and London: University of Texas Press, 1981.

Bammer, Angelika, ed. *Displacements: Cultural Identities in Question*. Bloomington and Indianapolis: Indiana University Press, 1994.

Bannerji, Himani, ed. *Returning the Gaze: Essays on Racism, Feminism and Politics*. Toronto: Sister Vision Press, 1993.

_____. "Re: turning the Gaze." *Beyond Political Correctness: Toward the Inclusive University*. Toronto: University of Toronto Press, 1995. 220-36.

_____. "Multiculturalism Is...Anti-anti-racism." *Kinesis* February 1997: 8-9.

"Barring of White Writers Denounced." *Vancouver Sun* June 4, 1994.

Bell, Lynne, and Carol Williams. "Geographical Memory, Island Space: An Interview with Melinda Mollineaux." *West Coast Line* 31.2, No. 23 (Fall 1997): 82-94.

Bennett, Donna. "English Canada's Postcolonial Complexities." *Essays on Canadian Writing* 51-52 (Winter 1993-Spring 1994): 164-210.

Bernstein, Charles. *Controlling Interests*. New York: Roof Books, 1980.

Bhabha, Homi K. "Postcolonial Authority and Postmodern Guilt." *Cultural Studies*. Ed. Lawrence Grossberg, Cary Nelson, Paula A. Treichler. New York: Routledge, 1992. 56-68.

_____. *The Location of Culture*. London and New York: Routledge, 1994.

Bissoondath, Neil. "I am Canadian." *Saturday Night* October 1994: 11-12, 16-20, 22.

Blanchot, Maurice. *The Space of Literature.* Trans. Ann Smock. Lincoln: University of Nebraska Press, 1989.

Bolan, Kim. "Liberal's Refusal to Redress Head Tax 'Betrays' Chinese-Canadians' Trust." *Vancouver Sun* December 15, 1994.

Bondi, Liz. "Locating Identity Politics." *Place and the Politics of Identity.* Ed. Michael Keith and Steve Pile. London and New York: Routledge, 1993. 84-101.

Bontogon, Eric. "Black Night." *Colour. An Issue.* Ed. Roy Miki and Fred Wah: 199.

Bourdieu, Pierre. *Language and Symbolic Power.* Ed. John B. Thompson. Trans. Gino Raymond and Matthew Adamson. Cambridge, Massachusetts: Harvard University Press, 1991.

Bowering, George. "Roy Kiyooka's Poetry (an appreciation)." *Roy K. Kiyooka: 25 Years.* Vancouver: Vancouver Art Gallery, 1975. np.

_____, ed. *Sheila Watson and* The Double Hook. Ottawa: Golden Dog Press, 1985.

Brand, Dionne. "Who Can Speak for Whom?" *Brick* 46 (Summer 1993): 13-20.

_____. "Notes to Structuring the Text and the Craft of Writing." *Front* 6.1 (September-October 1994): 12-15.

Brown, Wendy. "Wounded Attachments: Late Modern Oppositional Political Formations." *The Identity in Question.* Ed. John Rajchman. New York and London: Routledge, 1995. 199-227.

Browning, Janisse. "Self-Determination and Cultural Appropriation." *Fuse* 15.4 (Spring 1992): 31-35.

Brydon, Diana. "The White Inuit Speaks: Contamination as Literary Strategy." *Past the Last Post: Theorizing Post-Colonialism and Post-Modernism.* New York: Harvester Wheatsheaf, 1991. 191-203.

Butler, Judith. *Bodies That Matter: On the Discursive Limits of "Sex."* New York and London: Routledge, 1993.

_____. "Subjection, Resistance, Resignification: Between Freud and Foucault." *The Identity in Question.* Ed. John Rajchman. 229-49.

_____. *Excitable Speech: A Politics of the Performative.* New York and London: Routledge, 1997.

Butling, Pauline. "Interview with bpNichol." November 13, 1986. Unpublished.

Canada, Multiculturalism and Citizenship. *The Canadian Multiculturalism Act: A Guide for Canadians.* Ottawa: Communications Branch, 1990.

Cheung, Kong-Kok. "Attentive Silence: *Obasan.*" *Articulate Silences: Hisaye Yamamoto, Maxine Hong Kingston, Joy Kogawa.* Ithaca: Cornell University Press, 1993. 126-67.

Chinese Canadian National Council. "It Is Only Fair! Redress for the Head Tax and Chinese Exclusion Act." *In Justice: Canada, Minorities, and Human Rights.* Ed. Roy Miki and Scott McFarlane. Winnipeg: National Association of Japanese Canadians, 1996. 64-70.

Chow, Rey. *Writing Diaspora: Tactics of Intervention in Contemporary Cultural Studies.* Bloomington: Indiana University Press, 1993.

_____. "Film as Ethnography; or, Translation between Cultures in the Postcolonial World." *Primitive Passions: Visuality, Sexuality, Ethnography, and Contemporary Chinese Cinema.* New York: Columbia University Press, 1995. 173-202.

Chua, Cheng Lok. "Witnessing the Japanese Canadian Experience in World War II: Processual Structure, Symbolism, and Irony in Joy Kogawa's *Obasan.*" *Reading the Literatures of Asian America.* Ed. Shirley Geok-lin Lim and Amy Ling. Philadelphia: Temple University Press, 1992. 97-108.

"Conference Stirs Controversy." *Vancouver Sun* April 7, 1994.

Cooper, Afua. "Opinion: Writing thru Race." *Possibilitiis* 1.3 (1994): 5-6.

Crosby, Marcia. "Construction of the Imaginary Indian." *Vancouver Anthology: The Institutional Politics of Art.* Ed. Stan Douglas. Vancouver: Talonbooks, 1991. 267-91.

Dabydeen, Cyril. "Celebrating Difference." *Books in Canada* 23.6 (September 1994): 23-25.

Davey, Frank. "Surviving the Paraphrase." *Surviving the Paraphrase.* Winnipeg: Turnstone Press, 1983. 1-12.

_____. *Reading Canadian Reading.* Winnipeg: Turnstone Press, 1988.

_____. "Critical Response I: Canadian Canons." *Critical Inquiry* 16 (Spring 1990): 672-81.

_____. *Post-National Arguments: The Politics of the Anglophone-Canadian Novel Since 1967.* Toronto: University of Toronto Press, 1993.

Dawes, Kwame. "Re-Appropriating Cultural Appropriation." *Fuse* 16.5-6 (Summer 1993): 7-15.

de Man, Paul. "Criticism and Crisis." *Blindness and Insight.* Second Edition, Revised. Minneapolis: University of Minnesota Press, 1983. 3-19.

Deleuze, Gilles, and Félix Guattari. "What Is a Minor Literature?" *Out There: Marginalization and Contemporary Cultures.* Ed. Russell Ferguson, Martha Gever, Trinh T. Minh-ha, Cornel West. New York/Cambridge, Massachusetts: New Museum of Contemporary Art/MIT Press, 1990. 59-69.

Delgado, Richard, ed. *Critical Race Theory: The Cutting Edge.* Philadelphia: Temple University Press, 1995.

_____. "Words That Wound: A Tort Action for Racial Insults, Epithets, and Name-Calling." *Critical Race Theory: The Cutting Edge.* 159-68.

Derrida, Jacques. "Structure, Sign and Play in the Discourse of the Human Sciences." *Writing and Difference.* Trans. Alan Bass. Chicago: University of Chicago Press, 1978. 278-93.

_____. *The Ear of the Other: Otobiography, Transference, Translation.* Trans. Peggy Kamuf. Ed. Claude Levesque and Christie McDonald. Lincoln and London: University of Nebraska Press, 1985.

_____. *The Gift of Death.* Trans. David Wills. Chicago: University of Chicago Press, 1995.

Drainie, Bronwyn. "Controversial Writers' Meeting Is Both Meet and Right." *Globe and Mail* April 16, 1994.

Dutton, Paul, and Steve Smith, ed. *Read the Way He Writes: A Festschrift for bpNichol.* *Open Letter* 6th Series. 5-6 (Summer-Fall 1986).

Emberley, Julia V. *Thresholds of Difference: Feminist Critique, Native Women's Writings, Postcolonial Theory.* Toronto: University of Toronto Press, 1993.

"Excluding Whites." Editorial. *Toronto Star* April 5, 1994.

Flahiff, F. T. "Afterword." *The Double Hook,* by Sheila Watson. Toronto: McClelland & Stewart, 1989. 119-30.

Foster, Cecil. "An Infusion of Colour." *Quill and Quire* (September 1994): 12

Frye, Northrop. *The Bush Garden: Essays on the Canadian Imagination.* Toronto: Anansi, 1971.

Fujimoto, Yoko. "The Structure of Joy Kogawa's *Obasan.*" *Canada Bungaku Kenkyo* 2 (1989): 71-91.

Fujita, Gayle K. "'To Attend the Sound of Stone: The Sensibility of Silence in *Obasan.*" *MELUS* 12.3 (1985): 33-42.

Fulford, Robert. "George Orwell, Call Your Office." *Globe and Mail* March 30, 1994.

_____. "Down the Garden Path of Multiculturalism." *Globe and Mail* June 9, 1994.

Fung, Richard. "Working through Cultural Appropriation." *Fuse* 16.5-6 (1993): 16-24.

Gagnon, Monika Kin. "Writing thru Race in Vancouver: Landmarks and Landmines." *Front* 6.1 (September-October 1994): 6-8.

_____, and Scott Toguri McFarlane. "Writing thru Race." *Parallélogramme* 20.2 (1994): 6-9.

Gates, Henry Louis, Jr., ed. *"Race," Writing, and Difference*. Chicago: University of Chicago Press, 1986.

Geddes, Gary, and Phyllis Bruce, ed. *15 Canadian Poets Plus 5*. Toronto: Oxford University Press, 1978.

_____, ed. *20th Century Poetry and Poetics*. Third Edition. Toronto: Oxford University Press, 1985.

_____, ed. *15 Canadian Poets X2*. Toronto: Oxford University Press, 1988.

Godard, Barbara. "Structuralism/Post-Structuralism: Language, Reality and Canadian Literature." *Future Indicative: Literary Theory and Canadian Literature*. Ed. John Moss. Ottawa: University of Ottawa Press, 1987. 25-51.

Goellnicht, Donald C. "Minority History as Metafiction: Joy Kogawa's *Obasan*." *Tulsa Studies in Women's Literature* 7-8 (1988-99): 287-306.

Goldberg, David Theo, ed. *Anatomy of Racism*. Minneapolis: University of Minnesota Press, 1990.

Goldie, Terry. "Signs of the Themes: The Value of a Politically Grounded Semiotics." *Future Indicative*. Ed. John Moss. 85-93.

Goto, Hiromi. "The Body Politic." *Colour. An Issue*. Ed. Roy Miki and Fred Wah: 218-21.

Gottlieb, Erika. "The Riddle of Concentric Worlds in *Obasan*." *Canadian Literature* 109 (Summer 1986): 34-53.

Grant, George. *Lament for a Nation: The Defeat of Canadian Nationalism*. Toronto: McClelland and Stewart, 1965.

_____. *Technology and Empire: Perspectives on North America*. Toronto: Anansi, 1969.

Grossberg, Lawrence. "Cultural Studies and/in New Worlds." *Race, Identity, and Representation in Education*. Ed. Cameron McCarthy and Warren Crichlow. New York: Routledge, 1993. 89-105.

Hall, Stuart. "New Ethnicities." *'Race,' Culture and Difference*. Ed. James Donald and Ali Rattansi. London: Sage Publications, 1992. 252-59.

Harris, Mason. "Broken Generations in *Obasan*: Inner Conflicts and the Destruction of Community." *Canadian Literature* 127 (1990): 41-57.

Hawkings, Stephen. *A Brief History of Time: From the Big Bang to Black Holes*. New York: Bantam, 1990.

Hill, Richard. "One Part Per Million: White Appropriation and Native Voices." *Fuse* 15.3 (Winter 1992): 12-22.

Hunt, Erica. "Notes for an Oppositional Poetics." *The Politics of Form: Poetry and Public Policy*. Ed. Charles Bernstein. New York: Roof Books, 1990. 197-212.

Hutcheon, Linda. *Splitting Images: Contemporary Canadian Ironies*. Toronto: Oxford University Press, 1991.

Ismail, Jam. "From *Scared Texts*." *Many-Mouthed Birds: Contemporary Writing by Chinese Canadians*. Ed. Bennett Lee and Jim Wong-Chu. Vancouver: Douglas & McIntyre, 1991. 124-35.

Jones, D.G. *Butterfly on Rock: A Study of Themes and Images in Canadian Literature*. Toronto: University of Toronto Press, 1970.

Jones, Manina. "The Avenues of Speech and Silence: Telling Difference in Kogawa's *Obasan*." *That Art of Difference: 'Documentary-Collage' and English-Canadian Writing*. Toronto: University of Toronto Press, 1993. 120-39.

Jordan, Glenn, and Chris Weedon. *Cultural Politics: Class, Gender, Race and the Postmodern World*. Oxford: Blackwell, 1995.

Kallen, Evelyn. *Ethnicity and Human Rights in Canada.* Toronto: Gage, 1982.

Kitagawa, Muriel. *This Is My Own: Letters to Wes and Other Writings on Japanese Canadians, 1941-1948.* Ed. Roy Miki. Vancouver: Talonbooks, 1985.

Kiyooka, Roy. *Kyoto Airs.* Vancouver: Periwinkle Press, 1964.

_____. "Notes Toward a Book of Photoglyphs." *Capilano Review* Series 2.2 (Spring 1990): 76-94.

_____. "Dear Lucy Fumi." *West Coast Line* 24.3, No. 3 (Winter 1990): 125-6.

_____. "We Asian North Americanos." *West Coast Line* 24.3, No. 3 (Winter 1990): 116-18.

_____. *December / February 1987, 1988.* Toronto: Coach House Books, 1995.

_____. *Mothertalk: Life Stories of Mary Kiyoshi Kiyooka.* Ed. Daphne Marlatt. Edmonton: NeWest, 1997.

_____. *Pacific Windows: Collected Poems of Roy K. Kiyooka.* Ed. Roy Miki. Vancouver: Talonbooks, 1997.

Kobayashi, Audrey. "Multiculturalism: A Canadian Institution." *Place Culture Representation.* Ed. James Duncan and David Ley. London and New York: Routledge, 1993. 205-31.

Kogawa, Joy. *Obasan.* Penguin Books, 1983.

_____. *Woman in the Woods.* Oakville, Ontario: Mosaic, 1985.

Kristeva, Julia. *Desire in Language.* Ed. Leon S. Roudiez. Trans. Thomas Gora, Alice Jardine, and Leon S. Roudiez. New York: Columbia University Press, 1980.

Kroetsch, Robert. *What the Crow Said.* Toronto: General Publishing, 1978.

_____. *The Lovely Treachery of Words.* Toronto: Oxford University Press, 1989.

Lacapra, Dominick. *The Bounds of Race: Perspectives on Hegemony and Resistance.* Ed. Dominick Lacapra. Ithaca and London: Cornell University Press, 1991.

Lavie, Smadar, and Ted Swedenburg, ed. *Displacement, Diaspora, and Geographies of Identity.* Durham and London: Duke University Press, 1996.

Lecker, Robert. "The Canonization of Canadian Literature: An Inquiry into Value." *Critical Inquiry* 16 (Spring 1990): 656-71.

_____. "Critical Response II: Response to Frank Davey." *Critical Inquiry* 16 (Spring 1990): 682-89.

_____. "Privacy, Publicity, and the Discourse of Canadian Criticism." *Essays on Canadian Writing* 51-52 (1993-94): 32-82.

Lee, Bennett, and Jim Wong-Chu, ed. *Many-Mouthed Birds: Contemporary Writing by Chinese Canadians.* Vancouver: Douglas & McIntyre, 1991.

Lee, Dennis. "Cadence, Country, Silence: Writing in Colonial Space." *A Canadian Issue.* Ed. Robert Kroetsch. *Boundary2* 3.1 (Fall 1974): 151-68.

Lim, Shirley Geok-Lin. "Japanese American Women's Life Stories: Maternality in Monica Sone's *Nisei Daughter* and Joy Kogawa's *Obasan.*" *Feminist Studies* 16.2 (1990): 288-312.

Lionnet, Françoise. "Of Mangoes and Maroons: Language, History, and the Multicultural Subject of Michelle Cliff's *Abeng.*" *De/colonizing the Subject: The Politics of Gender in Women's Autobiography.* Ed. Sidonie Smith and Julia Watson. Minneapolis: University of Minnesota Press, 1992. 321-45.

Livesay, Dorothy. "Call My People Home." *Documentaries.* Toronto: Ryerson, 1968. 30-48.

_____. "The Documentary Poem: A Canadian Genre." *Contexts of Canadian Criticism.* Ed. Eli Mandel. Toronto: University of Toronto Press, 1971. 267-81.

López, Ian F. Haney. "White by Law." *Critical Race Theory: The Cutting Edge.* Ed. Richard Delgado. 542-50.

Lyotard, Jean-François. *The Postmodern Condition: A Report on Knowledge.* Trans. Geoff Bennington and Brian Massumi. Minneapolis: University of Minnesota Press, 1984.

Macdonald, Bruce. *Vancouver: A Visual History*. Vancouver: Talonbooks, 1992.

Maclear, Kyo. "Drawing Dividing Lines: An Analysis of Discursive Representations of Amerasian 'Occupation Babies.'" *RFR (Resources for Feminist Research)* 23.4 (Winter 1994-95): 20-34.

Magnusson, A. Lynne. "Language and Longing in Joy Kogawa's *Obasan*." *Canadian Literature* 116-117 (1988): 58-66.

Mandel, Eli. "Modern Canadian Poetry." *Another Time*. Erin, Ontario: Press Porcépic, 1977. 81-90.

_____. *Life Sentence: Poems and Journals 1976-1980*. Toronto and Victoria: Press Porcépic, 1981.

Maracle, Lee. "Ramparts Hanging in the Air." *Telling It: Women and Language Across Cultures*. Ed. The Telling It Collective. Vancouver: Press Gang, 1990. 161-72.

_____. "The 'Post-Colonial' Imagination." *Fuse* 16.1 (Fall 1992) 12-15.

Marlatt, Daphne. *Steveston*. Vancouver: Talonbooks, 1974.

_____. "musing with mothertongue." *Touch to My Tongue*. Edmonton: Longspoon, 1984. 45-49.

Mathur, Ashok. *Rhetoric of Approval: Theorizing Race through the Little Magazine and Other Places*. Burnaby, BC: The Production House, 1996.

Mayr, Suzette. *Moon Honey*. Edmonton: NeWest, 1995.

McAllister, Kirsten Emiko. "Confronting Official History with Our Own Eyes: Video-Documentary in the Japanese Canadian Community." *Colour. An Issue*. Ed. Roy Miki and Fred Wah: 66-84.

McCaffery, Steve. *Carnival: The First Panel, 1967-70*. Toronto: Coach House, 1973.

_____. *Carnival: The Second Panel: 1970-75*. Toronto: Coach House, 1978.

_____. *North of Intention: Critical Writings 1973-1986*. New York and Toronto: Roof Books and Nightwood Editions, 1986.

_____, and bpNichol. *Rational Geomancy: The Kids of the Book Machine, The Collected Research Reports of the Toronto Research Group 1973-1982*. Ed. Steve McCaffery. Vancouver: Talonbooks, 1992.

McCarthy, Cameron, and Warren Crichlow, ed. *Race, Identity, and Representation in Education*. New York and London: Routledge, 1993.

McEwen, Joan I. *Report in Respect of the Political Science Department of the University of British Columbia*. Prepared for the Dean of the Faculty of Arts and Graduate Studies. June 15, 1995.

McFarlane, Scott Toguri. "Covering *Obasan* and the Narrative of Internment." *Privileging Positions: The Sites of Asian American Studies*. Ed. Gary Y. Okihiro, Marilyn Alquizola, Dorothy Fujita Rony, K. Scott Wong. Pullman, Washington: Washington State University Press, 1995. 401-11.

_____. "The Haunt of Race: Canada's Multiculturalism Act, the Politics of Incorporation, and Writing thru Race." *Fuse* 18.3 (Spring 1995): 18-31.

Melnyk, George. "A Talk with Sheila Watson." *Quill and Quire*, September 1975: 14-15.

Merewether, Charles. "Zones of Marked Instability: Woman and the Space of Emergence." *Rethinking Borders*. Ed. John C. Welchman. Minneapolis: University of Minnesota Press, 1996. 101-24.

Miki, Roy. "Roy Kiyooka: An Interview." *Inalienable Rice: A Chinese and Japanese Canadian Anthology*. Vancouver: Powell Street Revue and the Chinese Canadian Writers Workshop, 1979. 58-64.

_____, ed. *Tracing the Paths: Reading ≠ Writing The Martyrology*. Vancouver: Talonbooks/Line, 1988.

_____, and Cassandra Kobayashi. *Justice in Our Time: The Japanese Canadian Redress Settlement*. Vancouver and Winnipeg: Talonbooks and National Association of Japanese Canadians, 1991.

_____. "Writing thru 'Race': A Mid-Stream Report." *The Writers' Union of Canada Newsletter* 21.8 (March 1994): 1-2, 13-14.

_____, and Fred Wah, ed. *Colour. An Issue. West Coast Line* 28.1-2, Nos. 13-14 (Spring-Fall 1994).

_____. "Why We're Holding the Vancouver Conference." *Globe and Mail* April 7, 1994.

_____, and Scott McFarlane, ed. *In Justice: Canada, Minorities, and Human Rights.* Winnipeg: National Association of Japanese Canadians, 1996.

_____. "Coruscations, Plangencies, and the Syllibant: After Words to Roy Kiyooka's *Pacific Windows. Pacific Windows: Collected Poems of Roy K. Kiyooka.* Vancouver: Talonbooks, 1997. 301-20.

Mitchell, Beverly. "Association and Allusion in *The Double Hook.*" *Sheila Watson and The Double Hook.* Ed. George Bowering. Ottawa: Golden Dog Press, 1985. 99-113.

Mookerjea, Sourayan. "Some Special Times and Remarkable Spaces of Reading and Writing thru 'Race.'" *West Coast Line* 28.3, No. 15 (Winter 1994-95): 117-29.

_____. *Crisis and Catachresis: Anti-Imperialist Pedagogy at the Limit of Identity Politics.* Burnaby, BC: The Production House, 1996.

·Moss, John, ed. *Future Indicative: Literary Theory and Canadian Literature.* Ottawa: University of Ottawa Press, 1987.

Mouffe, Chantal. *The Return of the Political.* London and New York: Verso, 1993.

_____. "Democratic Politics and the Question of Identity." *The Identity in Question.* Ed. John Rajchman. 33-45.

Mukerjee, Arun. *Oppositional Aesthetics.* Toronto: TSAR, 1994.

National Association of Japanese Canadians. *Democracy Betrayed: The Case for Redress.* Winnipeg: National Association of Japanese Canadians, 1984.

Newlove, John. "The Pride." *15 Canadian Poets X2.* Ed. Gary Geddes. 379-86.

Ng, Roxana. "Racism, Sexism, and Nation Building in Canada." *Race, Identity, and Representation in Education.* Ed. Cameron McCarthy and Warren Crichlow. 50-59.

Nichol, bp. *bp.* Toronto: Coach House, 1967.

_____. *The Martyrology: Books 3 and 4.* Toronto: Coach House, 1976.

_____. *The Martyrology: Books 1 and 2.* Toronto: Coach House, 1977.

_____. *The Martyrology: Book 5.* Toronto: Coach House, 1982.

_____. "The "Pata of Letter Feet, Or, the English Written Character as a Medium for Poetry." *Open Letter* 6th Series.1 (Spring 1985): 79-95.

_____. *The Martyrology: Book 6 Books.* Toronto: Coach House, 1987.

_____. "The Annotated, Anecdoted, Beginnings of a Critical Checklist of the Published Works of Steve McCaffery." *Steve McCaffery.* Ed. bpNichol. *Open Letter* 6th Series. 9 (Fall 1987): 67-92.

_____. "'IM: mortality play" [from Book 10]. *West Coast Line* 24.2, No. 2 (Fall 1990): 7-10.

_____. *Gifts: The Martyrology Book(s) 7 &.* Ed. Irene Niechoda. Toronto: Coach House, 1990.

Niranjana, Tejaswine. *Siting Translation: History, Post-Structuralism, and the Colonialist Context.* Berkeley: University of California Press, 1992.

Northey, Margot. "Symbolic Grotesque." *Sheila Watson and* The Double Hook. Ed. George Bowering. 55-61.

O'Neil, Peter. "Feds Won't Fund Writers' Workshop That Bars Whites." *Vancouver Sun* June 9, 1994.

Omi, Michael, and Howard Winant. *Racial Formation in the United States: From the 1960s to the 1980s.* New York and London: Routledge and Kegan Paul, 1986.

_____. "On the Theoretical Concept of Race." *Race, Identity, and Representation in Education*. Ed. Cameron McCarthy and Warren Crichlow. 3-10.

Outlaw, Lucius. "Toward a Critical Theory of 'Race.'" *Anatomy of Racism*. Ed. David Theo Goldberg. Minneapolis: University of Minnesota Press, 1990. 58-82.

Palumbo-Liu, David, ed. *The Ethnic Canon: Histories, Institutions and Interventions*. Minneapolis: University of Minnesota Press, 1995.

Perkins, Charmaine. *"Anymore Colourful and We'd Have to Censor It": Speaking of 'Race,' Subjectivity, and Institutionalized Violations*. Burnaby, BC: The Production House, 1996.

Philip, Marlene Nourbese. "The Absence of Writing, or How I Almost Became a Spy. " *She Tries Her Tongue, Her Silence Softly Breaks*. Charlottetown: Ragweed Press, 1989.

_____. *Frontiers: Essays and Writings on Racism and Culture*. Toronto: The Mercury Press, 1992.

Privy Council. Cunningham and Attorney-General for British Columbia and Tomey Homma and Attorney-General for the Dominion of Canada, On Appeal from the Supreme Court of British Columbia. *House of Lords and Privy Council*, December 17, 1902.

Racial Minority Writers' Committee. "What We Accomplished at the Planning Session." *The Appropriate Voice* 1.1 (Winter 1992): np.

Rajchman, John, ed. *The Identity in Question*. New York and London: Routledge, 1995.

Richer, Stephen and Lorna Weir, ed. *Beyond Political Correctness: Toward the Inclusive University*. Toronto: University of Toronto Press, 1995.

Rose, Marilyn Russell. "Politics into Art: Kogawa's *Obasan* and the Rhetoric of Fiction." *Mosaic* 21.2-3 (Spring 1988): 215-26.

Roy, Patricia. *A White Man's Province: British Columbia Politicians and Chinese and Japanese Immigrants, 1858-1914*. Vancouver: University of British Columbia Press, 1989.

Said, Edward W. *Culture and Imperialism*. New York: Vintage Books, 1993.

Sato, Ayako. "The Gentle Eyes of Mercy." *The Meiji Gakuin Review* 533 (1994): 75-84.

Sawhney, Sabina. "The Joke and the Hoax: (Not) Speaking as the Other." *Who Can Speak? Authority and Critical Identity*. Ed. Judith Roof and Robyn Wiegman. Urbana and Chicago: University of Illinois Press, 1995: 208-20.

Scobie, Stephen. *bpNichol: What History Teaches*. Vancouver: Talonbooks, 1984.

Scott, Gail. "Red Tin + White Tulle: On Memory and Writing." *Spaces Like Stairs*. Toronto: Women's Press, 1989. 17-18.

Scott, Joan W. "Multiculturalism and the Politics of Identity." Ed. John Rajchman. *The Identity in Question*. 3-12.

Shea, Victor. "Framing the 'Western Tradition' in Canadian PC Debates." *Beyond Political Correctness*. Ed. Stephen Richer and Lorna Weir. 88-117.

Shikatani, Gerry. *A Sparrow's Food: Poems 1971/82*. Toronto: Coach House, 1984.

_____. "Writing thru Race a Step Toward Shaping a Vision." *Globe and Mail* July 9, 1994.

Silvera, Makeda. *Her Head a Village*. Vancouver: Press Gang, 1994.

Spivak, Gayatri Chakravorty. *The Post-Colonial Critic: Interviews, Strategies, Dialogues*. Ed. Sarah Harasym. New York and London: Routledge, 1990.

_____. *Outside the Teaching Machine*. New York: Routledge, 1993.

_____. "Bonding in Difference: Gayatri Spivak Speaks." *An Other Tongue: Nation and Ethnicity in the Linguistic Borderlands*. Ed. Alfred Arteaga. 273-85.

_____. "Translator's Preface and Afterword to Mahasweta Devi, *Imaginary Maps*." *The Spivak Reader: Selected Works of Gayatri Chakravorty Spivak*. Ed.

Donna Landry and Gerald Maclean. New York and London: Routledge, 1996. 267-86.

Sunahara, Ann Gomer. *The Politics of Racism: The Uprooting of Japanese Canadians During the Second World War.* Toronto: James Lorimer, 1981.

_____. "The Abuse of Emergency Law in Canada: Is It Inevitable?" In *Justice: Canada, Minorities, and Human Rights.* Ed. Roy Miki and Scott McFarlane. 7-22.

Takashima, Shizuye. *A Child in Prison Camp.* Montreal: Tundra, 1971.

Tobias, Lenore-Keeshig. "Stop Stealing Native Stories." *Globe and Mail* January 26, 1990.

Todd, Loretta. "Notes on Appropriation." *Parallélogramme* 16.1 (Summer 1990): 24-33.

Tostevin, Lola Lemire. "Is this where the poem begins?: Points of Departure in bpNichol's 'A Book of Hours.'" *Subject to Criticism.* Toronto: The Mercury Press, 1995. 137-53.

Trinh T. Minh-ha. "Not You/ Like You: Post-Colonial Women and the Interlocking Questions of Identity and Difference." *Making Face, Making Soul: Creative and Critical Perspectives by Feminists of Color.* Ed. Gloria Anzalduá. 371-75.

_____. *When the Moon Waxes Red: Representation, Gender and Cultural Politics.* New York and London: Routledge, 1991.

_____. "An Acoustic Journey." *Rethinking Borders.* Ed. John C. Welchman. 1-17.

Valpy, Michael. "A Nasty Serving of Cultural Apartheid." *Globe and Mail* April 8, 1994.

Varley, Chris. "Intersections: From the Cassette Tape Interviews between Chris Varley and Roy Kiyooka." *Roy K. Kiyooka: 25 Years.* Vancouver: Vancouver Art Gallery, 1975. np.

"Victim-Writers Meeting the Stuff of Great Art." Editorial. *Vancouver Sun* April 9, 1994.

Wah, Fred. *Diamond Grill.* Edmonton: NeWest, 1996.

Ward, Peter W. *White Canada Forever: Popular Attitudes toward Orientals in British Columbia.* Montreal: McGill-Queen's University Press, 1990.

Watson, Sheila. *The Double Hook.* Toronto: McClelland and Stewart, 1959; 1989.

_____. *Deep Hollow Creek.* Toronto: McClelland and Stewart, 1992.

West, Cornel. "The New Cultural Politics of Difference." *Out There: Marginalization and Contemporary Cultures.* Ed. Russell Ferguson, Martha Gever, Trinh T. Minh-ha, Cornel West. New York/Cambridge, Massachusetts: New Museum of Contemporary Art/MIT Press, 1990. 19-36.

Wildman, Stephanie M., and Adrienne D. Davis. "Language and Silence: Making Systems of Privilege Visible." *Critical Race Theory: The Cutting Edge.* Ed. Richard Delgado. 573-79.

Williams, Patrick and Laura Chrisman, ed. *Colonial Discourse and Post-Colonial Theory: A Reader.* New York: Columbia University Press, 1994.

Willis, Gary. "Speaking the Silence: Joy Kogawa's *Obasan.*" *Studies in Canadian Literature* 12.2 (1987): 239-49.

Wong, Paul, ed. *Yellow Peril Reconsidered.* Vancouver: On Edge, 1990.

"Writhing thru Race." Editorial. *Globe and Mail* April 9, 1994.

Yocum, Demetrio. "Some Troubled Homecomings." *The Post-Colonial Question: Common Skies, Divided Horizons.* Ed. Iain Chambers and Lidia Curti. London and New York: Routledge, 1996. 221-27.